ANNUAL EDITIONS

Educating Children with Exceptionalities 10/11

Twentieth Edition

EDITOR

Karen L. Freiberg
University of Maryland, Baltimore County

Dr. Karen Freiberg has an interdisciplinary educational and employment background in nursing, education, and developmental psychology. She received her BS from the State University of New York at Plattsburgh, her MS from Cornell University, and her PhD from Syracuse University. She has worked as a school nurse, a pediatric nurse, a public health nurse for the Navajo Indians, an associate project director for a child development clinic, a researcher in several areas of child development, and a university professor. Dr. Freiberg is the author of an award-winning textbook, *Human Development: A Life-Span Approach,* which is now in its fourth edition. She is currently on the faculty at the University of Maryland, Baltimore County.

Mc Graw Hill

Connect
Learn
Succeed™

ANNUAL EDITIONS: EDUCATING CHILDREN WITH EXCEPTIONALITIES,
TWENTIETH EDITION

Published by McGraw-Hill, a business unit of The McGraw-Hill Companies, Inc., 1221 Avenue
of the Americas, New York, NY 10020. Copyright © 2010 by The McGraw-Hill Companies, Inc.
All rights reserved. Previous edition(s) 1989–2009. No part of this publication may be reproduced
or distributed in any form or by any means, or stored in a database or retrieval system, without the
prior written consent of The McGraw-Hill Companies, Inc., including, but not limited to, in any
network or other electronic storage or transmission, or broadcast for distance learning.

Some ancillaries, including electronic and print components, may not be available to customers outside the United States.

Annual Editions® is a registered trademark of the McGraw-Hill Companies, Inc.

Annual Editions is published by the **Contemporary Learning Series** group within the McGraw-
Hill Higher Education division.

1 2 3 4 5 6 7 8 9 0 QPD/QPD 0 9

ISBN 978–0–07–813587–3
MHID 0–07–813587–7
ISSN 0198–7518

Managing Editor: *Larry Loeppke*
Senior Managing Editor: *Faye Schilling*
Developmental Editor: *Dave Welsh*
Editorial Coordinator: *Mary Foust*
Editorial Assistant: *Cindy Hedley*
Production Service Assistant: *Rita Hingtgen*
Permissions Coordinator: *Deanna Dausener*
Senior Marketing Manager: *Julie Keck*
Marketing Communications Specialist: *Mary Klein*
Marketing Coordinator: *Alice Link*
Project Manager: *Joyce Watters*
Design Specialist: *Tara McDermott*
Senior Production Supervisor: *Laura Fuller*
Cover Graphics: *Kristine Jubeck*

Compositor: Laserwords Private Limited
Cover Image: © Richard Hutchings/Digital Light Source (inset); © Lars Niki (background)

Library in Congress Cataloging-in-Publication Data
Main entry under title: Annual Editions: Educating Children with Exceptionalities. 2010/2011.
  1. Educating Children with Exceptionalities—Periodicals. I. Freiberg, Karen L., *comp.* II. Title:
Educating Children with Exceptionalities.
658'.05

Editors/Academic Advisory Board

Members of the Academic Advisory Board are instrumental in the final selection of articles for each edition of ANNUAL EDITIONS. Their review of articles for content, level, and appropriateness provides critical direction to the editors and staff. We think that you will find their careful consideration well reflected in this volume.

ANNUAL EDITIONS: Educating Children with Exceptionalities 10/11
20th Edition

EDITOR

Karen L. Freiberg
University of Maryland, Baltimore County

ACADEMIC ADVISORY BOARD MEMBERS

Preface

In publishing ANNUAL EDITIONS we recognize the enormous role played by the magazines, newspapers, and journals of the public press in providing current, first-rate educational information in a broad spectrum of interest areas. Many of these articles are appropriate for students, researchers, and professionals seeking accurate, current material to help bridge the gap between principles and theories and the real world. These articles, however, become more useful for study when those of lasting value are carefully collected, organized, indexed, and reproduced in a low-cost format, which provides easy and permanent access when the material is needed. That is the role played by ANNUAL EDITIONS.

The No Child Left Behind Act (NCLB) of 2001 required schools to have "highly qualified" educators in place to teach "core subjects" such as English, reading, math and science. By 2006 all states had "high stakes" testing established in grades 3–8 for reading and math. Schools that failed to make "adequate yearly progress" (AYP) for two years were mandated by NCLB to make improvements and provide supplemental services. Failure to make AYP for five years required a "restructure" of the school. Restructuring could involve school closings, changes in staffing, becoming a charter school, or having the state run the school. The education of children with exceptionalities created problems for many schools attempting to meet the accountability standards of NCLB. While the law allowed accommodations and modifications for testing of students with disabilities, individualized education plans (IEPs) were supposed to reflect appropriate achievement. Problems with how to assess achievement in special education have been enormous since 2001.

The mandate of NCLB and the 2004 Individuals with Disabilities Education Improvement Act (IDEIA), require that assessment of children with exceptionalities be specific to each individual and translate into instructional practice, "authentic assessment." This compendium of articles includes several references to authentic assessment and how to meet the legal rights of children with special needs.

The Individuals with Disabilities Education Improvement Act of 2004 (IDEIA) was amended to be aligned with NCLB. Both NCLB and IDEIA relate to two other civil rights laws of the USA, the Rehabilitation Act Amendment (Section 504), and the Americans with Disabilities Act (ADA). The latter two laws prohibit disability discrimination while the NCLB and the IDEIA authorize funding to educate students with disabilities.

Under current U.S. law all children with disabilities are entitled to supportive educational services from diagnosis until age 21, and to reasonable accommodations and freedom from discrimination for life. Disability advocacy groups are continually alert to signs of exclusion of people with disabilities. Despite diverse attitudes, Congress set out four goals for them: equal opportunity, full participation, independent living, and economic self-sufficiency. IDEIA, as amended in 2004, stated that disability is a natural part of the human experience and in no way diminishes the right of individuals to participate in or contribute to society. IDEIA focuses on six principles of education to help achieve the congressional goals. These six fundamental legal educational policies are zero rejection from the educational system, nondiscriminatory evaluation, free and appropriate education in the public arena, the least-restrictive environment that meets the needs of the student, parental participation, and due process (right to sue if needs go unmet).

Annual Editions: Educating Children with Exceptionalities 10/11 includes multiple articles that deal with the legal rights of students with special needs, organized into categories of exceptionality. Many reports included in this compendium also discuss specific aspects of each category of exceptionality. Selections have been made with an eye to conveying information, giving personal experiences, offering suggestions for implementation, and stimulating meaningful discussions among future parents and teachers.

To help us improve future editions of this anthology, please complete and return the postage-paid article rating form on the last page. Your suggestions are valued and appreciated.

Karen Freiberg

Karen Freiberg
Editor

Contents

UNIT 1
Inclusive Education

The concepts in bold italics are developed in the article. For further expansion, please refer to the Topic Guide.

UNIT 2
Families/Early Intervention

UNIT 3
Learning Disabilities

The concepts in bold italics are developed in the article. For further expansion, please refer to the Topic Guide.

UNIT 4
Intellectual Disabilities/ Autistic Spectrum Disorders

UNIT 5
Emotional and Behavioral Disorders

The concepts in bold italics are developed in the article. For further expansion, please refer to the Topic Guide.

UNIT 6
Communication Disorders

UNIT 7
Hearing and Visual Impairments

The concepts in bold italics are developed in the article. For further expansion, please refer to the Topic Guide.

UNIT 8
Physical and Health Impairments

UNIT 9
Severe Disabilities/Multiple Disabilities

The concepts in bold italics are developed in the article. For further expansion, please refer to the Topic Guide.

UNIT 10
Gifted or Talented

The concepts in bold italics are developed in the article. For further expansion, please refer to the Topic Guide.

Correlation Guide

The *Annual Editions* series provides students with convenient, inexpensive access to current, carefully selected articles from the public press. **Annual Editions: Educating Children with Exceptionalities 10/11** is an easy-to-use reader that presents articles on important topics such as *fitting in, severe disabilities, gifted and talented,* and many more. For more information on *Annual Editions* and other *McGraw-Hill Contemporary Learning Series* titles, visit www.mhhe.com/cls.

This convenient guide matches the units in **Annual Editions: Educating Children with Exceptionalities 10/11** with the corresponding chapters in one of our best-selling McGraw-Hill Special Education textbooks by Taylor et al.

Annual Editions: Educating Children with Exceptionalities 10/11	**Exceptional Students, by Taylor et al.**
Unit 1: Inclusive Education	**Chapter 1:** An Overview of Special Education **Chapter 2:** The Special Education Process: From Initial Identification to the Delivery of Services
Unit 2: Families/Early Intervention	**Chapter 3:** School, Family, and Community Collaboration **Chapter 13:** Students Who Are At Risk: Early Identification and Intervention **Chapter 14:** Students with Attention Deficit/Hyperactivity Disorder
Unit 3: Learning Disabilities	**Chapter 4:** Students with Learning Disabilities
Unit 4: Intellectual Disabilities/Autistic Spectrum Disorders	**Chapter 5:** Students with Mental Retardation/Intellectual Disabilities **Chapter 11:** Students with Autism Spectrum Disorders
Unit 5: Emotional and Behavioral Disorders	**Chapter 6:** Students with Emotional or Behavioral Disorders
Unit 6: Communication Disorders	**Chapter 7:** Students with Communication Disorders
Unit 7: Hearing and Visual Impairments	**Chapter 8:** Students Who Are Deaf or Hard of Hearing **Chapter 9:** Students with Blindness or Low Vision
Unit 8: Physical and Health Impairments	**Chapter 10:** Students with Physical or Health Disabilities
Unit 9: Severe Disabilities/Multiple Disabilities	**Chapter 12:** Students with Severe Disabilities
Unit 10: Gifted or Talented	**Chapter 15:** Students Who Are Gifted and Talented

Topic Guide

This topic guide suggests how the selections in this book relate to the subjects covered in your course. You may want to use the topics listed on these pages to search the Web more easily.

On the following pages a number of websites have been gathered specifically for this book. They are arranged to reflect the units of this Annual Editions reader. You can link to these sites by going to *http://www.mhcls.com*.

All the articles that relate to each topic are listed below the bold-faced term.

Accommodations
1. The Issues of IDEA
3. Use Authentic Assessment Techniques to Fulfill the Promise of No Child Left Behind
10. Inclusion by Design: Engineering Inclusive Practices in Secondary Schools
12. Autism, the Law, and You
14. Understanding and Accommodating Students with Depression in the Classroom
22. Writing Explicit, Unambiguous Accommodations: A Team Effort
25. Monitor That Progress: Interpreting Data Trends for Assistive Technology Decision Making

Accountability
1. The Issues of IDEA
3. Use Authentic Assessment Techniques to Fulfill the Promise of No Child Left Behind
8. Dyslexia and the Brain: What Does Current Research Tell Us?
10. Inclusion by Design: Engineering Inclusive Practices in Secondary Schools
25. Monitor That Progress: Interpreting Data Trends for Assistive Technology Decision Making
27. Creating a Personal Technology Improvement Plan for Teachers of the Gifted

Assessment/Identification
3. Use Authentic Assessment Techniques to Fulfill the Promise of No Child Left Behind
8. Dyslexia and the Brain: What Does Current Research Tell Us?
9. Build Organizational Skills in Students with Learning Disabilities
10. Inclusion by Design: Engineering Inclusive Practices in Secondary Schools
14. Understanding and Accommodating Students with Depression in the Classroom
18. Assessment and Intervention for Bilingual Children with Phonological Disorders
19. A Speech-Language Approach to Early Reading Success
22. Writing Explicit, Unambiguous Accommodations: A Team Effort
25. Monitor That Progress: Interpreting Data Trends for Assistive Technology Decision Making
27. Creating a Personal Technology Improvement Plan for Teachers of the Gifted

Attention deficit hyperactive disorder
7. What Can You Learn from Bombaloo?
23. ADHD and the SUD in Adolescents

Autistic spectrum disorders
4. Does This Child Have a Friend?
11. Reading Disability and the Brain
12. Autism, the Law, and You

Vision problems
8. Dyslexia and the Brain: What Does Current Research Tell Us?

Brain development
8. Dyslexia and the Brain: What Does Current Research Tell Us?

Collaboration
2. Learn about Your New Students
10. Inclusion by Design: Engineering Inclusive Practices in Secondary Schools
11. Reading Disability and the Brain
12. Autism, the Law, and You
14. Understanding and Accommodating Students with Depression in the Classroom
21. Using Tactile Strategies with Students Who Are Blind and Have Severe Disabilities

Communication disorders
11. Reading Disability and the Brain
12. Autism, the Law, and You
18. Assessment and Intervention for Bilingual Children with Phonological Disorders
19. A Speech-Language Approach to Early Reading Success
20. The Debate over Deaf Education
21. Using Tactile Strategies with Students Who Are Blind and Have Severe Disabilities

Conflict resolution
10. Inclusion by Design: Engineering Inclusive Practices in Secondary Schools
17. Classroom Problems That Don't Go Away

Cultural diversity
18. Assessment and Intervention for Bilingual Children with Phonological Disorders

Deaf/Hard of hearing
20. The Debate over Deaf Education

Drug abuse
6. Children of Alcoholics

Early intervention
7. What Can You Learn from Bombaloo?
8. Dyslexia and the Brain: What Does Current Research Tell Us?
12. Autism, the Law, and You
15. Rethinking How Schools Address Student Misbehavior and Disengagement

Elementary school
2. Learn about Your New Students
18. Assessment and Intervention for Bilingual Children with Phonological Disorders

Emotional and behavioral disorders
7. What Can You Learn from Bombaloo?
13. Heading Off Disruptive Behavior
14. Understanding and Accommodating Students with Depression in the Classroom
15. Rethinking How Schools Address Student Misbehavior and Disengagement
16. Young Women in Jail Describe Their Educational Lives

Social skills

Technology

Internet References

The following Internet sites have been selected to support the articles found in this reader. These sites were available at the time of publication. However, because websites often change their structure and content, the information listed may no longer be available. We invite you to visit *http://www.mhcls.com* for easy access to these sites.

Annual Editions: Educating Children with Exceptionalities 10/11

General Sources

Appleseed
http://www.appleseednetwork.org

This site is for a national organization which provides information on education and the law and education policies for K–12. Appleseed advocates for social justice and equal education.

Consortium for Citizens with Disabilities
http://www.c-c-d.org

Included in this coalition organization is an Education Task Force that follows issues of early childhood special education, the president's commission on excellence in special education, issues of rethinking special education, 2001 IDEA principles, and many other related issues.

Family Village
http://www.familyvillage.wisc.edu/index.htmlx

Here is a global community of disability-related resources that is set up under such headings as library, shopping mall, school, community center, and others.

National Dissemination Center for Children with Disabilities (NICHCY)
http://www.nichcy.org/index.html

NICHCY provides information and makes referrals in areas related to specific disabilities, early intervention, special education and related services, individualized education programs, and much more. The site also connects to a listing of Parent's Guides to resources for children and youth with disabilities.

National Rehabilitation Information Center (NARIC)
http://www.naric.com

A series of databases that can be keyword-searched on subjects including physical, mental, and psychiatric disabilities. Vocational rehabilitation, special education, assistive technology, and more can be found on this site.

President's Commission on Excellence in Special Education (PCESE)
http://www.ed.gov/inits/commissionsboards/whspecialeducation/

The report stemming from the work of the PCESE, *A New Era: Revitalizing Special Education for Children and Their Families*, can be downloaded in full from this site.

School Psychology Resources Online
http://www.schoolpsychology.net

Numerous sites on special conditions, disorders, and disabilities, as well as other data ranging from assertiveness/evaluation to research, are available on this resource page for psychologists, parents, and educators.

Special Education Exchange
http://www.spedex.com/main_graphics.htm

SpEdEx, as this site is more commonly known, offers a wealth of information, links, and resources for everyone interested in special education.

Special Education News
http://www.specialednews.com/disabilities/disabnews/povanddisab031200.html

This particular section of this site discusses the problems of coping with both poverty and disability. Explore the rest of the site also for information for educators on behavior management, conflict resolution, early intervention, specific disabilities, and much more.

Teaching Tolerance
http://www.teachingtolerance.org/magazine

UNIT 1: Inclusive Education

Institute on Disability/University of New Hampshire
http://iod.unh.edu

This site includes Early Childhood, Inclusive Education, High School and Post-Secondary School, Community Living and Adult Life, Related Links, both state and national, and information on technology, health care, public policy, as well as leadership training and professional development.

Kids Together, Inc.
http://www.kidstogether.org

Based on the IDEA law about teaching children with disabilities in regular classrooms, this site contains all the information on inclusion you might need to know.

New Horizons for Learning
http://www.newhorizons.org

Based on the theory of inclusion, this site is filled with information on special needs inclusion, technology and learning, a brain lab, and much more, presented as floors in a building.

UNIT 2: Families/Early Intervention

Division for Early Childhood
http://www.dec-sped.org

A division of the Council for Exceptional Children, the DEC advocates for the improvement for conditions for young children with special needs. Child development theory, programming data, parenting data, research, and links to other sites can be found on this site.

Institute on Community Integration Projects
http://ici.umn.edu/projectcenters/

Research projects related to early childhood and early intervention services for special education are described here.

National Association for Child Development (NACD)
http://www.nacd.org

The NACD, an international organization, is dedicated to helping children and adults reach their full potential. Its home page presents links to various programs, research, and resources into such topics as learning disabilities, ADD/ADHD, brain injuries, autism, accelerated and gifted, and other similar topic areas.

Internet References

Special Education Resources on the Internet (SERI)
http://seriweb.com

SERI offers helpful sites in all phases of special education in early childhood, including disabilities, mental retardation, behavior disorders, and autism.

UNIT 3: Learning Disabilities

The Instant Access Treasure Chest
http://www.fln.vcu.edu/ld/ld.html

Billed as the Foreign Language Teacher's Guide to Learning Disabilities, this site contains a very thorough list of resources for anyone interested in LD education issues.

Learning Disabilities Association of America (LDA)
http://www.ldaamerica.org

The purpose of the LDA is to advance the education and general welfare of children of normal and potentially normal intelligence who show handicaps of a perceptual, conceptual, or coordinative nature.

Learning Disabilities Online
http://www.ldonline.org

This is a good source for information about all kinds of learning disabilities with links to other related material.

The Council for Exceptional Children, Division for Learning Disabilities
http://www.teachingld.org

The Division for Learning Disabilities of the CEC works to improve educational outcomes for students with LDs and to assist the professionals who serve them.

The National Center for Learning Disabilities
http://www.ncld.org

The NCLD is an organization devoted to working with individuals with LDs, their families, educators, and researchers. It promotes research on effective teaching and learning strategies, disseminates information, and advocates for policies to protect the rights of individuals with LDs.

UNIT 4: Intellectual Disabilities/ Autistic Spectrum Disorders

Appleseed
http://appleseednetwork.org

This website focuses on special education and the law.

Arc of the United States
http://www.thearc.org

Here is the website of the national organization of and for people with mental retardation and related disabilities and their families. It includes governmental affairs, services, position statements, FAQs, publications, and related links.

Disability-Related Sources on the Web
http://www.arcarizona.org

This resource's many links include grant resources, federally funded projects and federal agencies, assistive technology, national and international organizations, and educational resources and directories.

Gentle Teaching
http://www.gentleteaching.nl

Maintained by the Foundation for Gentle Teaching in the Netherlands, this page explains a nonviolent approach for helping children and adults with special needs.

UNIT 5: Emotional and Behavioral Disorders

Pacer Center: Emotional Behavioral Disorders
http://www.pacer.org/ebd/

Active in Minnesota for 8 years in helping parents become advocates for their EBD children, PACER has gone on to present workshops for parents on how to access aid for their child, explain what a parent should look for in a child they suspect of EBD, prepare a behavioral intervention guide, and link to resources, including IDEA's Partnership in Education site, and much more.

UNIT 6: Communication Disorders

Issues in Emergent Literacy for Children with Language Impairments
http://www.ciera.org/library/reports/inquiry-2/2-002/2-002.html

This site explores the relationship between oral language impairment and reading disabilities in children. It suggests that language impairment may be a basic deficit that affects language function in both its oral and written forms.

UNIT 7: Hearing and Visual Impairments

Info to Go: Laurent Clerc National Deaf Education Center
http://clerccenter.gallaudet.edu/InfoToGo/index.html

Important for parents and educators, this website from Gallaudet University offers information on audiology, communication, education, legal, and health issues of deaf people.

The New York Institute for Special Education
http://www.nyise.org/index.html

This school is an educational facility that serves children who are blind or visually impaired. The site includes program descriptions and resources for the blind.

UNIT 8: Physical and Health Impairments

Association to Benefit Children (ABC)
http://www.a-b-c.org

ABC presents a network of programs that includes child advocacy, education for disabled children, care for HIV-positive children, employment, housing, foster care, and day care.

An Idea Whose Time Has Come
http://www.boggscenter.org/mich3899.htm

The purpose of community-based education is to help students in special education to become more independent. Here is an excellent description of how it is being done in at least one community.

Resources for VE Teachers
http://www.cpt.fsu.edu/tree/ve/tofc.html

Effective practices for teachers of varying exceptionalities (VE) classes are listed here.

The Family Center on Technology and Disability
http://www.fctd.info

This national center is designed to support organizations and programs that work with children and families with disabilities that use assistive technology. Information on technological aides is free.

Internet References

UNIT 9: Severe Disabilities/Multiple Disabilities

Activity Ideas for Students with Severe, Profound, or Multiple Disabilities
http://www.palaestra.com/featurestory.html

The Fall 1997 issue of the *Palaestra* contains this interesting article on teaching students who have multiple disabilities. The complete text is offered here online.

Severe and/or Multiple Disabilities
http://www.nichcy.org/pubs/factshe/fs10txt.htm

This fact sheet offers a definition of multiple disabilities, discusses incidence, characteristics, medical, and educational implications, and suggests resources and organizations that might be of help to parents and educators of children with severe impairments.

UNIT 10: Gifted or Talented

Hoagies' Gifted: Educators
http://www.hoagiesgifted.org/educators.htm

This education page provides resources for teachers, counselors, psychologists, and administrators of the gifted including free resources, special topics, and academic programs.

The Council for Exceptional Children
http://www.cec.sped.org/index.html

This page will give you access to information on identifying and teaching gifted children, attention-deficit disorders, and other topics in gifted education.

The International Society for Technology Education
http://www.iste.org

This non-profit organization provides leadership and service to K–12 teachers and students who want to effectively use technology. It provides information, networking opportunities, and guidance in the use of technology.

UNIT 1

Inclusive Education

Unit Selections

Key Points to Consider

- What impact has IDEA had on the education of students with exceptionalities?

- How can a teacher be as prepared as possible to meet the education and social-emotional needs of a new student with a condition of exceptionality?

- Can authentic assessments fulfill the promise of No Child Left Behind (NCLB) and the Individuals with Disabilities Education Improvement Act (IDEIA)?

- Which instructional methods promote friendships in inclusive classrooms?

- What helps pave the way for students with disabilities to pursue college degrees?

Student Website

www.mhcls.com

Internet References

Institute on Disability/University of New Hampshire
   http://iod.unh.edu
Kids Together, Inc.
   http://www.kidstogether.org
New Horizons for Learning
   http://www.newhorizons.org
Teaching Tolerance
   http://www.teachingtolerance.org/magazine

A huge strength of American schools is the dedication and motivation of its professional teachers. The teaching responsibilities are carried out despite inadequate social, emotional, and financial support; a lack of sufficient inservice education; and few provisions for continuing education. Teachers need all the help they can get, to be the best they can possibly be, and to feel appreciated!

This unit on Inclusive Education highlights what's good in special education, and includes some suggestions for ways it can be improved.

Regular education teachers are expected to know how to provide special educational services to every child with an exceptional condition in their classroom, despite not having had coursework in special education. The numbers of students with exceptionalities who are being educated in regular education classes are increasing annually. The Individuals with Disabilities Education Improvement Act (IDEIA) has reduced the numbers of special needs students being educated in residential centers, hospitals, homes, or special schools to less than 5 percent. Children who once would have been turned away from public schools are now being admitted in enormous numbers. The No Child Left Behind Act (NCLB) has increased the emphasis on high expectations for all students from highly qualified teachers who do frequent proficiency assessments.

Recent Supreme Court legislation has emphasized the role of parental participation in planning for the free and appropriate public education (FAPE) of children with exceptionalities. Parents must be included in developing individualized education programs (IEPs). When public schools fail to provide appropriate instructional practices, parents are entitled to due process hearings. These entail attorneys, subpoenas, examinations, and cross-examinations of witnesses before an impartial hearing officer. If the plaintiffs are not satisfied with the ruling, they may appeal the case. Parents must try public schools, before enrolling their child with a disability in a private school. If public schools fail to provide FAPE, and parents prevail in due process hearings, the school is presented with an injunction to take specific actions to provide more appropriate education or to reimburse parents for tuition in a private school which will provide these services. In 2007, The Supreme Court in *Winkelman vs. Parma City School District,* reinforced IDEIA's mandate to allow parental participation and grant them enforceable rights to ensure that education is appropriate.

The trend toward inclusive education necessitates more knowledge and expertise on the part of the regular education teachers. They are entitled to receive meaningful and sustained inservice training in the newest, research-based methods and materials of special education. Educating children with exceptionalities can no longer be viewed as the job of special-education teachers. This trend also mandates knowledge about collaboration and advisory activities on the part of all special educators. Teamwork is essential as special education and regular education are becoming more and more intertwined.

The laws in Canada and the United States differ slightly. All public schools have an obligation to serve children with exceptional conditions in as normal an educational environment as

© David Toase/Getty Images

possible, or what is known as the least restrictive environment (LRE). Inclusive education is difficult. It works very well for some students with exceptionalities in some situations and marginally or not at all for other students with exceptionalities in other situations.

For inclusion to succeed within a school, everyone must be committed to being part of the solution: superintendent, principal, teachers, coaches, aides, ancillary staff, students, parents, and families. Special education teachers often find their jobs involving much more than instructing students with special needs. They serve as consultants to regular education teachers to assure that inclusion is meaningful for their students. They collaborate with parents, administrators, support personnel, and community agencies as well as with regular education teachers. They plan curriculum and oversee the writing of Individualized Family Service Plans (IFSPs), Individualized Education Plans (IEPs), and Individualized Transition Plans (ITPs). They schedule and make sure that services are provided by all team-involved persons. They keep up with enormous amounts of paperwork. They update parents even when parents are too involved, or not involved enough. They keep abreast of new resources, new legal processes, and new instructional techniques. They make projections for the futures of their students and set out ways to make good things happen. They also struggle to be accountable, both educationally and financially, for all they do.

The term "least restrictive environment" is often mistakenly understood as the need for all children to be educated in a regular education classroom. If students can learn and achieve better in inclusive programs, then they belong there. If students can succeed only marginally in inclusive education classrooms, some alternate solutions are necessary. A continuum of placement options exists to maximize the goal of educating every child. For some children, a separate class, or even a separate school, is still optimal.

Every child with an exceptional condition is different from every other child in symptoms, needs, and teachability. Each child is, therefore, provided with a unique individualized education plan. This plan consists of both long- and short-term goals for education, specially designed instructional procedures with related services, and methods to evaluate the child's progress. The IEP is updated and revised annually. Special education teachers, parents, and all applicable service providers must collaborate to make recommendations for goals and teaching strategies. The IEPs should always be outcomes-oriented with functional curricula.

Transitional services can help young children with disabilities who have been served by individualized family service programs (IFSPs) before school, make a smooth passage into the public school system. Transitional programs also help modulate the next stages when students with special needs transfer from elementary to middle school, from middle school to high school, from special classes into inclusionary classes, from one school district to another, or from high school to postsecondary academics.

Special educational services are required by law for students from the completion of their public school education through age 21 if they have a diagnosed condition of disability. The U.S. Individuals with Disabilities Education Improvement Act (IDEIA) has made terminal transitional services mandatory. Services are to help students transfer from their relatively protected life into the more aggressive world of work, driven by forces such as money and power.

Every student with a disability should have an individualized transition plan (ITP) added to his or her individualized education plan (IEP) by age 16, the upper limit for beginning transition planning. Transitional services are more difficult to design than educational plans because of the nearly unlimited possibilities for the rest of one's life compared to the defined academic subjects it is possible to learn while in school.

The first article in this Inclusive Education Unit gives an excellent overview of IDEA, one of the most important pieces of U.S. legislation providing for education for children with exceptionalities.

The second selection in this Inclusion Unit is an article by a leading expert on inclusive education. Dr. MaryAnn Byrnes gives twenty pieces of advice for beginning the school year with new students; those with, and without disabilities. These twenty ounces of prevention can be worth more than twenty pounds of remediation.

The third featured article discusses "authentic assessment" and gives twenty suggestions for making education and evaluation of achievement of children with disabilities more appropriate.

"Does This Child Have a Friend?" addresses the needs for social as well as academic support for students with conditions of exceptionality in inclusive classrooms in middle schools.

The final article, "Rethinking Inclusion: Schoolwide Applications," describes a pedagogical strategy that helps make regular and special educational collaboration succeed.

The Issues of IDEA

From funding to teaching to litigation, a look at what prevents the landmark special education law from meeting its core principles.

JOETTA SACK-MIN

In its 31-year history, the Individuals with Disabilities Education Act has pushed the complicated realm of special education into the mainstream of K–12 education. The benefits have been tremendous: Countless students with disabilities have reached a potential that even their greatest advocates did not think was possible.

But as with any law, there were unforeseen consequences and pitfalls, and the emotional aspect of special education has no doubt affected the way these have played out.

Here, we take a brief look at some of the pervasive issues that, despite the law's multiple reauthorizations, threaten the full implementation of IDEA and its core principles.

Funding

Just about any educator would say there is never enough money for K–12 programs, but paying for an appropriate education for each student with disabilities is the leading challenge for districts. Special education is almost always one of the largest line items in federal, state, and local K–12 budgets, yet the need for more funds weighs on nearly every other aspect of the law.

In the original 1975 Education for All Handicapped Children law, Congress promised to pay 40 percent of "excess costs" within seven years to provide an adequate education for students with disabilities, based on the national average for per-pupil expenditures. Even then, President Gerald R. Ford was quite cynical about the law and its funding requirement as he signed it unceremoniously: "Unfortunately, the bill contains more than the federal government can deliver. . . . Even the strongest supporters of this measure know that they are falsely raising the expectations of the groups affected by claiming authorization levels which are excessive and unrealistic."

States have never received more than 20 percent of those promised funds, even after Republican congressional leaders made it their top K–12 spending priority in the late 1990s. Special education enrollments have swelled, and treatments and technologies are far more advanced than in 1975, thus adding to the costs. Federal funding for IDEA has fallen slightly in the most recent budget cycles; this year's budget is $11.4 billion, or about 18 percent of the excess costs.

The funding quandary builds tensions between special education and other K–12 programs. School officials consistently lobby for more federal IDEA funds, saying they could free up many more local funds for other worthy education programs (which are not mandated by law) if the federal government paid its 40 percent share.

State funding for IDEA varies widely. And small districts that receive little state funding are particularly vulnerable—when one or more students' individualized education plans call for extremely expensive services, the entire K–12 budget can be affected.

The money available often has a dramtic *dramatic* impact on the placement and types of services a student with disabilities receives. Lacking sufficient funds, IDEA will never reach its full potential, many say.

Teachers

Nearly every district in the country is desperate for well-qualified special education teachers. The Center on Personnel Studies in Special Education at the University of Florida estimates that more than 50,000 new special education teachers are needed immediately, and it predicts the shortage will only get worse as federal requirements to ensure highly qualified teachers go into effect.

The departure rate of teachers who become certified and teach in special education is high: about 13.5 percent annually, according to COPSSE, compared to about 6.4 percent for general education. Much of this has to do with the demands of the job. Paperwork, large caseloads, lack of support and resources, threats of legal action, and the sometimes-grueling work wear on even the most enthusiastic teachers.

Rural and high-poverty urban districts have always seen the most severe shortages. And while all specialties are in high demand, the area of emotional disturbance has had the greatest shortages in recent years. Further, although more than one-third of special education students are minorities (and misdiagnosis

Key Dates in Special Education Law

Here are key dates and events in special education law over the past 40 years:

1967

Congress establishes the **Bureau of Education for the Handicapped,** which funds special techniques and programs for students with disabilities. These programs were generally segregated from regular classrooms and schools, and the quality was inconsistent. For years, the programs were usually the only option to students with disabilities who were able to gain access.

1972

Pennsylvania Association for Retarded Citizens (PARC) v. Pennsylvania and *Mills v. District of Columbia Board of Education:* These federal court decisions, which ruled that excluding children with disabilities from public education may be a violation of their due process and equal protection rights, helped lay the groundwork, along with the 1954 *Brown* desegregation ruling, for the Education for All Handicapped Children Act.

1973

The Rehabilitation Act becomes law: Section 504 of this law protects qualified individuals from discrimination based on their disability. The law applies to employers and organizations, including schools, which receive financial assistance from any federal department or agency. All students identified as disabled have rights under this law.

1975

President Gerald R. Ford signed the **Education for All Handicapped Children Act (PL 94-142),** the first law that guarantees that students with disabilities have a right to receive a free, appropriate public education (FAPE). Prior to this law, states and school districts decided where and how students with disabilities would be educated.

1982

Hendrick Hudson Central Board of Education v. Rowley: This landmark U.S. Supreme Court decision affirmed the rights of special education students to FAPE. Legal experts see the *Rowley* case as one of the most important in education because it created the standards by which schools decide what services they need to provide to students with disabilities, and it is still often cited in special education legal cases.

1984

Irving Independent School District v. Tatro: This was the first definitive case on schools' obligations to provide medical and related noneducational services within FAPE requirements. The Supreme Court ruled that if a child needed a service to benefit from the special education—unless that service had to be performed by a physician—it would be included in the school's obligation to FAPE. The court's decision was reaffirmed in the 1999 case *Cedar Rapids School District v. Garret F.*

1985

Burlington School Committee v. Department of Education: This case, along with the 1993 *Florence County School District v. Carter,* clarified tuition reimbursement and students' placement while going through legal disputes. The Supreme Court set a three-step process for determining whether the school district should pay for alternative services when a parent challenges the school's FAPE assignments. The rulings have spurred thousands of tuition-reimbursement cases.

1988

Honig v. Doe: In the first Supreme Court case to question the discipline and expulsion of students with disabilities, the Court ruled that districts cannot exclude a special education student for more then 10 days for conduct that was a manifestation of the disability.

1990

The **Individuals with Disabilities Education Act** is born: The reauthorization of the Education for all Handicapped Children Act changes the name to its current IDEA.

1990s

Autism: The 1990 IDEA reauthorization added this perplexing disability to the categories of student classification. Defined as "a developmental disability significantly affecting verbal and nonverbal communication and social interaction, generally evident before age 3," the students classified in this category increased exponentially through the 1990s, leading some parents and researchers to question whether environmental factors such as a child's vaccines could have caused the disability.

1997

IDEA reauthorization: Concerns over school safety and a few high-profile violent incidents by students with disabilities dominated many discussions, and lawmakers debated whether students with disabilities who committed violent acts should continue to be guaranteed an education. Congress added provisions for longer alternate placements but continued the guarantee of FAPE. This reauthorization also put in place new accountability and assessment requirements.

2002

No Child Left Behind Act: This reauthorization of the Elementary and Secondary Education Act brought some of the most sweeping changes ever to federal and state education policies, which in turn affected special education. The law mandates accountability and adequate yearly progress for all students, and dictates that all teachers must meet "highly qualified" criteria.

2004

IDEA reauthorization: This revamping aligned IDEA with the accountability measures under NCLB, making it the first time the education of students with disabilities would be held to high standards alongside their nondisabled peers.

2005

Schaffer v. Weast: In a test of the burden of proof for what constitutes an appropriate education, the Supreme Court ruled that IDEA forces parents, not schools, to prove that their children are not receiving FAPE in legal disputes.

can occur because of a lack of cultural understanding), the special education field tends to be overwhelmingly white.

In 2002, the No Child Left Behind Act mandated that states must ensure that all teachers meet the specifications for a "highly qualified teacher" under state regulations by 2006, although they later gave a one-year reprieve. The 2004 reauthorization of IDEA also adopted that language, which means that all special education teachers must hold full state certification, or pass a test for licensure, in special education and any other fields they teach. Under the proposed regulations, the federal government will set a timeline for all special education teachers to meet this standard, and it will require states to create recruitment and retention policies.

The "highly qualified" requirements will have a major impact on the numbers of teachers entering and staying in the field. In 2004, COPSSE reported that nearly one-third of special education teachers hired were uncertified, and that as many as 20 percent of special education teachers in some states were uncertified.

In addition to the teacher shortfall, districts also have reported growing shortages of special education administrators, paraprofessionals, and other school staff as well as disability specialists, such as speech/language pathologists.

Civil Rights vs. Education

The original IDEA was considered a major civil rights victory, the first time individuals with disabilities were guaranteed the right to receive an appropriate education. Many parents and advocates for children with disabilities—some who had been shut out of schools entirely—were thrilled that the law finally mandated that schools educate their children.

But the perception of IDEA as a civil rights law, many educators say, eventually led to an overemphasis on the process of providing educational services—ensuring that the orders in every student's individualized education plan were followed precisely—rather than evaluating the outcomes of those services. Those processes have contributed to the inherent bureaucracy that bogs down the spirit of the original law and has become a pervasive problem with its implementation.

There's no longer any debate over whether students with disabilities should have access to a classroom. Now, IDEA's focus has shifted from access to accountability to ensure that students with disabilities receive a quality education and show academic progress.

There's no longer any debate over whether students with disabilities should have access to a classroom. Now, IDEA's focus has shifted from access to accountability, to ensure that students with disabilities receive a quality education and show academic progress. In the past two reauthorizations, Congress has moved to instill more accountability into IDEA while decreasing bureaucracy and paperwork requirements, heeding the calls of many educators and school board members. Each school now must ensure that all students with disabilities are making progress toward specific goals set in their IEPs. These students also must be included in each school's annual assessments, with any necessary accommodations, or be assessed with an alternative measurement.

Many special education advocates say that including special education as a subgroup in the 2002 No Child Left Behind requirements for data collection, and the subsequent IDEA reauthorization in 2004, makes the quality of special education a national priority.

"NCLB has been the best thing that ever happened to special education," says Bill East, executive director of the National Association of State Directors of Special Education. Now, "no kids are hidden," he says.

However, implementation of NCLB's accountability provisions has been problematic because of a lack of funding and capacity for data collection and analysis. The new special education assessments and IDEA data collection will continue to be a challenge for states, many of which are already overwhelmed by NCLB's requirements.

Identification

Labeling a student as "special needs" is a profound decision that affects the rest of his or her educational career and life. While some disabilities are easily identifiable and many students are diagnosed before starting school, others do not manifest until a child is struggling in the classroom. School officials must then face often vexing decisions in determining whether that student is eligible for—and truly needs—special education services.

Since the original IDEA became law, special education enrollments have grown exponentially. Today, more than 6.7 million students are labeled as having a disability under 13 categories recognized by IDEA. Much of this growth is attributed to better identification, acceptance, and understanding of disabilities. Students with specific learning disabilities now comprise the largest category of the special education population—more than 48 percent.

Some experts argue that there are simply too many students in special education, and that many would not be classified—particularly those with learning disabilities—if they had been taught appropriately and received early intervention services in the regular classroom. Special educators have long feared that certain populations, particularly African-American males, are unnecessarily referred because teachers do not understand cultural and behavioral differences and can't provide the interventions they need in the regular classrooms. Others cite financial motives: Higher special education enrollments mean more federal and state funding. School administrators readily dismiss that claim and say that payments are so low that it costs the districts more to identify students.

The percentage of special education students in K–12 varies widely between districts, although the national average is about 14 percent. Some of the lowest enrollments are found in high-poverty areas, where environmental risk factors tend to be higher, while some of the highest enrollments are in well-to-do districts.

Some special education experts believe that affluent parents push for accommodations for their children, while low-income districts do not have the infrastructure needed to properly diagnose and educate their students. Others say that parents of children with disabilities move to districts that have the best programs for their child's disability, thus increasing enrollment.

The special education community is particularly intrigued about a relatively new process called "Response to Intervention," which some say will end the "wait-to-fail" mentality that has hindered academic progress and possibly labeled too many students as having learning disabilities. Using a tiered, research-based model, RtI goes through a series of educational or behavioral interventions to avoid labeling a child who might only need a different teaching technique or extra help. This treatment has the potential to dramatically reduce the number of students in special education, some say.

The new IDEA also adds steps to help guard against misdiagnosis. Regulations proposed following the 2004 reauthorization, but not yet approved, add procedures for recognizing specific learning disabilities, and require additional IEP team members who are qualified to provide a specific diagnosis.

But many researchers and educators note that much more research is needed to better understand the myriad of disabilities and find appropriate treatments for students.

Litigation

Overall, education litigation has subsided since the mid-1970s, but the lack of agreement on what constitutes an appropriate education for students with disabilities has resulted in a significant increase in special education lawsuits during that period. Legal issues and the litigious nature of IDEA are frequently cited as top deterrents to the law by both advocates for the disabled and school districts seeking to serve them.

Although disputes between parents and school districts rarely reach the court system, those that are challenged are prominent, and almost always sap money, time, and other resources from both sides.

The 2004 IDEA reauthorization attempted to ease the number of lawsuits filed, most notably by requiring states to offer mediation to parents and school officials. It's too soon to tell whether there will be a significant effect from the revamped law, which went into effect on July 1, 2005, says Perry A. Zirkel, a professor of law and education at Lehigh University.

Zirkel's latest research shows that the number of IDEA-related disputes decided by hearing officers or courts has quadrupled since 1991, with several large spikes followed by plateaus that, when only looking at recent years, appear to show the number of lawsuits subsiding. But Zirkel is not optimistic. The pervasive problem, he says, is that too many people stand to profit from IDEA disputes, from hearing officers to attorneys to publishers of books and newsletters on special education law.

Some legal experts feel the case numbers could even be higher, because districts often settle disputes even when they might have a fair chance at winning a court case, to avoid a costly confrontation. Under IDEA, districts must pay a parent's legal fees if the parent prevails in a court or due process hearing. And because of the often-emotional subject matter, school officials can be seen as "bad guys" during trials. Conversely, some parents may not be willing or able to challenge their children's IEPs.

The most recent rulings of the U.S. Supreme Court have clarified legal processes—which party is responsible for the burden of proof and legal fees—rather than educational needs. For instance, in the 2005 *Schaffer* v. *Weast* ruling, the Court said parents bear the legal burden of proving that a district did not provide an appropriate education for their children.

But the largest issue in special education litigation is FAPE, specifically, the appropriateness of a student's education. Because each case is based on individual matters, the case involving Amy Rowley has ensured that there will always be disputes, Zirkel says.

JOETTA SACK-MIN (jsack@nsba.org) is an associate editor of *American School Board Journal*.

Learn about Your New Students

MaryAnn Byrnes

Each September you meet new students. Knowing as much as possible about them helps the school year begin smoothly for teachers, students, and parents. Though evaluations and progress reports contain essential details, a wealth of information is waiting for you in the minds and files of last year's instructional team. Honest answers to these questions will help you build on the lessons learned last year and get this year off to a running start. My student, "Pat," stands for any student you are welcoming as your own.

1. What Supports Will Help Pat Succeed at the Beginning of this New Year?

Change is difficult for most people. After the "new" becomes familiar, we all settle down. Meanwhile, it is easy to misinterpret a new student's behavior during the first few days. What can last year's team tell you that would help? Will your new student need a visual schedule, an explanation of how this year's expectations differ from last year's, guidance traveling from room to room, encouragement to ask questions, a short-term behavior management program?

2. When Does Pat Need the Most Support?

Some students need support throughout the day. Other students experience times of particular stress. Does your new student require assistance most during independent learning times? Do unstructured activities, such as recess, passing time, or lunch, create a need for adult support?

3. What Can Pat Do Independently?

It is easy to focus on needs but equally important to know areas where a student can work without you. Acknowledging competence and independence communicates confidence in your student. When can you (and your student) anticipate success?

4. How Do You and Pat's Parents Communicate Best?

Establishing communications quickly forges a strong school/home partnership. Do your new student's parents respond best to telephone calls, e-mails, notes sent home? Do they prefer to be called at home, or can they be reached best at work?

5. Where in the Room Does Pat Learn Best?

Although you may prefer clusters or individual desks, there might be one critical area that helps your new student focus. Do windows refresh or distract? Is there a need for an individual carrel? A floor pillow?

6. What Are the Biggest Motivators for Pat?

How did last year's team encourage this student to succeed? Some students crave attention and praise. Others relish earned time with a valued adult. Still others react well to a homework pass or time on the computer.

7. How Does Pat React to Guidance or Correction?

Does this student accept constructive guidance well or become upset if everything is not perfect? Are there language and/or cultural traditions that you should consider?

8. What Is Pat's Favorite Part of School?

Is there a subject area that this student favors? Is group discussion the high point of the day? Are athletics the only reason your new student stays in school? Build on these positive experiences during the tough times to provide motivation and reinforcement.

9. What Is Pat's Least Favorite Part of School?

You can be guaranteed this will be the most difficult part of the day. Knowing ahead of time which activity is least favored will help you prepare.

10. What Frustrates Pat?

What bothers your new student so much that it interferes with school? Struggles with academic work? Interpersonal difficulties? Changes in routine? Family and home issues?

11. What Are the Signs That Pat Is Beginning to Feel Frustrated?

Although it is usually easy to tell when a student is totally frustrated, ask about behavioral cues that appear before a crisis arrives. Does this student fidget more? ask questions more frequently? look distressed? twist hair? stare out the window?

12. What Helps Pat Reduce Frustration?

Different learners respond to different techniques. What works for your new student?

- Collaboration with a peer or diversion to a quiet work space?
- Solitude to concentrate independently or offers of assistance?
- Words of support or time out with a counselor?

13. Who Are Pat's Friends?

Know the classmates with whom your new student is most closely connected. Nurture those friendships, and consider them in your seating arrangements. Do these friends work well together, or do they distract each other?

14. Who Are Pat's Adversaries?

Anticipated problems can be avoided. Use this information as you plan learning groups. Incorporate the issues behind some of these struggles in your class meetings or social skills activities with the entire class.

15. What Are Pat's Strengths?

Too often, we concentrate on learning and behavior problems. Each student has strengths that provide opportunities for you to praise accomplishments and stretch your new student's thinking.

16. What Are Pat's Biggest Learning Challenges?

What is the essence of your new student's learning difficulty? Which areas of learning are the most difficult? What strategies did last year's team try? What worked? Why?

17. What Is the Most Important Skill Pat Learned Last Year?

A prized accomplishment needs to be valued and reinforced. Was self-control during discussions a hard-won success? Did your new student unlock the mysteries of regrouping? What helped your student achieve this growth? Can you use the same strategy this year?

18. What Is the Most Important Skill for Pat to Learn This Year?

Accomplishments lead to new challenges. Of all the possibilities, what is the single most important? Is it academic, behavioral, or interpersonal? Why is this the most important? Does your new student (and his or her parents) agree? This information focuses your efforts and those of your student.

19. What Does Pat Like Best Outside of School?

Knowledge of your student's outside interests generates conversation starters and points of interest on which to build. Should you bone up on Harry Potter or add some books on soccer to your reading list? Can your student serve as an in-class expert on a particular topic?

20. What Did You Know about Pat in June That You Wish You Had Known Last September?

This final, but critical, question leaves the door open for last year's team to tell you what you haven't asked. The answer may be the most important piece of information you receive.

Each September is a fresh start. Learning from last year's instructional team ensures that you and your students make the most of this new year. Now, what would you like to share with those who will teach your former students?

MARYANN BYRNES, EdD, is an assistant professor at the University of Massachusetts Boston, after having been a special education administrator for 18 years. Her research interests include effective participation in standards-based curriculum and controversial issues in special education. Address: MaryAnn Byrnes, 17 Sherbourne Place, Waltham, MA 02451; e-mail: maryann.byrnes@umb.edu.

From *Intervention in School and Clinic,* by MaryAnn Byrnes, Vol. 41, No. 1, September 2005, pp. 13–15. Copyright © 2005 by Pro-Ed, Inc. Reprinted by permission.

Use Authentic Assessment Techniques to Fulfill the Promise of No Child Left Behind

Carol A. Layton and Robin H. Lock

The No Child Left Behind Act (NCLB) of 2001 mandates the nationwide development of state accountability assessment plans for all school districts and students. The bill also requires that the results of these assessments be made available in terms of individual, school, and statewide progress reports. School districts and schools failing to make adequate progress toward statewide proficiency goals must provide supplemental services for their students. These services may include free tutoring, afterschool assistance, and widespread instructional changes in the daily delivery of curriculum. In addition, each state is required to develop statewide curricular goals and objectives that are measured yearly using a state-developed achievement measure.

Progress for students with special needs is also included in this accountability system. In some states, specific guidelines for determining the use of the state-mandated assessment device contain provisions for on-grade-level assessment, below-grade-level assessment, the use of accommodations and modifications during assessment, and the need for student assessment of non-state-guided curricular expectations as delineated in the Individualized Education Program (IEP). While much attention has been given to the development of the state-mandated guidelines for determining accommodations and modifications, many states have encountered difficulty in establishing the appropriate level for assessing students with disabilities receiving special education services on the state-mandated assessment.

One state provides IEP teams with several choices when deciding upon the appropriate expected achievement level for students with disabilities receiving special education services. These choices include

- on-grade-level assessment with or without accommodations through the state-mandated assessment;
- below-grade-level assessment with or without accommodations using a state-developed alternative assessment; or

- a locally determined assessment designed by the IEP team.

IEP teams often report difficultly in pinpointing the appropriate assessment situation and indicate a need for more precise and explicit information for ascertaining the correct assessment.

Authentic assessment provides such a platform for making these types of assessment decisions on an individualized basis. Additionally, by including authentic assessment in the decision-making process, IEP teams honor both the mandates of NCLB and the Individuals with Disabilities Education Improvement Act of 2004, (IDEIA), which requires assessment practices that yield specific, individual results about student achievement that are easily translated into daily instructional practices. The following suggestions present authentic assessment techniques to validate and document the mandates of both NCLB and IDEIA.

1. Collect Daily Work Samples to Show the Student's Actual Progress

The IEP team will use this information to decide whether the student has a beginning, developing, or proficient knowledge of the particular state-mandated goal. This will help determine whether the student is performing on or below grade level on a daily basis.

2. Ensure That the IEP Reflects the Student's Instructional Level

Instructional level refers to beginning, developing, or proficient knowledge of a goal or objective. Goals and objectives should be tied to the state-mandated curriculum to ensure the student's access to the general education curriculum. This connection on the IEP is then documented through authentic assessment to provide specific examples of the student's growth from beginning mastery through proficiency.

3. Create Curriculum-Based Assessments to Link Student Performance to the Curriculum

Curriculum-based assessment (CBA) examines the student's performance on the standards mandated in general education by systematically increasing the difficulty in assignments and engaging in continuous assessments (Burns, 2002). This process links high expectations concerning the student's daily learning to accepted state-mandated indicators of student proficiency.

4. Establish a Baseline Using CBA

Use CBA to establish a baseline or present level of performance (PLOP) for the development of IEPs that coordinate with state-mandated standards and support state-developed assessment. The IEP team can depend on the results of CBA to isolate the suitable assessment level for the individual student with disabilities.

5. Rely on Curriculum-Based Measurement for Determining the Effectiveness of Instruction

Fuchs and Fuchs (2002) identified four factors for making data-based decisions by the IEP team to indicate progress in mastery of state-mandated standards. They are (a) shaping academic growth, (b) differentiating between unproductive instruction and undesirable student learning, (c) enlightening instructional planning, and (d) continually updating instructional effectiveness to increase student progress.

6. Use a Portfolio to Provide a Direct Bond between Instruction and the General Education Classroom Curriculum

The portfolio provides an efficient and convenient system for logging and compiling examples of a student's comprehensive growth over time. The IEP team applies the results of the portfolio to decisions concerning the appropriate assessment based on the student instructional level. Losardo and Notari-Syverson (2001) identified the following components of portfolios, which empower the IEP team with specific information for decision making. Portfolios

- allow for ongoing assessment across environments;
- pass from teacher to teacher or grade to grade, supplying information to ease the student's transition;
- provide many ways of examining a student's performance from a variety of perspectives; and

- improve self-advocacy for students by encouraging their participation in the selection of products and communication about their work.

7. Maintain Classroom Portfolios to Create a Detailed and Complex Picture of the Student's Mastery Over Time

The IEP team will then have concrete examples of the student's actual instructional level (Stiggins, 2001) to make decisions about the student's progress from beginning to proficient mastery and to identify appropriate state-mandated assessment levels.

8. Perform Direct Observations to Record Behavior

Behavioral observations provide the IEP team with a close-up look at on-task behavior and skill performance in a variety of settings. The IEP team makes more valid instructional and assessment decisions when data confirm the results of standardized or previous test scores (Salvia and Ysseldyke, 2001).

9. Employ Direct Observations to Document the Inclusion of Research-based Strategies

In addition to observing the student's behavior, instructional delivery, classroom practices, and student response to research-based strategies can also be monitored. Details about the arrangement of the classroom, grouping for instruction, and teacher response rates and expectations, as well as other daily routines and strategies, are easily obtained through direct observations (Cohen & Spenciner, 2003).

10. Draw on Environmental Assessments to Analyze the Instructional Cycle

Environmental assessments are key elements in improving the curriculum, intervention goals, and procedures (McLean, Wolery, & Bailey, 2004). A fit between individual need and the delivery of instruction, as well as the need for and use of accommodation and modifications in the environment, aids the IEP team in selecting the appropriate state-mandated assessment.

11. Examine Environmental Assessments to Identify Staff Training Needs

Environmental assessments provide documentation of program quality and the types of improvements needed in particular settings (Salvia & Ysseldyke, 2001). Recording research-based practices and evaluating their implementation aids the IEP team in verifying their use and effectiveness in the least restrictive environment. These data direct the IEP team in determining assessment levels and the need for change in instructional practices.

12. Generate Questionnaires to Gather Different Perspectives

By having a variety of individuals complete the same questionnaire, the IEP team obtains multiple sources to document progress (Bauer & Shea, 2003). This information allows the team to become familiar with the student's generalization of the goal and achievement proficiency level.

13. Interview All Stakeholders in the Student's Academic Life

Interviews permit the teacher or examiner to gain insight into the student's life in and beyond the classroom (Spinelli, 2002). They supply the IEP team with facts concerning the use and generalization of academic skills at home and in environments beyond the classroom.

14. Explore the Results of Checklists Based on State-mandated Goals

Checklists should be used frequently to monitor the progress on state-mandated assessment goals. Checklists help determine whether the student is at risk for particular problems. They also document slow or nonexistent achievement to establish the need for changes in the instructional process.

15. Survey the Success and Use of Modifications and Accommodations in a Variety of Environments

Teacher-made checklists reveal the student's existing behaviors in the classroom setting (Gallagher, 1998). Documentation of consistent use of modifications or accommodations provides the IEP team with the rationale for including them in the state-mandated assessment process.

16. Capture Student Achievement Over Time through Rating Scales

Rating scales portray the breadth and depth of student achievement over time (Prestidge & Williams Glaser, 2000). The IEP team evaluates readiness for a particular achievement level on the state-mandated assessment by examining both examples of

daily work and attitudinal dispositions indicating movement toward proficiency.

17. Develop Communication Notebooks to Inform Parents

The communication notebook emphasizes the dual responsibility for student learning (Williams & Cartledge, 1997) by all participants in the system including parents and teachers, students and teachers, and general and special education teachers, as well as others. Communication notebooks enable parents to make more informed decisions about their student's current programming. Frequent interaction between the home and school facilitates the understanding of a student's present level of performance. This awareness improves decision making with respect to the selection and implementation of research-based instructional strategies and determination of appropriate assessment techniques.

18. Journal to Corroborate Student Progress on IEP Goals and Objectives

By providing a connection between participants to record what is happening in the classroom, at home, and in everyday life, journals enhance the quality of the data by providing a holistic observation of the student's progress (English & Gillen, 2001). Journals present an avenue for open lines of communication.

19. Document the Correct Choice for the Level of State-mandated Assessment

Authentic assessment supplies specific examples of student achievement in a variety of settings. These data support the team's decision making concerning the level of assessment as well as appropriate modifications and accommodations for the testing environment.

20. Base Assessment Decisions on NCLB and IDEIA Mandates

NCLB and IDEIA require assessment decisions reflective of the student's strengths and needs rather than relying solely on curricular goals. Authentic assessment bridges the gap between the state-mandated assessment process and NCLB by accurately identifying strengths and needs for more individualized assessment decision making.

References

Bauer, A. M., & Shea, T. M. (2003). *Parents and schools: Creating a successful partnership for students with special needs.* Upper Saddle River, NJ: Merrill/Prentice Hall.

Burns, M. K. (2002). Comprehensive system of assessment to intervention using curriculum-based assessments. *Intervention in School and Clinic, 38*(1), 8–13.

Cohen, L. G., & Spenciner, L. J. (2003). *Assessment of children and youth with special needs.* Boston, MA: Pearson Education, Inc.

English, L. M., & Gillen, M. A. (2001). Journal writing in practice: From vision to reality. *New Directions for Adult and Continuing Education, 90,* 87–94.

Fuchs, L. S., & Fuchs, D. (2002). Curriculum-based measurement: Describing competence, enhancing outcomes, evaluating treatment, effects, and identifying treatment nonresponders. *Peabody Journal of Education, 77*(2), 64–84.

Gallagher, J. D. (1998). *Classroom assessment for teachers.* Upper Saddle River, NJ: Merrill/Prentice Hall.

Individuals with Disabilities Education Improvement Act of 2004, 20 U.S.C. § 1400 *et seq.* (2004) (reauthorization of the Individuals with Disabilities Education Act of 1990).

Losardo, A., & Notari-Syverson, A. (2001). *Alternative approaches to assessing young children.* Baltimore, MD: Paul H. Brookes.

McLean, M., Wolery, M., & Bailey, D. B., Jr. (2004). *Assessing infants and preschoolers with special needs* (3rd ed.). Upper Saddle River, NJ: Prentice Hall.

No Child Left Behind Act of 2001, 20 U.S.C. § 6301 *et seq.* (2002).

Prestidge, L. K., & Williams Glaser, C. H. (2000). Authentic assessment: Employing appropriate tools for evaluating students' work in 21st-century classrooms. *Intervention and School and Clinic, 35*(3), 178–182.

Salvia, J., & Ysseldyke, J. E. (2001). *Assessment* (8th ed.). Boston, MA: Houghton Mifflin.

Spinelli, C. G. (2002). *Classroom assessment for students with special needs in inclusive settings.* Upper Saddle River, NJ: Prentice Hall.

Stiggins, R. J. (2001). *Student-involved classroom assessment* (3rd ed.) Upper Saddle River, NJ: Prentice Hall.

Williams, V. I., & Cartledge, G. (1997). Passing notes-to parents. *Teaching Exceptional Children, 30*(1), 30–35.

CAROL A. LAYTON, EdD, associate professor, is an assessment specialist at Texas Tech University. Her interests include the authentic assessment of intrinsic processing disorders and the synthesis of evaluation results in planning successful interventions. **ROBIN H. LOCK,** PhD, is an associate professor at Texas Tech University. Her research interests include the role of intrinsic processing disorders in the diagnosis of learning disabilities and the provision of effective interventions and accommodations for students. Address: Carol A. Layton, Texas Tech University, College of Education, Box 41071, Lubbock, TX 79409-1071; e-mail: carol.layton@ttu.edu.

From *Intervention in School and Clinic,* by Carol A Layton and Robin H. Lock, Vol. 42, No. 3, January 2007, pp. 169–173. Copyright © 2007 by Pro-Ed, Inc. Reprinted by permission via Rightslink.

Does This Child Have a Friend?

Segregated into separate classrooms for much of the day, left out at gym, not invited to the weekend slumber party—by middle school, students with disabilities can face overwhelming peer exclusion, even in schools with inclusive classrooms. Innovative social inclusion programs are turning the tide, reducing the social isolation of students with disabilities, ending harassment and stereotyping, and improving life opportunities.

MARY M. HARRISON

Laughing and snapping pictures, students make their way around tables in the noisy, crowded rooms at Margarita's Mexican Grill in Santa Clarita, Calif. They stop to talk to friends, as well as the teachers and administrators who have joined them for dinner this Wednesday evening. The 40 or so students, from junior and senior high schools in the William S. Hart Union High School District, are participants in a program called "Yes I Can."

J.J., a sophomore with brown hair falling over his ears, stops to hug the district's speech and language specialist. He pauses to mug for a photo with Elliot, another sophomore, whose smile stretches across his face. Spying other friends at tables across the room, J.J. takes off. "I'm loving this!" he calls out.

The dinner at Margarita's helps raise funds for the students' year-end rock concert. But the outing has another purpose—to give students with and without disabilities a chance to have a good time together. About half the students here tonight have a significant disability that in the past has isolated them, socially and sometimes physically, from their peers. J.J. has a form of autism called Asperger's syndrome, sometimes more problematic because it is unnoticeable in appearance.

Emily Iland is one of many parents here tonight, laughing and talking among themselves. Iland's son Tom, now a college student, also has Asperger's syndrome. In 2001, hoping to alleviate the harassment and social isolation Tom had experienced, Iland helped to bring the Yes I Can program to the Hart district. (See "Case Study.")

Iland says parents understand the effects of social isolation at school—the often total absence of phone calls from classmates and activities with peers—in ways that teachers often cannot. At gatherings like the one at Margarita's, she says, "It's such a relief to see your kid happy, accepted, part of the group."

The Causes and the Costs

Social isolation and the harassment of students with disabilities are closely related problems that occur in schools throughout the country. Often, both problems begin in middle school, as children's elementary school friends fade from the picture.

Developmentally, says Martha Snell, a professor of education at the University of Virginia, middle school students possess the tendency to mock differences, whether racial, economic or ability-related. As a result, Snell says, "you can predict that a person with a disability will be made fun of unless there are some things in those kids' lives to counter that, to say this is not a good thing."

Social isolation and harassment can feed each other—without meaningful interaction with students with disabilities, other students are more likely to make hurtful remarks based on stereotypes. In return, faced with the threat of being teased, students with disabilities are less likely to assert themselves. Without deliberate interventions, the cycle can be never-ending—sometimes with extreme personal and academic consequences.

If not addressed, social isolation can deprive students of important social skills needed for post-secondary school, jobs and happy lives—skills most other students pick up naturally as they enjoy give-and-take with peers. And harassment and loneliness undoubtedly contribute to a dropout rate that is double that of students without disabilities.

Students without disabilities lose out, too, when their peers remain isolated: They become more likely to absorb the stereotypes and fears about people with disabilities that pervade American society, and they miss opportunities to learn new perspectives from people with different life experiences.

Barbara Trader is the executive director of TASH, an international disability advocacy association at the forefront of social inclusion efforts. Trader believes that one of the most destructive

14

attitudes in society is that people with disabilities are somehow less—less human, less likely to be aware of what's going on around them, less sensitive.

"Until a person establishes a personal relationship with another person who has a disability, they don't understand how wrong that is, how mean-spirited, how prejudicial," Trader says.

Inclusion Makes the Difference

Many schools use inclusive classrooms—the placement of students with disabilities in general education classes—as a tool for integrating students into the school community. This is a good first step. Fewer schools, though, offer social inclusion efforts in or beyond the classroom.

Yet disability experts agree that informal interaction between students with and without disabilities is a necessary antidote to isolation and teasing.

Some school districts are taking heed, creating programs so students with and without disabilities can spend casual time together as peers, sharing common interests and socializing.

Called social inclusion programs, these efforts vary in design and structure, but the most successful programs reflect best practices identified by disability experts:

- opportunities for fun activities in relaxed settings outside of the classroom;
- one-on-one relationships between students with and without disabilities, based on equality and common interests;
- school-wide effort to promote respect for differences among all students—not a project relegated only to one class;
- expectations that young people with disabilities will express everything they need to engage in activities and that their needs will be met;
- discussions about disabilities that dispel myths and stereotypes;
- continuation of relationships/program involvement for a full school year.

In a twist that seems equally ironic and hopeful, young teens—the age group most likely to bully mercilessly—often seem the most enthusiastic about participating in social inclusion programs.

At Palmetto Middle School in Williamston, S.C., for example, teacher Jennifer Dorriety introduced an inclusion program called Gym Friends last fall. (See "Case Study.") Seventy-five students volunteered—far more than she had expected. Fifty more volunteers have since asked to be included.

Recently, one of the 6th-grade participants encountered a group of 8th graders making snide remarks to a student with a disability in the boys' bathroom. The 6th grader put a quick stop to it by saying, "You wouldn't treat your friends that way, and I don't like when you treat my friend that way." Then he walked the student back to Dorriety's classroom and explained what had happened.

Case Study
California

Yes I Can

In the mid-1990s, after parents in Minnesota begged for help for their teens' social isolation, staff at the Institute on Community Integration at the University of Minnesota developed the Yes I Can Social Inclusion Curriculum. Today, the program is used in secondary schools across the country as a class for credit, an after-school program or a part of service-learning initiatives.

In Santa Clarita, Calif., the 20-lesson curriculum helps students with and without disabilities get to know one another, learn specifics about disabilities and the misconceptions that surround them, learn communication and friendship skills, and work as teams to identify and eliminate barriers to inclusion in their schools and communities.

The students pair up, based on common interests, and plan activities outside of class. A student with strong social skills, with or without a disability, takes the role of mentor. A student who wants to build social skills, usually a student with a disability, is the partner.

At West Ranch High School, freshman Evan calls himself a "Yes I Can success story" whose grades went from straight F's to straight A's through the boost in confidence and new interest in school he received from mentors.

"Mentors give us a reason to come to school," Evan says. "We know when we come that we'll have some friends here. (They) accept us for the person we are. They always have our back."

Snell, the education professor, isn't surprised by the response of students at Palmetto. She says intervention with students in middle school can affect rapid change—especially when it involves doing things that are novel and fun.

A positive experience, which Snell calls "the biggest antidote to bullying," can cause middle school students to cease bullying and quickly turn into advocates, she says. "And from then on," she adds with a laugh, "they can almost get into fights as defenders."

Social inclusion programs can have spillover effects, too, slowly changing attitudes not just among participating students, but challenging the climate of the entire school. Aileen, a senior at St. Paul, Minn.'s private Cretin-Derham Hall, participates in the school's Friendship Club program. (See "Case Study.")

Her experience has made her reflect on peers' use of words like "retarded" as commonplace put-downs.

"At one point in life, I threw it around, as well," Aileen says. "But now, (with) my friends, I say, 'Hey, use a different word. You're taking something that's bothersome to you and putting a word to it that describes people. And they're my friends.'"

Case Study
South Carolina

Gym Friends

At Palmetto Middle School in Williamston, S.C., special education teacher Jennifer Dorriety noticed how other students would smirk or giggle at her students' appearance when she walked them to the cafeteria.

Dorriety knew that the five students in her self-contained classroom, who have intellectual disabilities and mostly non-verbal communication skills, had gifts and talents to share with others.

"I don't want people to feel sorry for my kids," Dorriety says. "I want them to understand the disabilities and the limitations they may have and adapt their dealings to (those). But I also want people to know that (my students) are more than somebody who just needs to be taken care of."

Hoping to achieve those goals and reduce the teasing, and with the help of a Teaching Tolerance grant, Dorriety launched a program called Gym Friends. The idea is pretty simple: student volunteers spend their after-lunch recess in the gym, helping the school's 22 students with disabilities enjoy new sports.

The whole group interacts, but Dorriety also partners each of her students one-on-one with a volunteer, to deepen the peer-to-peer understanding.

The program's impact has spread beyond the students involved, Dorriety says. Volunteers have taken steps to challenge and change attitudes of peers not involved in the program. Most of all, it's hard not to notice the high-fives and hugs — not smirks — her students now receive in the halls and cafeteria.

Case Study
Minnesota

Friendship Clubs

Math teacher Paul Nyberg, whose sister, now deceased, had Down syndrome, was concerned that students at his private Catholic school, Cretin-Derham Hall in St. Paul, Minn., had few opportunities to get to know peers with significant disabilities.

After speaking with his principal, Nyberg reached out to parent Pat Leseman. Two of her sons attended Cretin-Derham, while a third son, who had developmental disabilities, attended a nearby public school.

The timing was perfect: Leseman and another Cretin-Derham mother, Rosemary Fagrelius, had recently formed a new community organization, the Highland Friendship Club, to provide much-needed summer recreation opportunities for their sons and other young people with disabilities.

Now that school had started, their club wanted to socialize with students without disabilities, and they needed a place to meet.

The Cretin-Derham Hall Friendship Club was launched a year later, and, today, it meets frequently with the Highland club for art and music classes and other activities. Together, the groups host an annual interdenominational spiritual retreat and a dance. During basketball season, they meet for pizza and go to games together.

The partnership gives Highland club members the opportunity "to do what every other high school student does on Friday and Saturday night," Fagrelius says. "It's a godsend for our whole community."

One Passionate Teacher

People with disabilities have experienced a long history of exclusion from public schools. Prior to 1975, states could lawfully refuse to serve students with disabilities. That year, when Congress passed the first law guaranteeing an education to students with disabilities, an estimated one million students were being left out of the public education system.

The landmark law, now known as the Individuals with Disabilities Act, mandates a free and appropriate public education for students with disabilities, with an emphasis on inclusive classrooms.

Yet in 2000, a report to Congress showed that less than half of all students with disabilities experienced inclusive classroom settings for 80 percent or more of each school day. The rates for students with significant disabilities were much lower.

Experts say the No Child Left Behind Act's emphasis on testing has compounded the classroom isolation. Expensive testing means social programs are put on the back burner in many schools.

"Right now, no one is asking the question, 'Does this child have a friend?'" says Brian Abery, who helped developed

the Yes I Can curriculum. "Research clearly suggests that for kids with significant disabilities, an ability to develop lasting friendships and a close circle of support has a lot more to do with their success later in life than how well they can balance a checkbook."

In this environment, how can social inclusion programs get off the ground?

Abery advises starting small and being flexible. If one passionate teacher gains the support of administrators, he says, "the program will sell itself."

Resources

The *Yes I Can Social Inclusion Curriculum for Students With and Without Disabilities* ($49), is a yearlong, 20-lesson curriculum that fosters the social inclusion of secondary students with disabilities in their schools and communities. Instructions for use are included; on-site training and follow-up by program staff also is available.

The Institute on Community Integration is seeking schools to pilot a related service-learning program for elementary, middle and high schools.

Yes I Can Program
Institute on Community Integration,
University of Minnesota
www.ici.umn.edu/yesican

TASH (formerly The Association for the Severely Handicapped) is an international membership organization of people working to build inclusive communities through research, education and advocacy. TASH offers professional development to educators and publishes the peer-reviewed journal, *Research and Practice for Persons with Severe Disabilities*. www.tash.org

Easter Seals offers a wealth of information that could be used in social inclusion programs, including "Understanding Disability," "Myths and Facts about People with Disabilities," and "Friends Who Care." www.easterseals.com

Teaching Tolerance offers grants of up to $2,500 to help educators develop and implement innovative anti-bias projects in their classrooms and schools. www.teachingtolerance.org/grants

MARY M. HARRISON, a regular contributor to *Teaching Tolerance*, is a freelance writer in St. Charles, Mo.

Rethinking Inclusion

Schoolwide Applications

"Inclusion" is usually regarded as the placement of special education students in general education settings. But Mr. Sailor and Ms. Roger present a new vision of integrated education, in which previously specialized adaptations and strategies are used to enhance the learning of all students.

WAYNE SAILOR AND BLAIR ROGER

As a field, special education presents an excellent case study of the paradox of differentiation and integration, wherein we seek solutions through increased specialization but, in so doing, we redefine a problem in terms of discrete parts at the expense of the whole. As Thomas Skrtic pointed out more than a decade ago, a large and ever-widening gap exists between the purpose of special education—to provide needed supports, services, adaptations, and accommodations to students with disabilities in order to preserve and enhance their educational participation in the least restrictive environment—and its practice.[1] And that practice has evolved over three decades into a parallel and highly differentiated educational structure, often with only loosely organized connections to the general education system.[2]

Having disengaged from general education early on, special education began to undergo a process that, at times, has seemed to mimic cell division. At one point in its ontogeny, the field could list some 30 distinct eligibility categories for special education services (e.g., learning disabilities, behavioral disorders, severe disabilities, autism, and so on).[3] Many of these early categories further subdivided, with autism, for example, splitting into a host of subcategories lumped under "autism spectrum disorders."[4]

How has all of this come about? The paradox of differentiation and integration—with its tensions in practice and contradictions in policy—offers a reasonable hypothesis. In our efforts to better meet the educational needs of specific identifiable groups, we have promoted differentiation at the expense of integration. If such a policy produced exemplary outcomes, the only remaining questions would concern how to direct scarce resources to meet the needs of a few individuals, and the values underlying special education would no doubt resolve the tension in favor of customization and differentiation. But the positive outcomes don't seem to be there.[5]

In its early days, special education embraced the diagnostic/prescriptive model characteristic of modern medicine, and disability was viewed as pathology. Psychology, with its partner the test industry, became the "gatekeeper" for special education. Students referred by teachers and parents were diagnosed in one of the categories of disability and tagged for separate (highly differentiated) treatment. Indeed, special education policy handbooks at the district level came to resemble the *Diagnostic and Statistical Manual* of the American Psychiatric Association.

Then in the 1980s, the U.S. Department of Education began to advance policy reforms designed to slow the growth in the number of special education categorical placements and practices. These initiatives occurred against a backdrop of publications citing positive outcomes from integrated practices and a corresponding barrage of studies associating separate classrooms and pullout practices with negative outcomes.[6]

The first of these reforms was called the Regular Education Initiative and was designed to stimulate the provision of special education supports and services in general education classrooms. It generated enormous controversy within special education. Indeed, a special issue of the *Journal of Learning Disabilities* was devoted entirely to an attempt to refute the research underlying the policy.[7] Framing the reform of special education policy as general education policy ("regular" education initiative) failed completely within the community of special education.

More recently, federal policy has advanced "inclusion" as recommended practice and has expended significant funds for training, research, and demonstration purposes. This initiative, too, has failed to significantly change special education placement and service configurations, over about a 15-year period. Again, the policy has drawn fire from within special education and has failed to attract interest and enthusiasm from general education.[8]

The No Child Left Behind (NCLB) legislation, for all its problems, does offer special education an opportunity to pursue once again the pathway to integration. First, NCLB makes clear that *all children* in public education are general education students. Second, the law is firmly anchored in accountability, even going so far as to define "evidence" and to restrict scientific inquiry to approved methodologies. If students identified for special education are placed in general education settings and provided with specialized services and supports, and if evidence for academic and social outcomes is to be evaluated according to approved methodologies, then there is an opportunity to achieve a measure of integrated education policy. And the sum of available evidence overwhelmingly supports integrated instructional approaches over those that are categorically segregated,[9] regardless of the categorical label or severity of the disability.[10]

A Schoolwide Approach

That inclusion policy has failed to garner much support from general education can be partially attributed to the way "inclusion" has been defined. Virtually all definitions begin with a general education classroom as the unit of interest and analysis for the provision of supports and services. The problem with a general-classroom-based model is that it doesn't seem credible to the general education teacher, whose job is usually seen as moving students as uniformly as possible through the curriculum. Students whose disabilities impede them from progressing at the expected rate and who, as a result, fall whole grade levels behind their classmates on various components of the curriculum seem to belong elsewhere. Special education has usually been there to oblige with separate categorical placements, particularly when "inclusion" has been tried and has "failed."

Alternatively, when inclusion is a core value of the school program, students with IEPs (individualized education programs) who cannot function in various components of the classroom curriculum often find themselves at tables, usually in the back of the classroom, with paraprofessionals who, in a one-on-one approach, work with them on "something else." This practice not only segregates special education students within the general education classroom but also creates a distraction that has a detrimental effect on general and special education students alike.[11]

But does inclusion need to be tied to a classroom-based model? If the objective is to avoid separate, categorical placements as the chief alternative to general education placements, then can we shift the unit of analysis from the classroom to the school? So if Joey is a student who, because of his disabilities, cannot progress at grade level in the third grade, then we can ask, For those portions of the third-grade curriculum that Joey cannot successfully engage, even with support, where should he be? With whom? And doing what? The problem then becomes one of scheduling, personnel deployment, and the use of space, not one of alternative placement.

A schoolwide approach is not a variation on the older "pull-out" model. Under emerging schoolwide models, students with IEPs are not removed from general education classrooms to receive one-on-one therapies and tutorials or to go to "resource rooms." Following the logic of integration, all services and supports are provided in such a way as to benefit the maximum number of students, including those not identified for special education. Indeed, in recent years, special education has developed evidence-based practices that have been shown to work for general education students as well. Learning strategies, positive behavior support, and transition planning are three excellent examples.[12] Here's a good summary of this new kind of thinking:

> In a transformed urban school, then, learning and other educational supports are organized to meet the needs of all students rather than historical conventions or the way the rooms are arranged in the building. Creative reallocation of even limited resources and innovative reorganization of teachers into partnerships and teams offer ways to break old molds and create the flexibilities needed to focus on student learning and achievement. Previously separate "programs," like special education, Title I, or bilingual education, come together to form a new educational system that delivers necessary additional supports and instruction in the same spaces to diverse groups of students. The new system anchors both organizational and professional effort in student content, performance, and skill standards that are owned by local communities and families while informed by national and state standards, curriculum frameworks, and effective assessment strategies.[13]

The Individuals with Disabilities Education Act (IDEA) contains language in its "incidental benefits" section that encourages applications of special education that hold promise for general education students. This approach enables special educators to support students with special needs by means of integrated arrangements.

Three decades of comprehensive special education have produced an extraordinary wealth of pedagogical adaptations and strategies to enhance learning. This unique set of conditions came about through the provision of set-aside funds for research under IDEA, and much of that research has focused on problem-solving strategies that can benefit any hard-to-teach students. Today, NCLB exhorts us to teach all students to the highest attainable standards. Special education has designed instructional enhancements that can facilitate this outcome, but for these research-based enhancements to benefit all students, special education needs to be integrated with general education. Emerging schoolwide approaches and the call for a "universal design for learning"[14] represent early efforts in this direction.

When a schoolwide approach is applied to "lowperforming" schools, such as those sometimes found in isolated rural settings or in inner-city areas affected by conditions of extreme poverty, mounting evidence suggests that integrated applications of special education practices can yield positive outcomes for all students. For example, when fully integrated applications of learning strategies designed originally for students with specific learning disabilities have been implemented, scores on NCLB-sanctioned accountability measures for all students have increased. Where social development is at issue, the use of schoolwide positive behavior support has led to higher standardized test scores for general education students in low-performing schools.[15]

SAM

To illustrate how an integrated model works in practice, we describe below our own version of such an approach, called SAM for Schoolwide Applications Model, which is being implemented and evaluated in eight California elementary and middle schools and in one elementary school in Kansas City, Kansas. We describe this model in terms of six "guiding principles," which can be broken down into 15 "critical features." Each feature can be evaluated over time using SAMAN (Schoolwide Applications Model Analysis System), an assessment instrument designed to enable schools themselves to link specific interventions to academic and social outcomes for all students. While this approach can appear to mimic comprehensive school reform in some ways, it is specifically designed to be integrated into the existing values and culture of each individual school. In other words, under SAM, a school that wishes to unify its programs and resources is presented with the 15 critical features and instructed to use team processes to implement them according to its own culture and time lines. Across our nine research sites, we are seeing great diversity and creativity on the part of school teams.

Guiding Principles and Critical Features

Guiding principle 1. General education guides all student learning. As a fully integrated and unified model, SAM proceeds on the key assumption that all student learning is guided by a district's framework for curriculum, instruction, and assessment and is thus aligned with state standards. Four critical features support this principle: 1) all students attend their regularly assigned school; 2) all students are considered general education students; 3) general education teachers are responsible for all students; and 4) all students are instructed in accordance with the general education curriculum.

Most teacher training programs today continue to encourage general education teachers to expect special education teachers to assume primary responsibility for students with IEPs. Special education departments at colleges and universities reinforce this notion by training special education teachers in self-contained classrooms and by having little overlap with general education departments, such as departments of curriculum and instruction.[16] An integrated schoolwide model, on the other hand, essentially requires teachers to see their role differently. At SAM schools, the general education teacher is the chief agent of each child's educational program, with support from a variety of others. Using SAM, general education teachers have primary responsibility for all students, consider themselves responsible for implementing IEPs, and collaborate with special education professionals to educate students with disabilities.

Furthermore, this guiding principle encourages schools to avoid such alternative placements as special schools for students who need extensive services and supports. Through SAM, schools welcome these students and configure any funding that comes with them to benefit a variety of students through integrated applications.

At our research sites, it is school policy to encourage parent participation and involvement, and parents are given extensive information about the schoolwide model. In those rare cases when parents feel strongly that their child requires a separate, self-contained placement—and the district concurs—the student may be referred to a comparable non-SAM school that offers self-contained classes for students with disabilities.

SAM does not allow for separate classes for students with disabilities at the school site, so the challenge is to focus on how such students can be supported in the general education classroom, how they can be supported in other environments, and how specialized therapies and services can be provided. The use of space, the deployment of support personnel, and scheduling issues become significant. At SAM schools, very little attention is focused on the existence of disabilities among some students. Every effort is made to foster friendships and positive relationships among students with and without disabilities.

SAM differs from traditional inclusion models by ensuring that students with IEPs are pursuing goals and objectives matched to and integrated with the curriculum being implemented in the general education classroom. Under SAM, no student with disabilities would be found at the rear of a classroom, engaged with a paraprofessional on some task that is unrelated to what the rest of the class is doing. If the class is engaged in a higher level curricular activity, say, algebra, and a student with disabilities cannot engage that material with measurable benefit, then that student might be assigned to an integrated grouping outside of the classroom for that period. In that case, instruction in remedial math would take place with general education students who are also operating at the same curricular level.

There are times, of course, when one-on-one instruction is appropriate in the general education classroom, but this option would be available to any student who could benefit rather than restricted solely to students identified for special education. For example, any child who needs intensive instruction in reading might receive a 30-minute tutorial session in the school's learning center while the rest of the class is engaged in a reading exercise.

Guiding principle 2. All school resources are configured to benefit all students. Three critical features support this principle: 1) all students are included in all activities; 2) all resources benefit all students; and 3) the school effectively incorporates general education students in the instructional process.

In traditional schools, students in special education often do not accompany general education students on field trips; attend sporting events, assemblies, performances, and after-school programs; or take part in specialized reading, math, and science programs or enrichment programs in the arts. SAM schools seek to overcome such barriers to inclusion in all regular school events. All students with IEPs are members of age-appropriate, grade-level classrooms, and they attend all non-classroom functions with their classmates.

Large SAM schools, particularly secondary schools, also make use of small-group arrangements at the classroom level and small learning communities at the school level. Cooperative learning groups, student-directed learning, peer tutorials, peer-mediated instructional arrangements, and so on can greatly enhance outcomes for all students in integrated instructional settings. In addition, particularly in large middle schools and high schools, teams of general and support teachers skilled in math or literacy can use learning centers to support any student's needs. The learning center becomes flexible space for tutorial services offered by teachers or volunteer members of the National Honor Society, as well as a place to make up tests, complete homework with assistance, see a missed film, find resources for a paper or project, and so forth.

Guiding principle 3. Schools address social development and citizenship forthrightly. A single critical feature undergirds this principle: the school incorporates positive behavior support (PBS) at the individual, group, and schoolwide levels. PBS was originally developed as specialized instruction in social development for students with behavioral disabilities. But it has demonstrated its efficacy for all students, particularly those in schools challenged by urban blight and poverty.[17] SAM schools incorporate schoolwide PBS as a comprehensive intervention package to help meet the social development needs of all students.

Guiding principle 4. Schools are democratically organized, data-driven, problem-solving systems. Four critical features support this principle: 1) the school is data-driven and uses team processes; 2) all personnel take part in the teaching/learning process; 3) the school employs a noncategorical lexicon; and 4) the school is governed by a site leadership team.

SAM schools are encouraged to upgrade district software to enable the leadership team to make use of all available databases that affect the social and academic performance of students. Through a process called schoolcentered planning, SAM schools use a variety of performance data fields, disaggregated at the district level, to make decisions regarding priorities related to school improvement.

SAM schools recognize that all salaried personnel at a school can contribute to the teaching/learning process. A custodian may have hidden talents for vocational training, or a speech therapist may be skilled in musical composition. The trick is to enable all school personnel to contribute to the primary mission of the school and not to be completely constrained by bureaucratic specifications of roles. SAM schools also seek to move away from such categorical descriptors as "learning disabilities," "inclusion," "specials," and so on. There are just two kinds of teachers in a SAM school: classroom teachers and support teachers.

The trick is to enable all school personnel to contribute to the mission of the school.

A site leadership team is established at each SAM school. It represents all school personnel and may include parents and members of the local community. This team undertakes the process of school-centered planning to evaluate data related to student academic and social performance, to prioritize specific interventions to improve outcomes, and to advance the mission of the school through full implementation of SAM.

Guiding principle 5. Schools have open boundaries in relation to their families and communities. Two critical features support this guiding principle: 1) schools have working partnerships with their students' families; and 2) schools have working partnerships with local businesses and service providers.

SAM schools go beyond the traditional structure of parent/teacher organizations and solicit the active participation of family members in the teaching/learning process. Some SAM sites have made the establishment of a family resource center at the school a top priority. Some have even created a "parent liaison" position.

SAM schools also reach beyond the "business partnership" relationship that has characterized some school reform efforts. Schools undertake a "community mapping" process to understand their respective communities. Under many circumstances, the school community may not be geographically defined. But the point is to engage the school's constituents in the life of the school.

Furthermore, effective community partnerships set the stage for meaningful service-learning opportunities and open up possibilities for community-based instruction for any student. Students with IEPs, for example, who cannot engage a secondary-level, classroom-based math curriculum, might take part in "community math" in real-life applied settings such as banks and stores. Other students who are chronically unmotivated by school may reconnect with the learning process through community-based learning opportunities.

Guiding principle 6. Schools enjoy district support for undertaking an extensive systems-change effort. Just one critical feature is necessary here: schoolwide models such as SAM that offer a significant departure from traditional bureaucratic management and communication processes must have district support. One way to garner such support is to set up pilot projects with the understanding that expansion to additional sites is contingent on documented gains in measured student academic and social outcomes. District-level support may be expected to increase following successful demonstrations and sharing results across schools over time.

Measurement Strategies

Each SAM school employs a package of psychometrically established instruments with which to assess progress related to the priorities that were established through the school-centered planning process. These instruments include a schoolwide evaluation tool to assess support for positive behavior,[18] SAMAN to assess the 15 critical features of SAM, and EVOLVE to assess the training of paraprofessionals and the ways they are deployed.[19]

Districts are encouraged to use the COMPASS Data Analyzer[20] as an adjunct to the districtwide data system to enable each SAM school to receive feedback about its own priorities and specific data of interest. The program also facilitates reporting to the other teams and committees at the school.

Structural Elements of SAM

SAM is a fully integrated and unified approach to the education of all students. As a process, it is intended to enable schools to engage in collaborative, team-driven decision making that is focused on interventions designed to enhance academic and social outcomes for students. The process of educating all students together presents both challenges and opportunities. The SAM approach requires certain structural elements to be in place. As touched upon earlier, two elements, a site leadership team and school-centered planning, must be present at the school level. And two more elements, a district leadership team and a district resource team, must be present at the district level.

Site leadership team. The SLT, usually with between eight and 12 members, evaluates schoolwide data on student progress; sets priorities, goals, and objectives for each school term; and networks with and reports to the other teams and committees that function at the school. The principal is usually a member of the SLT but does not need to be its chair. Membership on SLTs is usually determined by a combination of internal teacher nominations, with elections for one-year renewable terms; principal appointments; and invitations to specific parents and community members. Expenses incurred by parent and community participants, the cost of substitutes for participating teachers who attend out-of-class meetings, the cost of supplies, and so on, can become budget items for SLTs. SLTs follow strict team procedures with regard to agenda, floor time, minutes, and so on, so that precious time is not wasted. SLTs meet at least biweekly and undergo full-day "retreats" at least twice a year, prior to the beginning of each new term. The school-centered-planning process takes place during these retreats.

School-centered planning. The SCP process is patterned after empowerment evaluation.[21] Using this process, a facilitator, supplied by the district or arranged through a university partnership, assists the SLT to begin with a vision for why the school decided to become a SAM school. A set of goals is derived to make the vision real, and a set of specific objectives for the coming term is spelled out for the various school/ community personnel. Measurement strategies are identified for each objective so that subsequent planning and objective setting can take account of data on pupil performance that are linked to specific measurable processes. The SLT holds interim meetings to review progress in the implementation of each SCP action plan for the term.

District leadership team. The DLT consists of district personnel with an interest in implementing SAM. The superintendent may well be a member but usually will not be the chair. DLTs are frequently chaired by the head of curriculum and instruction, since SAM processes are driven primarily by general education. Other members of the DLT typically include the head of pupil support services, the special education director, the Title I director, and the director of programs for second-language learners. The superintendent may appoint other members as needed. The DLT usually meets three or four times a year to review SAM school-site plans and to consider requests for approval of policy and budget items arising from these plans.

District resource team. The final structural component is the DRT. This team is usually made up of district-level staff members who work closely with the schools, such as regional special education personnel, grade-level specialists, the parent support coordinator, and transportation officials. The function of the DRT is to help the DLT consider requests for resources from each school site for the coming term. If, for example, a SAM site requests two additional paraprofessionals to implement one or more objectives on its plan for the coming term, the DRT will consider the request, balance the needs of that site against the collective needs of all district schools, and make recommendations to the DLT. Typically, DRTs with several SAM sites in the district will meet on a fairly frequent basis to help the district stay ahead of the curve of systems change.

The Schoolwide Applications Model is a work in progress. It represents an effort to integrate all aspects of comprehensive school reform with a new and innovative approach to the delivery of special education supports and services. Research must continue if we are to determine whether the premise of SAM holds: namely, that dedifferentiated educational practices can support personalized learning—in and outside of classrooms—while creating a sense of unity and a culture of belonging in the school.

References

1. Thomas M. Skrtic, *Behind Special Education: A Critical Analysis of Professional Culture and School Organization* (Denver: Love Publishing, 1991).
2. Steven J. Taylor, "Caught in the Continuum: A Critical Analysis of the Principle of the Least Restrictive Environment," *Journal of the Association for Persons with Severe Handicaps,* vol. 13, 1988, pp. 41–53.
3. Wayne Sailor and Doug Guess, *Severely Handicapped Students: An Instructional Design* (Boston: Houghton Mifflin, 1983).
4. Johnny L. Matson, *Autism in Children and Adults: Etiology, Assessment, and Intervention* (Pacific Grove, Calif.: Brookes/ Cole, 1994).
5. See for example, Wayne Sailor, testimony before the Research Agenda Task Force of the President's Commission on Excellence in Special Education, 18 April 2002.
6. See, for example, Diane Lea Ryndak and Douglas Fisher, eds., *The Foundations of Inclusive Education: A Compendium of Articles on Effective Strategies to Achieve Inclusive Education,* 2nd ed. (Baltimore: TASH, 2003), available at www.tash .org; and Margaret Wang, Maynard C. Reynolds, and Herbert J. Wahlberg, eds., *Handbook of Special Education: Research and Practice Vol. 1: Learner Characteristics and Adaptive Education* (Oxford: Pergamon Press, 1987).
7. See *Journal of Learning Disabilities,* vol. 21, 1988.
8. James M. Kauffman, Kathleen McGee, and Michele Brigham, "Enabling or Disabling? Observations on Changes in Special Education," *Phi Delta Kappan,* April 2004, pp. 613–20;

and Larry M. Lieberman, "Special Education and Regular Education: A Merger Made in Heaven?," *Exceptional Children,* vol. 51, 1985, pp. 513–16.

9. An exception can be made for students with a hearing problem. Some recent research suggests that instruction delivered in American Sign Language results in better academic outcomes than interpreted instruction in general education classrooms.

10. Wayne Sailor and Kathy Gee, "Progress in Educating Students with the Most Severe Disabilities: Is There Any?," *Journal of the Association for Persons with Severe Handicaps,* vol. 13, 1988, pp. 87–99.

11. Michael F. Giangreco and M. B. Doyle, "Students with Disabilities and Paraprofessional Supports: Benefits, Balance, and Band-Aids," *Exceptional Children,* vol. 68, 2002, pp. 1–12.

12. Sailor and Gee, op. cit.; George Sugai and Rob H. Homer, "Including Students with Severe Behavior Problems in General Education Settings: Assumptions, Challenges, and Solutions," in Alice J. Marr, George Sugai, and Gerald A. Tindal, eds., *The Oregon Conference Monograph 6* (Baltimore: Paul H. Brookes, 1994), pp. 102–20; and Mary Morningstar, Jeannie Kleinhammer-Tramill, and Dana Lattin, "Using Successful Models of Student-Centered Transition Planning and Sevices for Adolescents with Disabilities," *Focus on Exceptional Children,* vol. 31, no. 9, 1999, pp. 1–19.

13. Dianne L. Ferguson, Elizabeth B. Kozleski, and Anne Smith, "Transformed, Inclusive Schools: A Framework to Guide Fundamental Change in Urban Schools," National Institute for Urban School Improvement: The Office of Special Education Programs, August 2001, available from www.inclusiveschools.org/publicat.htm#transformed.

14. Cynthia Curry, "Universal Design: Accessibility for All Learners," *Educational Leadership,* October 2003, pp. 55–60; "Principles of Universal Design," Center for Universal Design, North Carolina State University, 1997, available at www.design.ncsu.edu/cud; James Rydeen, "Universal Design," available at http://industryclick.com//magazinearticle.asp?magazinearticleid=33035&mode=print; and David H. Rose, Sheela Sethuraman, and Grace J. Meo, "Universal Design for Learning," *Journal of Special Education Technology,* vol. 15, no. 2, 2000, pp. 56–60.

15. Steve R. Lassen, Michael M. Steele, and Wayne Sailor, "The Relationship of School-wide Positive Behavior Support to Academic Achievement in an Urban Middle School," manuscript in preparation.

16. Claude Goldenberg, "School-University Links: Settings for Joint Work," in *Successful School Change* (New York: Teachers College Press, 2004), pp. 138–62.

17. Cheryl Utley and Wayne Sailor, eds., *Journal of Positive Behavior Interventions,* vol. 4, 2002.

18. Robert H. Horner et al., "The School-wide Evaluation Tool (SET): A Research Instrument for Assessing School-wide Positive Behavior Support," *Journal of Positive Behavior Interventions,* vol. 6, 2004, pp. 3–12.

19. Giangreco and Doyle, op. cit.

20. Robert Harsh, "COMPASS Data Management System," available at http://sbiweb.kckps.org:2388/common/default.asp.

21. David M. Fetterman, "Empowerment Evaluation: An Introduction to Theory and Practice," in idem, Sakeh J. Kafterian, and Abraham Wandersman, eds., *Empowerment Evaluation: Knowledge and Tools for Self-Assessment and Accountability* (Thousand Oaks, Calif.: Sage, 1997), pp. 1–46.

WAYNE SAILOR is a clinical psychologist, a professor of special education, and an associate director of the Beach Center on Disability, University of Kansas, Lawrence. **BLAIR ROGER** is an educational consultant based in Oakland, Calif. They wish to thank the administrators, teachers, staff, students, and families of the Ravenswood (Calif.) School District, East Palo Alto, and of USD 500, Wyandotte County, Kansas City, Kan. The authors also thank Leonard Burrello of Indiana University, Bloomington, and the Forum on Education (www.forumoneducation.org) for initiating a forum on the paradox of differentiation, which led to this article. Preparation of this article was supported, in part, by the National Center on Positive Behavior Interventions and Supports (Grant no. 113265980003).

UNIT 2

Families/Early Intervention

Unit Selections

6. **Children of Alcoholics: Risk and Resilience,** Cara E. Rice et al.
7. **What Can You Learn from Bombaloo?,** Debby M. Zambo

Key Points to Consider

• It is currently estimated that 25% of U.S. children have experienced alcohol abuse or dependency in their families. What problems do these children face? Is there anything you can do to help these children before they become teens and adults?

• What can books do for young children in early intervention programs?

Student Website

www.mhcls.com

Internet References

Division for Early Childhood
   http://www.dec-sped.org
Institute on Community Integration Projects
   http://ici.umn.edu/projectscenters/
National Association for Child Development (NACD)
   http://www.nacd.org
Special Education Resources on the Internet (SERI)
   http://seriweb.com

In 1986 the U.S. Congress established a grant incentive aimed at providing services for young children at risk of disability beginning at the age of three. In 1991 this early intervention became part of the Individuals with Disabilities Education Act (IDEA). Early intervention operates through "Child Find," organizational groups that look for babies, toddlers, and preschoolers with conditions of disability. These young children can receive special educational services according to IDEA's mandate for "a free and appropriate education for all in the least-restrictive environment." Many more infants and young children are being found who are at "high risk" of developing educational disabilities (for example, low vision, hearing impairments, developmental delays) unless education begins before the age of six. This outreach is having a profound impact on the care of families and children.

The United States is faced with multiple questions about the education of its future citizens—its young children. Many American babies are born preterm, small for gestational age, or with extremely low birth weight. This is a direct result of the United States' high rate of teenage pregnancy (nearly double that of most European countries and Canada) and its low rate of providing adequate prenatal care, especially for the young, the poor, or recent immigrant mothers. These infants are at high risk for developing disabilities and conditions of educational exceptionality. Early intervention can help these babies.

Early intervention is as much a parent/family program as it is a service for infants and toddlers. As "home" is the most natural environment, education begins there. All caregivers become recipients of assistance. They learn about the disability and what educational programs help. They have procedures modeled by special educators or health professionals (e.g., physical therapists' speech-language clinicians) and in turn do them, then teach to others. As the child becomes a preschooler, intervention may move to a part-time or full-time program outside the home. There parents not only continue to work with their child, but also work with other children and engage in group meetings with other parents.

All services to be provided for any infant, toddler, or preschooler with a disability, and for his or her family, are to be articulated in an individualized family service plan (IFSP). The IFSP is to be written and implemented as soon as the infant or young child is determined to be at risk. IFSPs specify what services will be provided for the parents, for the diagnosed child, for siblings, and for all significant caregivers. Children with pervasive disabilities (such as autism, traumatic brain injuries, blindness, deafness, orthopedic impairments, severe health impairments, or multiple disabilities) may require extensive and very expensive early childhood interventions.

IFSPs are written in collaboration with parents, experts in the area of the child's exceptional condition, teachers, home-service providers, and other significant providers. They are updated every 6 months until the child turns three and then are annually updated. A case manager is assigned to oversee each individual child with an IFSP to ensure high-quality and continuous intervention services.

Despite the care taken, many children who qualify for, and would benefit from, early intervention services are missed. Child

© 2009 Jupiterimages Corporation

Find associations are not well funded. There are constant shortages of time, materials, and multidisciplinary professionals to do assessments. Finding translators for parents who speak uncommon foreign languages adds to the problems. Occasionally the availability of funds for early childhood interventions encourages the overdiagnosis of risk factors in infants from low-income, minority, immigrant, or rural families.

A challenge to all professionals providing early childhood special services is how to work with diverse parents. Some parents welcome any and all intervention, even if it is not merited. Other parents resist any labeling of their child as "disabled" and refuse services. Professionals must make allowances for cultural, economic, and educational diversity, multiple caregivers, and single parents. Regardless of the situation, parental participation is the sine qua non of early childhood intervention.

When a child with a disability enters public school, parents continue to be involved in writing annually updated individualized education programs (IEPs). They are encouraged to keep participating in the education of their child in many other ways as well. For each transition their child makes (e.g., preschool to elementary school, special class to regular education class, elementary to middle school, middle to high school) parents help develop individualized transition plans (ITPs). These are outcome-oriented activities which make the life changes easier for all involved.

During adolescence, the student, together with family, teachers and counselors, begins an ITP for terminal education. It is mandated that the ITP be included in the IEP by age 16. These ITPs help students with disabilities prepare for living as independently as possible, finding meaningful employment, and balancing work with recreation and leisure as adults. Parents, teachers, and career counselors must remember to allow students to dream, to think big, and to have optimistic visions of themselves. They also need to inculcate the idea that persistence pays: It takes a lot of little steps to achieve a goal.

The first article in this unit, "Children of Alcoholics," examines the risk factors of alcoholism and the outcomes in children of alcoholics as well as possible interventions to assist these children.

The second article discusses the benefits of books in early intervention programs. Families and children learn together as they read, look at pictures, and discuss the plot lines. Books about emotions are especially useful for young children with disabilities who may have difficulties regulating their moods (e.g., children with attention deficits, developmental, and emotional disorders).

Children of Alcoholics
Risk and Resilience

CARA E. RICE ET AL.

In 2002, over 17 million people in the United States were estimated to suffer from alcohol abuse or alcohol dependence (NIAAA, 2006). These alcohol disorders have devastating effects on the individuals, their families, and society. It has been reported that one in four children in the United States has been exposed to alcohol abuse or dependence in the family (Grant, 2000). A 1992 survey revealed that over 28 million children in the United States lived in households with one or more adults who had an alcohol disorder at some time in their lives, while nearly 10 million children lived with adults who reported alcohol disorders in the past year (Grant, 2000). Children of alcoholics (COAs) are at increased risk for a variety of negative outcomes, including fetal alcohol syndrome, substance use disorders, conduct problems, restlessness and inattention, poor academic performance, anxiety, and depression (West & Prinz, 1987). Furthermore, children of alcoholics are more likely to be exposed to family stressors such as divorce, family conflict, parental psychopathology, and poverty, which, in turn, may contribute to their negative outcomes.

In particular, COAs show increased risk of alcoholism and other substance use disorders. Genetic factors have been identified as increasing the risk of developing substance use problems among COAs (Schuckit, 2000). However, the risk faced by COAs is best understood as resulting from the interplay of both genetic and environmental factors (McGue, Elkins, & Iacano, 2000). We will discuss the factors that influence the development of substance abuse and other negative outcomes in COAs. We will also review three models in the development of substance disorders for COAs. These models are not mutually exclusive, and all three may influence a child. We will also discuss protective factors that may decrease COAs' risk for the development of future negative outcomes.

Prenatal Risk

One pathway for increased risk among COAs is through prenatal exposure to alcohol. Fetal alcohol syndrome (FAS), which can occur if a woman drinks alcohol during pregnancy, is a condition characterized by abnormal facial features, growth retardation, and central nervous system problems. Children with FAS may have physical disabilities and problems with learning, memory, attention, problem solving, and social/behavioral problems (Bertrand et al., 2004).

Pathways of Risk for the Development of Substance Disorders

Multiple pathways have been studied in the development of substance use disorders. Three important ones are the deviance proneness model, the stress/negative affect model, and the substance use effects model (Sher, 1991). Although these models were originally proposed to explain the development of alcohol disorders among COAs, they can also be extended to a consideration of other negative outcomes.

Deviance Proneness Pathway

The deviance proneness pathway theorizes that parental substance abuse produces poor parenting, family conflict, difficult child temperament and cognitive dysfunction. Poor parenting along with conflicted family environment are thought to interact with a child's difficult temperament and cognitive dysfunctions, which raises the child's risk for school failure and for associating with peers who themselves have high levels of conduct problems. Affiliation with these antisocial peers then increases the likelihood of antisocial behavior by COAs, including substance use (Dishion, Capaldi, Spracklen, & Li, 1995). Conduct problems in childhood and later adolescence predict the development of substance use disorders in young adulthood (Chassin et al., 1999; Molina, Bukstein, & Lynch, 2002).

One component of the deviance proneness model is difficult temperament or personality. The temperament and personality traits that are associated with adolescent substance use include sensation seeking, aggression, impulsivity, and an inability to delay gratification (Gerra et al., 2004; Wills,

Windle, & Cleary, 1998). For example, 3-year-old boys observed to be distractible, restless, and impulsive were more likely to be diagnosed with alcohol dependence at the age of 21 (Caspi, Moffitt, Newman, & Silva, 1996). Importantly, these characteristics, which are associated with adolescent substance use, have also been shown to be more common among COAs and children of drug users. (e.g., Carbonneau et al., 1998). This suggests that COAs may be at risk for substance use, in part, because of their personality traits.

One in four children in the United States has been exposed to alcohol abuse or dependence in the family.

Another component of the deviance proneness model is a deficit in cognitive function. Children of alcoholics may also be at risk for substance abuse because of deficits in cognitive functioning that have been called "executive" functions. Executive functioning refers to the ability to adjust behavior to fit the demands of individual situations and executive functioning includes planning, working memory and the ability to inhibit responses (Nigg et al., 2004). COAs have demonstrated poor response inhibition (Nigg et al., 2004), and impairments in executive functioning have found to predict drinking among young adult COAs (Atyaclar, Tarter, Kirisci, & Lu, 1999).

The deviance proneness pathway also suggests that COAs may be at risk because of the poor parenting that they receive. Decreased parental monitoring of the child's behavior, inconsistent discipline, and low levels of social support from parents are associated with increased levels of adolescent substance use and conduct problems (Brody, Ge, Conger, Gibbons, Murry, Gerrard, & Simons, 2001; Wills, McNamara, Vaccaro, & Hirky, 1996). These negative parenting behaviors have been found in substance-abusing families (Chassin, Curran, Hussong, & Colder, 1996; Curran & Chassin, 1996), suggesting that alcoholic parents may engage in poor parenting practices, which may in turn place their children at risk for substance use and/or conduct problems.

Most researchers have assumed that poor parenting leads to behavior problems in children, making it the basis for many prevention and intervention programs. However, developmental researchers have suggested that child behavior also affects parenting (Bell & Chapman, 1986). For example, Stice and Barrera (1995) found that low levels of parental control and support predicted adolescent substance use. However, adolescent substance use, in turn, predicted decreases in parental control and support. Therefore, the link between parenting and adolescent conduct problems and substance use may best be thought of as a system in which parents affect children, and children affect parents.

Stress and Negative Affect Pathway

The stress and negative affect pathway suggests that parental substance abuse increases children's exposure to stressful life events such as parental job instability, familial financial difficulty, parental legal problems, etc. (Chassin et al., 1993; Sher, 1991). These potentially chronic stressors may lead to emotional distress in COAs such as depression and/or anxiety. Substance use may then be used to control this distress.

Research has shown a link between negative affect and substance use in adolescence (see Zucker, 2006, for a review). For example, depression has been found to co-occur with adolescent substance abuse (Deykin, Buka, & Zeena, 1992) and heavy alcohol use (Rohde, Lewinson, & Seely, 1996). Moreover, negative life events have been associated with adolescent substance use (Wills, Vaccaro, & McNamara, 1992). However, not all findings support a negative affect pathway to adolescent substance use problems.

One explanation for the conflicting findings is that not all adolescents with negative affect will be at risk for substance use. Rather, adolescents who suffer from negative affect may only use alcohol and drugs if they also lack good strategies to cope with their negative moods and/or if they believe that alcohol or drugs will help them cope. Therefore, helping COAs to develop coping strategies can potentially serve as an intervention. There may also be gender differences in the extent to which COAs use substance use to cope with stress and negative mood (Chassin et al., 1999).

Substance Use Effects Model

The substance use effects model focuses on individual differences in the pharmacological effects of substances. It is hypothesized that some individuals are more sensitive to the pleasurable effects of alcohol and substance use and/or less sensitive to the adverse effects. For example, Schuckit and Smith (1996) found that male COAs with extremely low levels of negative responses to alcohol were more likely be to diagnosed with alcohol abuse/dependence almost a decade later. It is possible that individuals who do not experience negative effects from drinking may lack the "natural brakes" that limit drinking behavior. Some researchers have also suggested that COAs receive greater stress reduction effects from drinking alcohol (Finn, Zeitouni, & Pihl, 1990). Thus, COAs would be expected to engage in more stress-induced drinking than non-COAs because they derive greater physiological benefit from it. It is important to note, however, that not all studies have supported this finding and more research is needed to draw concrete conclusions concerning COAs' physiological response to alcohol (see Sher, 1991, for a review).

Resilience/Protective Factors

Despite the risks presented by genetic, social, and psychological variables, not all COAs experience negative outcomes. These individuals who, despite high-risk status, manage to defeat the odds, are labeled resilient (Garmezy & Neuchterlein, 1972). Resilience has been extensively studied in a variety of populations, but resilience among COAs remains an area that needs further research (Carle & Chassin, 2004). Sher (1991) hypothesized that factors that can help protect COAs from developing alcoholism include social class, preservation of family rituals, amount of attention received from primary caregivers, family harmony during infancy, parental support, personality, self-awareness, cognitive-intellectual functioning, and coping skills.

COAs show increased risk of alcoholism and other substance use disorders.

Carle and Chassin (2004) examined competence and resilience of COAs and found a significant difference between COAs and non-COAs in competence with regards to rule-abiding and academic behaviors, but no differences in social competence. A small subset of resilient COAs demonstrated at or above average levels of academic and rule-abiding competence. These resilient COAs also had fewer internalizing symptoms and reported increased levels of positive affect than did the general COA population (Carle & Chassin, 2004). This suggests that COAs with average or above average academic and rule-abiding competence as well as low levels of internalizing symptoms and high positive affect may be resilient to the risk associated with having an alcoholic parent.

Another potential source of resilience for COAs may be the recovery of the alcoholic parent. Hussong and colleagues (2005) found support for this idea in a study of social competence in COAs. Results from this study indicated that children of recovered alcoholics demonstrated comparable levels of social competence when compared to children of nonalcoholic parents, suggesting again that not all COAs are at equivalent levels of risk.

Along with recovery of parental alcohol symptoms, previous research has also demonstrated the importance of a number of familial factors in buffering the risk associated with parental alcoholism. For example, parental social support, consistency of parental discipline, family harmony, and stability of family rituals have all been shown to protect COAs from the development of alcohol and drug use and abuse (King & Chassin, 2004; Marshal & Chassin, 2000; Stice, Barrera, & Chassin, 1993).

Although there is evidence to suggest that family factors play a protective role in children's risk for substance use and substance use disorders, there is evidence to suggest that this protection may not be equal for all children (Luthar, Cicchetti, & Becker, 2000). In other words, the protective family factor may reduce the negative effect of parental alcoholism for some children, but may lose its effectiveness at the highest levels of risk. For example, King and Chassin (2004) found that parental support reduced the negative effect of family alcoholism for children with low and average levels of impulsivity and sensation seeking, but not for children with high levels of impulsivity and sensation seeking. In other words, parental support was protective for most children, but not for those with the highest levels of risk. Similarly, Zhou, King, and Chassin (2006) found that the protective effect of family harmony was lost for those children with high levels of family alcoholism. Together these studies provide evidence that consistent and supportive parenting and family harmony are protective for many children of alcoholics, but those children at especially high risk may not benefit from these familial protective factors.

Family relationships, though clearly an important aspect of resilience in COAs, are not the only relationships that appear to contribute to positive outcomes in children of alcoholics. There is also evidence to suggest that, for older children, peer relationships may be as influential as family relationships on adolescents' decision to use substances (Mayes & Suchman, 2006). Therefore, peer relationships may also provide protection against the risk associated with having an alcoholic parent. For example, Ohannessian and Hesselbrock (1993) found that COAs with high levels of social support from friends drank at levels similar to non-COAs, indicating that friendships may also work to reduce the negative effects of parent alcoholism.

Conclusion

Although much work remains to be done in understanding both risk and resilience among COAs, the work that has been done provides important implications for preventive interventions. For example, family factors appear to protect many COAs from negative outcomes. This knowledge supports the need for family-based preventive interventions, which seek to improve both parenting practices and family relationships among families of alcoholics. As research in this area continues to uncover the complex interplay of both the genetic and environmental factors that contribute to COA risk and resilience, prevention researchers will be afforded the opportunity to design and implement interventions to assist this prevalent and heterogeneous population of children.

References

Atyaclar, S., Tarter, R.E., Kirisci, L., & Lu, S. (1999). Association between hyperactivity and executive cognitive functioning in childhood and substance use in childhood and substance use in early adolescence. *Journal of the American Academy of Child and Adolescent Psychiatry, 38,* 172–178.

Bell, R.Q., & Chapman, M. (1986). Child effects in studies using experimental or brief longitudinal approaches to socialization. *Developmental Psychology, 22,* 595–603.

Bertrand, J., Floyd, R.L., Weber, M.K., O'Connor, M., Riley, E.P., Johnson, K.A., Cohen, D.E., National Task Force on FAS/FAE.

(2004). *Fetal Alcohol Syndrome: Guidelines for Referral and Diagnosis.* Atlanta, GA: Centers for Disease Control and Prevention. Available online at http://www.cdc.gov/ncbddd/fas/documents/FAS_guidelines_accessible.pdf

Brody, G.H., Ge, X., Conger, R., Gibbons, F.X., Murry, V.M., Gerrard, M., & Simons, R.L. (2001). The influence of neighborhood disadvantage, collective socialization, and parenting on African American children's affiliation with deviant peers. *Child Development, 72*(4), 1,231–1,246.

Carbonneau, R., Tremblay, R.E., Vitaro, F., Dobkin, P.L., Saucier, J.F., & Pihl, R.O. (1998). Paternal alcoholism, paternal absence, and the development of problem behaviors in boys from age 6 to 12 years. *Journal of Studies on Alcohol, 59,* 387–398.

Carle, A.C., & Chassin, L. (2004) Resilience in a community sample of children of alcoholics: Its prevalence and relation to internalizing symptomatology and positive affect. *Applied Developmental Psychology, 25,* 577–595.

Caspi, A., Moffitt, T., Newman, D., & Silva, P. (1996). Behavioral observations at age 3 years predict adult psychiatric disorders. *Archives of General Psychiatry, 53,* 1,033–1,039.

Chassin, L., Curran, P., Hussong, A., & Colder, C. (1996). The relation of parent alcoholism to adolescent substance use: A longitudinal follow-up study. *Journal of Abnormal Psychology, 105,* 70–80.

Chassin, L., Pillow, D., Curran, P., Molina, B., & Barrera, M. (1993). The relation between parent alcoholism and adolescent substance use: A test of three mediating mechanisms. *Journal of Abnormal Psychology, 102,* 1–17.

Chassin, L., Pitts, S.C., DeLucia, C., & Todd, M. (1999). A longitudinal study of children of alcoholics: Predicting young adult substance use disorders, anxiety, and depression. *Journal of Abnormal Psychology, 108,* 106–118.

Curran, P.J., & Chassin, L. (1996). Longitudinal study of parenting as a protective factor for children of alcoholics. *Journal of Studies on Alcohol, 57,* 305–313.

Deykin, E.Y., Buka, S.L., & Zeena, T.H. (1992). Depressive illness among chemically dependent adolescents. *American Journal of Psychiatry, 149,* 1,341–1,347.

Dishion, T.J., Capaldi, D., Spracklen, K.M., & Li, F. (1995). Peer ecology of male adolescent drug use. *Development and Psychopathology. Special Issue: Developmental Processes in Peer Relations and Psychopathology, 7*(4), 803–824.

Finn, P., Zeitouni, N., & Pihl, R.O. (1990). Effects of alcohol on psychophysiological hyperreactivity to nonaversive and aversive stimuli in men at high risk for alcoholism. *Journal of Abnormal Psychology, 99,* 79–85.

Garmezy, N., & Neuchterlein, K. (1972). Invulnerable children: The fact and fiction of competence and disadvantage. *American Journal of Orthopsychiatry, 42,* 328–329.

Gerra, G., Angioni, L., Zaimovic, A., Moi, G., Bussandri, M., Bertacca, S., Santoro, G., Gardini, S., Caccavari, R., & Nicoli, M.A. (2004). Substance use among high-school students: Relationships with temperament, personality traits, and personal care perception. *Substance Use & Misuse, 39,* 345–367.

Grant, B.F. (2000). Estimates of U.S. children exposed to alcohol use and dependence in the family. *American Journal of Public Health, 90,* 112–115.

Hussong, A.M., Zucker, R.A., Wong, M.M., Fitzgerald, H.E., & Puttler, L.I. (2005). Social competence in children on alcoholic parents over time. *Developmental Psychology, 41,* 747–759.

King, K.M., & Chassin, L. (2004). Mediating and moderated effects of adolescent behavioral under control and parenting in the prediction of drug use disorders in emerging adulthood. *Psychology of Addictive Behaviors, 18,* 239–249.

Luthar, S.S., Cicchetti D., & Becker, B. (2000). The construct of resilience: A critical evaluation and guidelines for future work. *Child Development, 71*(3), 543–562.

Marshal, M.P., & Chassin, L. (2000). Peer influence on adolescent alcohol use: The moderating role of parental support and discipline. *Applied Developmental Science, 4,* 80–88.

Mayes, L.C., & Suchman, N.E. (2006). Developmental pathways to substance use. In D. Cicchetti & D.J. Cohen (Eds.), *Developmental Psychopathology: Vol. 3. Risk, Disorder, and Adaptation* (2nd ed., pp. 599–619). New Jersey: John Wiley & Sons.

McGue, M., Elkins, I., Iacono, W.G. (2000). Genetic and environmental influences on adolescent substance use and abuse. *American Journal of Medical Genetics, 96,* 671–677.

Molina, B.S.G., Bukstein, O.G., & Lynch, K.G. (2002). Attention-deficit/hyperactivity disorder and conduct disorder symptomatology in adolescents with alcohol use disorder. *Psychology of Addictive Behaviors, 16,* 161–164.

National Institute on Alcohol Abuse and Alcoholism. (2006). NIAAA 2001–2002 NESARC [Data File]. Accessed August 1, 2006. from http://niaaa.census. gov/index.html.

Nigg, J.T., Glass, J.M., Wong, M.M., Poon, E., Jester, J.M., Fitzgerald, H.E., Puttler, L.I., Adams, K.A., & Zucker, R.A., (2004). Neuropsychological executive functioning in children at elevated risk for alcoholism: Findings in early adolescence. *Journal of Abnormal Psychology, 113,* 302–314.

Ohannessian, C.M., & Hesselbrock, V.M. (1993). The influence of perceived social support on the relationship between family history of alcoholism and drinking behaviors. *Addiction, 88,* 1,651–1,658.

Rohde, P., Lewinson, P.M., & Seeley, J.R. (1996). Psychiatric comorbidity with problematic alcohol use in high school students. *Journal of the American Academy of Child and Adolescent Psychiatry, 35,* 101–109.

Schuckit, M.A. (2000). Genetics of the risk for alcoholism. *The American Journal on Addictions 9,* 103–112.

Schuckit, M.A., & Smith, T.L. (1996). An 8-year follow-up of 450 sons of alcoholic and control subjects. *Archives of General Psychiatry, 53*(3), 202–210.

Sher, K.J. (1991). *Children of Alcoholics: A Critical Appraisal of Theory and Research.* Chicago: University of Chicago Press.

Stice, E., & Barrera, M. (1995). A longitudinal examination of the reciprocal relations between perceived parenting and adolescents' substance use and externalizing behaviors. *Developmental Psychology, 31*(2), 322–334.

Stice, E., Barrera, M., & Chassin, L. (1993). Relation of parental support and control to adolescents' externalizing symptomatology and substance use: A longitudinal examination of curvilinear effects. *Journal of Abnormal Child Psychology, 21,* 609–629.

West, M.O., & Prinz, R.J. (1987). Parental alcoholism and childhood psychopathology. *Psychological Bulletin, 102*(2), 204–218.

Wills, T.A., McNamara, G., Vaccaro, D., & Hirky, A.E. (1996). Escalated substance use: A longitudinal grouping analysis from early to middle adolescence. *Journal of Abnormal Psychology, 105,* 166–180.

Wills, T.A., Vaccaro, D., & McNamara, G. (1992). The role of life events, family support, and competence in adolescent substance use: A test of vulnerability and protective factors. *American Journal of Community Psychology, 20,* 349–374.

Wills, T.A., Windle, M., & Cleary, S.D. (1998). Temperament and novelty seeking in adolescent substance use: Convergence of dimensions of temperament with constructs from Cloninger's theory. *Journal of Personality and Social Psychology, 74*(2), 387–406.

Zhou, Q., King, K.M., & Chassin, L. (2006). The roles of familial alcoholism and adolescent family harmony in young adults' substance dependence disorders: mediated and moderated relations. *Journal of Abnormal Psychology, 115,* 320–331.

Zucker, R.A. (2006). Alcohol use and the alcohol use disorders: A developmental-biopsychosocial systems formulation covering the life course. In D. Cicchetti & D.J. Cohen (Eds.), *Developmental Psychopathology: Vol 3. Risk, Disorder, and Adaptation* (2nd ed., pp. 620–656). New Jersey: John Wiley & Sons.

CARA E. RICE, MPH, is Project Director of the Adult and Family Development Project at Arizona State University. **DANIELLE DANDREAUX,** MS, is a doctoral student in applied developmental psychology at the University of New Orleans and is currently employed by the Department of Psychology at Arizona State University. **ELIZABETH D. HANDLEY,** MA, is a doctoral student in clinical psychology at Arizona State University. Her research and clinical training are focused on at-risk children and families. **LAURIE CHASSIN,** PhD, is Professor of Psychology at Arizona State University. Her research focuses on longitudinal, multigenerational studies of risk for substance use disorders and intergenerational transmission of that risk.

Preparation of this article was supported by grant AA16213 from the National Institute of Alcohol Abuse and Alcoholism to Laurie Chassin.

What Can You Learn from Bombaloo?

Using picture books to help young students with special needs regulate their emotions.

DEBBY M. ZAMBO

In the picture book *When Sophie gets Angry—Really, Really Angry . . .* by Molly Bang (1999), Sophie gets mad at her sister and loses control. "She kicks. She screams. She wants to smash the world to smithereens." Sophie's emotions are reflected in the text typeface and accompanying illustrations. Words like "roar," "explode," "smash," and "pabam" are written in hot colors and bold scripts that help the reader understand how angry Sophie feels. The illustrations in the book include a dragon's red fire coming out of Sophie's mouth and a volcano's molten lava surrounding Sophie as she explodes. Sophie's face and body express her anger with furrowed brow, frowning mouth, clenched fists, and kicking feet. But then, with a turn of the page, things change. Sophie begins to run and run and she begins to cry. Sophie is sad because her anger got the best of her and she realizes she needs to regain control.

Imagine a teacher using this book to help young students with disabilities understand their emotions and how to regulate them. The students could be encouraged to listen carefully to the story to understand how someone feels when they are really, really angry. They also could be encouraged to use their visual literacy, to look closely and carefully at the illustrations to interpret and label how the character feels. The story and illustrations in this book could be used to initiate conversations about similar emotional experiences, how they were handled, and their consequences. The teacher could model strategies to help students learn about emotional regulation, and students could set goals and plans for strategy use. From this scene it is easy to see how a well chosen picture book like *When Sophie Gets Angry—Really, Really Angry . . .* (Bang, 1999) could be a powerful learning tool (Hansen & Zambo, 2005; Zambo, 2005, 2006).

Emotional Regulation and Why It Matters

Emotions are the physiological and psychological feelings we have in response to events in our world. Emotions are important to help young children focus their attention, energize their bodies, and organize their thinking in ways that are adaptive to their needs (LeDoux, 1996). For example, happiness is an emotion with an adaptive function. Children's smiles are infectious, drawing adults nearer to share in their joy; these interactions form the basis of positive relationships and loving bonds (Diamond & Hobson, 1998). Likewise, when situations are stressful, children signal their fear to caregivers, who respond with soothing words and touches that help bring strong feelings under control (Thompson, 1994).

Emotional regulation is the ability to understand emotions and develop strategies to modulate them (LeDoux, 1996). Diamond and Hobson (1998) note that emotional regulation is the most challenging aspect of development. Both positive and negative emotions must be regulated. For example, even though it is a positive emotion, happiness must be regulated. Exuberance is welcome on the playground but not in the classroom. Likewise, sadness is an appropriate emotion in unfortunate situations but not all the time. Regulating emotions is important for children because it enables them to focus their attention, approach and learn in new situations, and form lasting and sincere friendships. Emotional regulation contributes to success in the classroom, with one's peers, and in every aspect of life (Rothbart & Ahadi, 1994).

Emotional Regulation and Students with Disabilities

Unfortunately, not all children develop emotional regulation easily, and this is compounded for students with special needs. For example, children with attention deficit/hyperactivity disorder (ADHD) have difficulty with behavioral inhibition, which in turn causes difficulty in self-regulation of emotion, or affect (Barkley, 1998). When they feel strong emotions, children with ADHD have trouble inhibiting their reactions and keeping themselves under control. Their display of excessive feelings leads to peer rejection and low social status in groups, and they often become outcasts and experience emotional distress (National Research Council, 2000). Armstrong (2000) suggests taking a psychoaffective perspective in the diagnosis of ADHD by looking at how much attention difficulties stem from emotional trauma or anxiety.

Another group that has difficulty with emotional regulation is children with emotional disorders (ED). These children comprise the fourth largest group receiving special education services; more boys than girls are diagnosed with ED (Hardman, Drew, & Egan, 2002). Children with ED have extreme difficulty regulating how they feel; they are either overly emotional or not emotional enough. In other words, children with ED may exhibit externalizing behaviors in the form of aggression and noncompliance, or they may internalize their feelings and show flat affect (Lambrose, Ward, Bocian, MacMillan & Gresham, 1998). For both externalizers and internalizers, emotions become detrimental and cause difficulty in relationships. Young children with ED have a hard time sharing toys, making friends, and cooperating with adults. Situations that produce strong feelings are very uncomfortable for them because they misunderstand their emotions and display them in the wrong manner, with the wrong intensity, and at the wrong time (Hardman et al.). Fortunately, research shows that directly teaching skills can help children with ED understand their feelings and develop friends (Theodore, Bray, Kehle, & Jensen, 2001), Children with ED who learn to manage their emotions have an easier time with frustrations, disappointments, and hurt feelings. They relate better to others and are happier all around (National Research Council, 2000).

Everyone experiences emotions, and the ability to label emotions is an important skill that comes from interactions with caregivers. Caregivers help children learn words for their feelings, and these words help children develop a more accurate and elaborate understanding of how they feel. Conversations between caregivers and children are especially important for children with developmental disabilities like Down syndrome. Beeghley and Cicchetti (1997) investigated conversations between caregivers and children and found that caregivers of children with Down syndrome were significantly less likely to refer to inner states (feelings) than caregivers of normally developing children. This means that children with Down syndrome are less likely to gain a vocabulary for their emotions and, in turn, talk about their feelings less—even though they have just as many, varied, and intense emotions as anyone else (Wallis, 2006).

It is important for teachers to realize that emotional regulation is necessary for all children, children in special education and children not labeled with special needs.

It is important for teachers to realize that emotional regulation is necessary for all children, children in special education and children not labeled with special needs. In the world today many children are experiencing emotional distress. More children than ever are being exposed to environmental stressors like divorce, drugs, violence, and absence of loving care. Stressors cause strong feelings, and without adults to model how to modulate these feelings they can become detrimental to their mental health. The American Academy of Child and Adolescent Psychiatry notes that the number of children and adolescents with problems like depression, panic attacks, phobias, and somatic symptoms is rising and will likely continue to rise (National Research Council, 2000). Being able to manage arousal and affect influences the ability to function in personal and social spheres for both children without and with special needs. Identifying emotions and intervening when help is needed is important because when emotions are not regulated they can become extreme (Lewis & Doorlag, 2003). Temper tantrums, excessive or prolonged sadness, unjustified fear, and anxiety are a few examples of what can happen when emotions are not regulated.

Emotional regulation is the most challenging aspect of development, and many children do not understand emotions or easily develop emotional regulation (Diamond & Hobson, 1998). Answers as to why some children develop regulation with ease whereas others face a long and difficult journey are complex and in reality may stem from a constellation of factors including nature, nurture, or both (Bronson, 2000). Teachers and caregivers need to find constructive ways to coach and support children with emotional needs. Achieving content standards and being successful in school depends on emotional regulation (LeDoux, 1996). Fortunately, positive and structured experiences using picture books can play a key role (Zambo, 2006).

Why Picture Books?

Picture books are easily accessible, cognitively stimulating and motivating, and have affective value—and they are therefore a reasonable medium to use with students with disabilities or when teaching students emotional regulation strategies. Many children and adults are familiar with picture books, and their characters often become friends and teachers. Favorite characters help children, especially those with disabilities, understand that they are not alone in their emotional challenges and concerns (Ouzts, 1991). Riordan and Wilson (1989) found bibliotherapy (using books for therapeutic purposes) to be a successful adjunct to counseling, social skills training, and behavioral support. For young children with disabilities picture books can be used, in conjunction with a social skills program like Skill-streaming (McGinnis & Goldstein, 2003) to reinforce skills being learned. Characters in picture books can help students make connections between the desired skills and themselves. When students identify with a character they can relate the character's feelings to themselves, talk more openly about their feelings, and discuss their feelings in a constructive way. Students are more willing to listen to alternate solutions and ideas when they are placed in the context of a character's life (Hansen & Zambo, 2005; Ouzts, 1991; Zambo, 2006).

When students identify with a character they can relate the character's feelings to themselves, talk more openly about their feelings, and discuss their feelings in a constructive way.

Another reason to use picture books with students with disabilities is because of the stories and illustrations they contain (Evans, 1998; Sadoski & Paivio, 2001). The stories in picture books promote all aspects of literacy development from automaticity in decoding to vocabulary and comprehension skills. Stories help children develop skills and learn important concepts in a natural, nonthreatening way (Hirsh-Pasek & Golinkoff, 2003). Adults in every culture tell stories to pass on important information to future generations, and children typically enjoy listening to these narrative tales. Story is a powerful way to learn and has been used as long as humans have had language (Leu & Kinzer, 2003; Schank, 1995). When teachers place ideas they want students to learn in the context of a story they can challenge current ideas, advance students' reasoning skills, and make a point without lecturing (Koc & Buzzelli, 2004). When teachers ask open-ended questions, value all replies, and involve students through various activities, they nurture emotional regulation in a nonauthoritarian way (Damon, 1988). Stories help students feel how characters feel; this gains their attention, evokes their emotions, and encourages deeper processing. Students are more likely to internalize the material and make connections to what they know. Using stories to help students understand emotions can result in more empathetic and educated human beings (Leu & Kinzer).

In addition to the value of story, picture books also provide a visual representation of a character's emotions and experience. The illustrations in picture books depict a character's facial expressions, emotional reactions, and body posture, and these visuals help children learn. Young children look at the faces and body language of their caregivers to learn about emotions and understand how they should feel (Walden & Baxter, 1989). In one experiment conducted by Boccia and Campos (1989), young children were noticeably friendlier toward a stranger when their mothers exhibited friendly facial expressions in the stranger's presence. Young children learn by looking at real faces, and as they develop they gain the ability to learn from symbols in the form of signs and images (Piaget, 1963). This *visual literacy* is a vital skill but one in which some students with disabilities lag behind (Falk, 2005; Greenspan, 1998). Fortunately, the illustrations in picture books can be used to help students develop their visual literacy; the books can be used to show students representative emotions on faces and in body language.

Children who cannot read intentionality from faces and body language are likely to interpret behaviors as negative even when they are not (National Research Council, 2000). Using pictures and text simultaneously, or coding information visually and verbally, helps children better understand and retain information. Dual-coding information increases the likelihood of recall because students can use both visual and verbal cues (Sadoski & Paivio, 2001).

Picture books are a valuable teaching tool. Their illustrations provide a visual of emotions, and their stories help place emotions in context. Picture books also connect to reading standards and recommendations made by groups such as the Center for the Improvement of Early Reading Achievement (CIERA). In *Put Reading First: The Research Building Blocks for*

Teaching Children to Read (Armbruster, Lehr, & Osborn, 2001), CIERA suggests that reading to children and engaging children in conversations builds new words and concepts. CIERA also recommends the use of visual imagery to help children form mental pictures of what is being read. These ideas are promoted, extended, and supported with the suggestions offered here, which align with good reading practice and with the spirit of the Individuals With Disabilities Education Improvement Act (IDEA, 2004). IDEA promotes the use of positive behavioral support for students with special needs; the use of picture books can help scaffold learning of prosocial skills (Zambo, 2005).

Collecting Data and Developing a Plan

For a variety of reasons, some children with special needs may not understand emotions nor develop strategies to regulate the emotions that they feel. Fortunately, there is much teachers can do to help all their students develop this important skill (Diamond & Hobson, 1998). To understand how this can be achieved, let's step into a fictitious second-grade classroom. There are 26 students in this newly formed inclusive classroom. Nineteen students have no special needs; seven are students with special needs and include one child with a learning disability, two children with an emotional disability, one child with Down syndrome, and three children with ADHD. To facilitate inclusion of the children with special needs, the classroom teacher is collaborating with the special education teacher. Together they have been collecting observational and interview data from students about their experiences, using a checklist of basic emotions and their outward signs, which they developed based on the work of Paul Ekman (2003; see Table 1).

In addition to their observations, the teachers conduct interviews to understand if the students with special needs are fitting in and how students not classified with special needs are interacting with their classmates. The teachers have noticed several interesting things from data collected. Students not classified with special needs say that they want to include their new classmates but that it is difficult; they say that their classmates do not gracefully join groups and interrupt and get pushy instead of being patient and tactful. Likewise, the students with special needs say that they want to be part of the group. They actively seek to be included, but from interview data it is evident they do not know how to join groups diplomatically. When groups reject their attempts, these students display outward signs of anger and anxiety—and when these emotions occur they have difficulty regulating how they feel. This has become a major problem because when the students display these emotions they say cruel things and when a teacher hears them they are placed in time-out. Being in time-out typically calms the students down but instead of rejoining the class they typically withdraw to the back of the classroom, put down their heads, and resist talking constructively about how they feel. As a result students with special needs are missing valuable social and instructional time.

Table 1 Basic Emotions, Outward Signs, and Picture Book Connections

Emotion	Outward Signs	Picture Books about Emotions
Anger	Downturned mouth and angry expression. Body is tense and fists clenched: accelerated heart rate and rapid breathing.	*When Sophie Gets Angry—Really, Really Angry . . .* (Bang, 1999) *Sometimes I'm Bombaloo* (Vail, 2002) *Franklin's Bad Day* (Bourgeois & Clark, 1997)
Anxiety	Worried expression. Hand-wringing and pacing.	*Parts* (Arnold, 1997) *Owen* (Henkes, 1993) *Wemberly Worried* (Henkes, 2005) *Knuffle Bunny: A Cautionary Tale* (Willems, 2004)
Disgust	Pursed lips, wrinkled nose, remarks such as "yuck." Moves away from source.	*Everyone Poops* (Gomi & Stinchecum, 1993) *Walter the Farting Dog* (Kotzwinkle & Murray, 2001) *That's Disgusting* (Pittau & Gervais, 2004)
Fear	Eyes and mouth wide open. Rapid heart rate, sweating, tremors, and weak knees.	*There's a Nightmare in My Closet* (Mayer, 1968) *Shiela Rae the Brave* (Henkes, 2003) *Hooway for Wodney Wat* (Lester, 1999)
Guilt	Self-conscious expression—looks around, lack of eye contact.	*Jamaica Tag-Along* (Havill, 1990) *Lilly's Purple Plastic Purse* (Henkes, 1996) *It Wasn't My Fault* (Lester, 1985)
Happiness	Face sparkles, eyes bright and alert, smiling. Overall sense of lightheartedness and play.	*ABC I Like Me!* (Carlson, 1997) *Chrysanthemum* (Henkes, 1991) *Skippyjon Jones* (Schachner, 2003)
Pride	Head held high, chest stuck out. Overall look of happiness with self.	*Stand Tall, Molly Lou Melon* (Lovell, 2001) *The Rainbow Fish* (Pfister, 1992) *Quick as a Cricket* (Wood, 1982)
Sadness	Frowning, eyes looking down; may be crying. Child is upset and withdrawn.	*Koala Lou* (Fox, 1988) *Tough Boris* (Fox, 2000) *Two Cool Coyotes* (Lund, 1999)
Shame	Blushing, embarrassment, and withdrawal. Lack of eye contact; eyes diverted, looking down or away.	*The Sissy Duckling* (Cole, 2002) *Leo the Late Bloomer* (Kraus, 1971) *No, David!* (Shannon, 1998)

With insight from these data and requirements for positive behavioral support from IDEA, the teachers decide to focus on helping students with special needs to learn the prosocial skills presented in *Skillstreaming in Early Childhood* (McGinnis & Goldstein, 2003). Specifically, they will focus on making friendships, dealing with feelings, identifying alternatives to aggression, and dealing with stress. The teachers decide to use picture books to introduce and reinforce these ideas (see Table 1), and Pressley and Woloshyn's (1995) work to help keep lessons focused and applicable for students with various needs. The teachers decided to:

- Focus on a few strategies at a time.
- Model and explain new strategies with picture books and in classroom contexts.
- Re-model and re-explain as necessary with picture books and in classroom contexts.

- Explain where and when to use the strategy, with picture books and in the classroom.
- Provide opportunities for practice and ways to monitor progress.

Lewis, Sugai, and Colvin (1998) note that all students can benefit from strategies and instruction in social skills, and these teachers decide to present the strategies to all the students in the class. Students who do not have special needs will receive the same training and be asked to model the strategies, provide feedback, and be patient with classmates when mistakes are made. Taking varied goals and ability differences into consideration, the teachers develop a lesson plan (see Figure 1), which incorporates ideas from Tomlinson's (2005) book *How to Differentiate Instruction in Mixed-Ability Classrooms*.

Lesson Title: Learning emotional regulation

Books to Be Used:

Reference: Skillstreaming in Early Childhood

Picture book: Sometimes I'm Bombaloo

Social/Affective Skills Link (mark all that apply)

_____ friendship-making

__X__ alternatives to aggression

__X__ dealing with feelings

_____ dealing with stress

Standards/Link to IDEA: Vocabulary, verbal expression, concept development, and prosocial skills

Lesson Delivery: Whole group moving into smaller workgroups.

Insight From Data: Students with special needs want to be included but they do not know how to join groups. When this happens they get angry, do not regulate their emotions, and end up in time-out. When they get out they pout and lose social and instructional time.

Students in general education want to let students with special needs join their groups but they do not know what to do.

Learner Outcome: Students will learn about emotions, strategies to develop emotional regulation, and set goals to control their emotions.

Lesson Description:

Prereading: Have students guess what book will be about by looking at the cover.

While reading: Read pages 1–8 in the story, then ask students to share good times when they felt happy—and why.

Read pages 9–15 (Bombaloo behaviors), point out illustrations while reading to help students see emotions being expressed in facial expressions and body language. Also note colors used to express emotions.

Model a time when you lost control (what it looked like, sounded like, felt like). Ask students to do the same. Have them show and discuss what they look, sound, feel like when they get angry.

Finish reading the book. End with a discussion on alternatives to acting out.

Connect to Skillstreaming activity. Demonstrate steps.

After reading: Break into small work groups. Students work in pairs to set 1–2 goals. After goals are set students meet with a teacher to develop ways to monitor them and rewards for success. In addition to setting goals, students in general education are required to model strategies and give feedback and praise to their classmates with special needs.

Differentiation/Accommodations for Learning Profiles:

Group orientation: Large group to small.

Cognitive style: Auditory, visual, kinesthetic, interpersonal/introspective, easily distracted/long attention span, and cognitive processing styles.

Learning environment: Lesson begins quiet then moves to noise

Intelligence preference: Focus on bodily/kinesthetic, interpersonal, intrapersonal.

Assessment Learner Outcomes: Goals will be tracked for 2 weeks. Students will consult with the teacher on progress. Observations and interviews will also be gathered again.

Additional Adaptations: Preferential seating/alternative positions for student's with special needs.

Figure 1 Lesson plan template linking social skills training with picture books.

Putting the Plan Into Action

Data collected indicate an immediate need to help students understand each other, and a need to help students with special needs regulate the strong emotions they feel. The teachers decide that the anger the students with special needs are feeling occurs when they do not feel included. To address this important issue they decide that they will take turns reading and discussing picture books, and decide to start with *Sometimes I'm Bombaloo* by Patricia Vail (2002), whose main character experiences a challenge with emotional regulation. The special education teacher begins by holding up the book and asking students to predict what it might be about. After a few responses, she begins to read. The book begins with Katie Honors explaining how she is a happy, compliant, and cooperative little girl.

> My name is Katie Honors and I'm a really good kid. I smile a lot because usually I'm happy, and I give excellent hugs.

The illustrations show Katie smiling and contently interacting with others. The colors are bright and light: Katie is wearing a soft orange dress and is pictured against a background of soft pink, white, green, and yellow. The teacher focuses the students' attention on these facts and the students are asked to share their own memories of happy feelings. All responses are valued, and the teachers provide constant feedback and praise. After adequate sharing the teacher goes on to read how things begin to change for Katie: her brother knocks over her castle of bricks and even though she tries with all her might to remain composed, Katie loses control of her emotions and becomes, in her own words, *Bombaloo*. When this happens Katie starts to growl, her face scrunches like a monster's, and she uses her fists and feet instead of her words. The illustrations depict a large, angry Katie shouting; the backgrounds have sharp edges and dark muted colors. The pages turn to black and there is a small Katie sitting in darkness talking about how difficult it is for her to regulate how she feels.

> But when I'm Bombaloo, I don't want to think about it. I want to smash stuff.

While the students study these pages, the teacher talks about a time she lost control. She uses her face and body to model and exaggerate the emotions: She scrunches her face into a frown, stomps her feet, and tightens her hands into fists. Students are then asked to share a time they lost control, and several mention how they sometimes end up in time-out. The teacher asks the students to use their bodies and faces to express how they sound, look, and feel when this happens. After this sharing, the teacher continues to read the story; Katie is in time-out in her bedroom.

> I have to go take time for myself and think about it.

This makes Katie's anger flare and she demolishes her room. Fortunately, for Katie a pair of underpants lands on her head, which makes her laugh.

> When I laugh I'm Katie Honors again.

The teachers discuss ways to deal with angry feelings, and encourage the students to talk about how they feel when they get angry. Students talk about how scary it is to be Bombaloo and how hard it is to regain control. After this sharing the teacher goes on to finish the story. Katie gains control, apologizes for her behavior, and builds a new castle with her brother. The teachers ask students to discuss the positive things Katie did to rejoin her family and strategies they could use to join groups or rejoin them after embarrassing situations when they get angry and lose control; this also enables the teachers to foster connections to Skill-streaming (McGinnis & Goldstein, 2003). Students are instructed that when they want to join groups they should move closer to the activity and the children, watch and wait for a pause, then at the opportune moment should politely ask if they can join in. The teachers then go on to discuss what to do when attempts are not successful and strong emotions arise, suggesting strategies like counting to 10 to calm down, looking for another group, and thinking of a solitary activity. After ample time to discuss their ideas, students break into small groups to work together to set goals for using the skills they have learned. Each child sets one or two goals; the teachers determine ways to track progress and rewards that can be gained for success.

Fortunately, the students have an opportunity to try out their new goals because it is recess time and several children have decided to form a team to play kickball. One child with a disability decides that he wants to join in and he tries his strategy so he can meet his goal. He moves closer to the group, looks them in the eyes, and at an opportune moment he asks if he can play. His attempt results in acceptance and happy feelings all around.

To date, the teachers in our fictitious scenario can expect to see this type of positive change in their classroom. The students in general education become more aware of their emotions, and there are fewer discipline referrals overall. At the same time, they are learning about their classmates' struggles to fit in and how emotional and upset they can feel when they are left out. This insight helps the students in general education develop a sense of empathy and care. Likewise, students with special needs gain insight into joining groups gracefully, learn how to recognize and label the emotions that they feel, and also acquire some strategies to use to regulate themselves. In addition, they set personal goals to implement those strategies.

Well-chosen picture books give students a behind-the-scenes glimpse into the lives of characters who also face challenges regulating their emotions.

Students can master emotional regulation when taught strategies in a structured format and when these ideas are reflected in the context of a picture book. Well-chosen picture books give students a behind-the-scenes glimpse into the lives of characters who also face challenges regulating their emotions. Picture books can be used to help students understand what Katie and Sophie also learn: that emotions may seem overwhelming, sometimes to the point of exploding or becoming Bombaloo. Students can learn to manage, control, and effectively mobilize their emotions when provided with insight into their own feelings and with strategies to regulate them. This is a valuable lesson that will help students get along in the classroom and throughout their lives.

References

References marked with an asterisk indicate children's picture books about emotions.

Armbruster, B., Lehr, F., & Osborn, J. (2001). *Put reading first: The research building blocks for teaching kindergarten through grade three.* Washington, DC: National Institute for Literacy.

Armstrong, T. (2000). *ADD/ADHD alternatives in the classroom.* Alexandria, VA: Association for Curriculum and Instruction.

*Arnold, T. (1997). *Parts.* New York: Scholastic.

*Bang, M. (1999). *When Sophie gets angry—Really, really angry . . .* New York: Blue Sky/Scholastic.

Barkley, R. A. (1998). *Attention deficit hyperactivity disorder: A handbook for diagnosis and treatment.* New York: Guilford.

Beeghly, M., & Cicchetti, D. (1997). Talking about self and others: Emergence of an internal state lexicon in young children with Down Syndrome. *Development and Psychopathology, 9*(4), 729–748.

Boccia, M., & Campos, J. J. (1989). Maternal emotional signals, social referencing, and infants' reactions to strangers. In N. Eisenberg (Ed.), *New directions for child development: No. 44. Empathy and related emotional responses* (pp. 25–49). San Francisco: Jossey-Bass.

*Bourgeois, B., & Clark, B. (1997). *Franklin's bad day.* New York: Scholastic.

Bronson, M. B. (2000). *Self-regulation in early childhood: Nature and nurture.* New York: Guilford.

*Carlson, N. (1997). *ABC I like me!* New York: Scholastic.

*Cole, H. (2002). *The sissy duckling.* New York: Aladdin.

Damon, W. (1988). *The moral child: Nurturing children's natural moral growth.* New York: Free Press.

Diamond, M., & Hobson, J. (1998). *Magic trees of the mind: How to nurture your child's intelligence, creativity, and healthy emotions from birth through adolescence.* New York: Penguin Books.

Ekman, P. (2003). *Emotions revealed: Recognizing faces and feelings to improve communication and emotional life.* New York: Times Books.

Evans, J. (1998). *What's in the picture? Responding to illustrations in picture books.* London: Paul Chapman.

Falk, L. (2005). Paintings and stories: Making connections. *Arizona Reading Journal, 31*(2), 19–21.

*Fox, M. (1988). *Koala Lou.* San Diego, CA: Voyager Books.

*Fox, M. (2000). *Tough Boris.* New York: Harcourt Brace & Company.

*Gomi, T., & Stinchecum, A. (1993). *Everyone poops.* La Jolla, CA: Kane/Miller.

Greenspan, S. I. (1998). *The growth of the mind and the endangered origins of intelligence.* Cambridge, MA: Perseus Books.

Hansen, C., & Zambo, D. (2005). Piaget, meet Lilly: Understanding child development through picture book characters. *The Early Childhood Education Journal, 33*(1). Retrieved November 16, 2005, from http://dx.doi.org/10.1007/s10643-005-0020-8

Hardman, M. L., Drew, C. J., & Egan, M. W. (2002). *Human exceptionality: Society, school and family* (7th ed.). Boston: Allyn & Bacon.

*Havill, J. (1990). *Jamaica tag-along.* New York: Houghton Mifflin.

*Henkes, K. (1991). *Chrysanthemum.* New York: Mulberry Books

*Henkes, K. (1993). *Owen.* New York: Greenwillow Books.

*Henkes, K. (1996). *Lilly's purple plastic purse.* New York: Scholastic.

*Henkes, K. (2003). *Shiela Rae the brave.* New York: Greenwillow Books.

*Henkes, K. (2005). *Wemberly worried.* New York: Scholastic.

Hirsh-Pasek, K., & Golinkoff, R. M. (2003). *Einstein never used flash cards: How our children really learn—and why they need to play more and memorize less.* New York: Rodale.

Koc, K., & Buzzelli, C. A. (2004). The moral of the story is . . . Using children's literature in moral education. *Young Children, 59*(1), 92–97.

*Kotzwinkle, W., & Murray, G. (2001). *Walter the farting dog.* Berkeley, CA: Frog Ltd.

* Kraus, R. (1971). *Leo the late bloomer.* New York: Windmill.

Lambrose, K. M., Ward, S. L., Bocian, K. M., MacMillan, D. L., & Gresham, F. M. (1998). Behavioral profiles of children at risk for emotional and behavioral disorders: Implications for assessment and classification. *Focus on Exceptional Children, 30*(5), 1–16.

LeDoux, J. (1996). *The emotional brain.* New York: Touchstone.

* Lester, H. (1985). *It wasn't my fault.* New York: Scholastic.

* Lester, H. (1999). *Hooway for Wodney Wat.* Boston: Houghton Mifflin.

Leu, D. J., & Kinzer, C. K. (2003). *Effective literacy instruction: Implementing best practices* (5th ed.). Upper Saddle River, NJ: Merrill Prentice Hall.

Lewis, R. B., & Doorlag, D. H. (2003). *Teaching special students in general education classrooms* (6th ed.). Upper Saddle River, NJ: Merrill Prentice Hall.

Lewis, T. J., Sugai, G., & Colvin, B. G. (1998). Reducing problem behavior through a school-wide system of behavioral support: Investigation of a school-wide social skills training program and contextual intervention. *School Psychology Review, 27*, 446–459.

* Lovell, P. (2001). *Stand tall, Molly Lou Melon.* New York: Scholastic.

* Lund, J. (1999). *Two cool coyotes.* New York: Dutton Children's Books.

* Mayer, M. (1968). *There's a nightmare in my closet.* New York: Penguin Books.

McGinnis, E., & Goldstein, A. (2003) *Skillstreaming in early childhood: New strategies and perspectives for teaching prosocial skills.* Champaign, IL: Research Press.

National Research Council Institute of Medicine (2000). *From neurons to neighborhoods: The science of early childhood development.* Washington, DC: National Academies Press.

Ouzts, D. T. (1991). The emergence of bibliotherapy as a discipline. *Reading Horizons, 31*(3). 199–206.

* Pfister, M. (1992). *The rainbow fish.* New York: North-South Books.

Piaget, J. (1963). *Origins of intelligence in children.* New York: Norton.

* Pittau, F., & Gervais, B. (2004). *That's disgusting!* New York: Black Dog & Leventhal.

Pressley, M., & Woloshyn, V. (1995). *Cognitive strategy instruction that really improves children's academic performance.* Cambridge, MA: Brookline Books.

Riordan, R. J., & Wilson, L. S. (1989). Bibliotherapy: A tool for helping preschool children deal with developmental change related to family relationships. *Early Child Development and Care, 47,* 107–129.

Rothbart. M. K., & Ahadi, S. A. (1994). Temperament and the development of personality. *Journal of Abnormal Psychology, 103,* 55–66.

Sadoski, M., & Paivio, A. (2001). *Imagery and text: A dual-coding theory of reading and writing.* Mahwah, NJ: Lawrence Erlbaum.

* Schachner, J. (2003). *Skippyjon Jones.* New York: Dutton Children's Books.

Schank, R. C. (1995). *Tell me a story: Narrative intelligence.* Evanston, IL: Northwestern University Press.

* Shannon, D. (1998). *No, David!* New York: Scholastic.

Theodore, L. A., Bray, M. A., Kehle, T. J., & Jensen, W. R. (2001). *Instructional conversation: Teaching and learning in social activity.* Washington, DC: National Center for Research on Cultural Diversity and Second Language Learning.

Thompson, R. A. (1994). Emotional development: A theme in search of development. In N. A. Fox (Ed.), *The development of emotion regulation and dysregulation: Biologic and behavioral aspects.* Monographs of the Society for Research in Child Development.

59 (2/3): 25–52 (Serial no. 240). Ann Arbor, MI: Society for Research in Child Development.

Tomlinson, C. A. (2005). *How to differentiate instruction in mixed-ability classrooms* (2nd ed.). Upper Saddle River, NJ; Merrill Prentice Hall.

*Vail, R. (2002). *Sometimes I'm bombaloo.* New York: Scholastic.

Walden. T. A., & Baxter, A. (1989). The effect of context and age on social referencing. *Child Development, 60,* 1511–1518.

Wallis, C. (2006, July 24). A very special wedding. *Time, 168*(4), 44–45.

*Willems, M. (2004). *Knuffle bunny: A cautionary tale.* New York: Hyperion Books for Children.

*Wood, A. (1982). *Quick as a cricket.* New York: Scholastic.

Zambo, D. (2005). Using the picture book *Thank you, Mr. Falker* to understand struggling readers. *Journal of Adolescent and Adult Literacy, 48*(6), 502–512.

Zambo, D. (2006) Learning from picture book characters in readaloud sessions for students with ADHD. *TEACHING Exceptional Children Plus 2*(4). Retrieved March 2006, from http://escholarship.bc. edu/education/tecplus/vol2/iss4/art4/

DEBBY M. ZAMBO (CEC AZ Federation), Assistant Professor of Elementary Education, Department of Education, Arizona State University, Phoenix.

Address correspondence to Debby Zambo, Department of Education (3151), Arizona State University, Phoenix, AZ 85069-7100 (e-mail: debby.zambo@asu.edu).

UNIT 3
Learning Disabilities

Unit Selections

Key Points to Consider

- What have brain imaging studies told us about dyslexia?

- Can students with LDs learn better organizational skills? How?

- Do engineering principles apply to special education? How?

Student Website
www.mhcls.com

Internet References

The Instant Access Treasure Chest
http://www.fln.vcu.edu/ld/ld.html

Learning Disabilities Association of America (LDA)
http://www.ldaamerica.org

Learning Disabilities Online
http://www.ldonline.org

The Council for Exceptional Children, Division for Learning Disabilities
http://www.teachingld.org

The National Center for Learning Disabilities
http://www.ncld.org

Learning how to learn is one of life's most important tasks. For students with learning idiosyncrasies it is a most critical lesson. Today general education teachers and special educators must seriously attend to the growing numbers of students who have a wide range of different learning disabilities (LDs). LD enrollments in inclusive, regular education classes have skyrocketed. They are the fastest growing and largest category of exceptionalities in elementary, middle, and high schools. Children with LDs now make up over 50 percent of those receiving special educational services.

The ways in which students with LDs are identified and served have been radically transformed with the IDEIA (Individuals with Disabilities Education Improvement Act). New assessment methods have made the identification of students with LDs easier and far more common. Many lawmakers and educators, however, feel that students who have other problems (for example, behavior disorders, poor learning histories, or dysfunctional families) are erroneously being diagnosed with LDs. IDEIA requires states to place students with disabilities in regular classrooms as much as possible or lose their federal funding. A landmark U.S. Supreme Court case in November of 1993 (*Carter v. Florence Co., S.C.*) ruled that public schools must give appropriate educational services to students with LDs or pay the tuition for private schools to do so. This ruling opened a floodgate of new litigation by parents. In 2007, The U.S. Supreme Court ruled in *Winkelman vs. Parma City School District* that parental participation is crucial to ensuring that children with disabilities receive a free and appropriate public school education. If parents are not satisfied they have enforceable rights under the law. This re-definition of parental importance will bring more pressure to bear on school districts to provide special education with meaningful benefits.

The Individuals with Disabilities Education Act has turned out to be much more expensive than Congress envisioned when it enacted this education bill 26 years ago. The passage of No Child Left Behind in 2001 required that schools be held accountable for appropriate education of all students.

Is the rapid increase in students assessed as having learning disabilities an artifact of misdiagnoses, exaggeration, and a duping of the system that makes funding available for special needs? Neonatal medical technology and achievements in preventive medicine and health maintenance have greatly reduced the numbers of children who are born deaf, blind, severely physically disabled, or with multiple exceptional conditions. The very same medical technology has greatly increased the numbers of children kept alive who are born prematurely, small for gestational age, with low birth weight, and "at-risk" for less-severe disabilities such as LDs.

A learning disability is usually defined by the lay public as difficulty in reading or calculating. IDEIA defines it as a disorder in the processes involved in understanding or in using language, spoken or written, that may manifest itself in an imperfect ability to listen, speak, read, write, spell, or do mathematical calculations. Learning disabilities are identified differently outside of education. *The Diagnostic and Statistical Manual of Mental Disorders* (4th edition) divides LDs into academic skills disorders

© Gary S. Chapman/Getty Images

(reading, mathematics, written expression) and attention deficit hyperactive disorder (ADHD). The National Joint Committee for Learning Disabilities (NJCLD) separates LDs into specific problems related to the acquisition and use of listening, speaking, reading, writing, reasoning, or mathematical abilities. Attention deficit hyperactive disorder, if not accompanied by any specific learning problem or any specific behavioral/emotional disorder, can be assessed as a health disability by both IDEIA and NJCLD especially if it can be ameliorated with medication. Due to parental pressures, the IDEIA definition of LDs has been amended administratively to include ADHD if the deficit in attention leads to difficulty in learning. In this compendium, ADHD is treated as a health disability.

The rest of the definition of an LD is an exclusionary definition. It helps clarify the nature of LDs. They are not developmental disabilities. They are not deficiencies in any of the sensory systems (vision, hearing, taste, touch, smell, kinesthetics, vestibular sensation). They are not problems associated with health or physical mobility. They are not emotional or behavioral disorders. They are not disabilities of speech or language. They can be assessed as true LDs only if there is a discrepancy between the child's ability to learn and his or her actual learning.

IDEIA's and No Child Left Behind's strong emphases on a free and appropriate educational placement for every child with a disability has forced schools to be more cautious about all assessments and labeling. Increasing numbers of children are now being assessed as LD who once might have been labeled developmentally disabled or disabled by speech, language, emotions, behavior, or one of the senses. A child with an LD may concurrently have a disability in any of these other areas, but if this occurs, both the LD and any other disabilities must be addressed in an individualized education plan (IEP) designed especially for that unique child.

Recent research suggests that reading disabilities may affect about 15 percent of elementary school-aged children. If this is accurate, many LD children are not yet being identified and serviced. The causes of LDs are unknown. Usually some central nervous system glitches are believed to underlie the disabilities, even if their existence cannot be demonstrated. Other suspected causes include genetic inheritance, poor nutrition, or exposure to toxic agents. The NJCLD definition of LD presumes biological causation and lifetime chronicity.

This unit on learning disabilities addresses both the successes and the frustrations of educating children with LDs. There are many myths about learning disabilities which frustrate both students and their adult teachers. The first article in this unit discusses the common misunderstandings about students with dyslexia. It gives accurate, up-to-date information from brain research on diagnosing the disorder. The authors give recommendations for parents and teachers on how to help students avoid the lifelong consequences of poor reading.

The second article in the section deals with 20 ways to build better organizational skills in students with LDs. Knowing how to systematically approach assignments and how to apply methods to finish the tasks helps improve both work quality and self-esteem of the students.

In the final article Charles Dukes and Pamela Lamar-Dukes use engineering as a metaphor for creating individualized education programs that really work for high school students with learning disabilities in inclusive classrooms.

Dyslexia and the Brain: What Does Current Research Tell Us?

The identification of a child with dyslexia is a difficult process, but there are ways that parents and teachers can learn more about the reading difficulty and support the child's learning.

ROXANNE F. HUDSON, LESLIE HIGH, AND STEPHANIE AL OTAIBA

Developmental dyslexia and how it relates to brain function are complicated topics that researchers have been studying since dyslexia was first described over a hundred years ago. W. Pringle Morgan (cited in Shaywitz, 1996), a doctor in Sussex, England, described the puzzling case of a boy in the *British Medical Journal:* "Percy . . . aged 14 . . . has always been a bright and intelligent boy, quick at games, and in no way inferior to others of his age. His great difficulty has been—and is now—his inability to read" (p. 98).

Almost every teacher in the United States has at least one student who could fit the same description written so many years ago. This situation leads many school personnel to wonder why their articulate, clearly bright student has so many problems with what appears to be a simple task—reading a text that everyone else seems to easily comprehend. Having information about the likely explanation for and potential cause of the student's difficulties often relieves teachers' fears and uncertainties about how to teach the student and how to think about providing instruction that is relevant and effective. Current research on dyslexia and the brain provide the most up-to-date information available about the problems faced by over 2.8 million school-aged children.

When talking with teachers about their students who struggle with reading, we have encountered similar types of questions from teachers. They often wonder, What is dyslexia? What does brain research tell us about reading problems and what does this information mean for classroom instruction? The purpose of this article is to explain the answers to these questions and provide foundational knowledge that will lead to a firmer understanding of the underlying characteristics of students with dyslexia. A greater understanding of the current brain research and how it relates to students with dyslexia is important in education and will help teachers understand and evaluate possible instructional interventions to help their students succeed in the classroom.

What Is Dyslexia?

Dyslexia is an often-misunderstood, confusing term for reading problems. The word *dyslexia* is made up of two different parts: *dys* meaning not or difficult, and *lexia* meaning words, reading, or language. So quite literally, dyslexia means difficulty with words (Catts & Kamhi, 2005). Despite the many confusions and misunderstandings, the term *dyslexia* is commonly used by medical personnel, researchers, and clinicians. One of the most common misunderstandings about this condition is that dyslexia is a problem of letter or word reversals (b/d, was/saw) or of letters, words, or sentences "dancing around" on the page (Rayner, Foorman, Perfetti, Pesetsky, & Seidenberg, 2001). In fact, writing and reading letters and words backwards are common in the early stages of learning to read and write among average and dyslexic children alike, and the presence of reversals may or may not indicate an underlying reading problem. See Table 1 for explanations of this and other common misunderstandings.

One of the most complete definitions of dyslexia comes from over 20 years of research:

> Dyslexia is a specific learning disability that is neurobiological in origin. It is characterized by difficulties with accurate and/or fluent word recognition and by poor spelling and decoding abilities. These difficulties typically result from a deficit in the phonological component of language that is often unexpected in relation to other cognitive abilities and the provision of effective classroom instruction. (Lyon, Shaywitz, & Shaywitz, 2003, p. 2)

Dyslexia is a specific learning disability in reading that often affects spelling as well. In fact, reading disability is the most widely known and most care fully studied of the learning disabilities, affecting 80% of all those designated as learning disabled.

Table 1   Common Misunderstandings about Students with Reading Disabilities

Writing letters and words backwards are symptoms of dyslexia.

Writing letters and words backwards are common in the early stages of learning to read and write among average and dyslexic children alike. It is a sign that orthographic representations (i.e., letter forms and spellings of words) have not been firmly established, not that a child necessarily has a reading disability (Adams, 1990).

Reading disabilities are caused by visual perception problems.

The current consensus based on a large body of research (e.g., Lyon et al., 2003; Morris et al., 1998; Rayner et al., 2001; Wagner & Torgesen, 1987) is that dyslexia is best characterized as a problem with language processing at the phoneme level, not a problem with visual processing.

If you just give them enough time, children will outgrow dyslexia.

There is no evidence that dyslexia is a problem that can be outgrown. There is, however, strong evidence that children with reading problems show a continuing persistent deficit in their reading rather than just developing later than average children (Francis, Shaywitz, Stuebing, Shaywitz, & Fletcher, 1996). More strong evidence shows that children with dyslexia continue to experience reading problems into adolescence and adulthood (Shaywitz et al., 1999, 2003).

More boys than girls have dyslexia.

Longitudinal research shows that as many girls as boys are affected by dyslexia (Shaywitz, Shaywitz, Fletcher, & Escobar, 1990). There are many possible reasons for the overidentification of males by schools, including greater behavioral acting out and a smaller ability to compensate among boys. More research is needed to determine why.

Dyslexia only affects people who speak English.

Dyslexia appears in all cultures and languages in the world with written language, including those that do not use an alphabetic script such as Korean and Hebrew. In English, the primary difficulty is accurate decoding of unknown words. In consistent orthographies such as German or Italian, dyslexia appears more often as a problem with fluent reading—readers may be accurate, but very slow (Ziegler & Goswami, 2005).

People with dyslexia will benefit from colored text overlays or lenses.

There is no strong research evidence that intervention using colored overlays or special lenses has any effect on the word reading or comprehension of children with dyslexia (American Optometric Association, 2004; Iovino, Fletcher, Breitmeyer, & Foorman, 1998).

A person with dyslexia can never learn to read.

This is simply not true. The earlier children who struggle are identified and provided systematic, intense instruction, the less severe their problems are likely to be (National institute of Child Health and Human Development, 2000; Torgesen, 2002). With adequately intensive instruction, however, even older children with dyslexia can become accurate, albeit slow readers (Torgesen et al., 2001).

Because of this, we will use the terms *dyslexia* and *reading disabilities* (RD) interchangeably in this article to describe the students of interest. It is neurobiological in origin, meaning that the problem is located physically in the brain. Dyslexia is not caused by poverty, developmental delay, speech or hearing impairments, or learning a second language, although those conditions may put a child more at risk for developing a reading disability (Snow, Burns, & Griffin, 1998). Children with dyslexia will often show two obvious difficulties when asked to read text at their grade level. First, they will not be able to read as many of the words in a text by sight as average readers. There will be many words on which they stumble, guess at, or attempt to "sound out." This is the problem with "fluent word recognition" identified in the previous definition. Second, they will often show decoding difficulties, meaning that their attempts to identify words they do not know will produce many errors. They will not be very accurate in using letter–sound relationships in combination with context to identify unknown words. These problems in word recognition are due to an underlying deficit in the sound component of language that makes it very difficult for readers to connect letters and sounds in order to decode. People with dyslexia often have trouble comprehending what they read because of the great difficulty they experience in accessing the printed words.

What Areas of the Brain Relate to Language and Reading?

The human brain is a complex organ that has many different functions. It controls the body and receives, analyzes, and stores information. The brain can be divided down the middle lengthwise into a right and a left hemisphere. Most of the areas responsible for speech, language processing, and reading are in the left hemisphere, and for this reason we will focus all of our descriptions and figures on the left side of the brain. Within each hemisphere, we find the following four brain lobes (see Figure 1).

- The frontal lobe is the largest and responsible for controlling speech, reasoning, planning, regulating emotions, and consciousness. In the 19th century, Paul

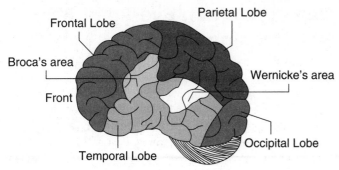

Figure 1 Left hemisphere of the brain showing lobes and two areas important for language.

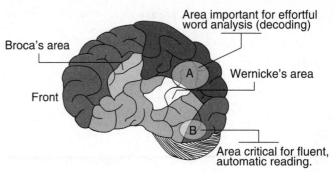

Figure 2 Brain areas in the left hemisphere found to be important for skilled reading (based on the research of B.A. Shaywitz, S.E. Shaywitz, and colleagues).

A = parietotemporal, B = occipitotemporal.

Broca was exploring areas of the brain used for language and noticed a particular part of the brain that was impaired in a man whose speech became limited after a stroke. This area received more and more attention, and today we know that Broca's area, located here in the frontal lobe, is important for the organization, production, and manipulation of language and speech (Joseph, Noble, & Eden, 2001). Areas of the frontal lobe are also important for silent reading proficiency (Shaywitz et al., 2002).

- The parietal lobe is located farther back in the brain and controls sensory perceptions as well as linking spoken and written language to memory to give it meaning so we can understand what we hear and read.

- The occipital lobe, found at the back of the head, is where the primary visual cortex is located. Among other types of visual perception, the visual cortex is important in the identification of letters.

- The temporal lobe is located in the lower part of the brain, parallel with the ears, and is involved in verbal memory. Wernicke's area, long known to be important in understanding language (Joseph et al., 2001), is located here. This region, identified by Carl Wernicke at about the same time and using the same methods as Broca, is critical in language processing and reading.

In addition, converging evidence suggests that two other systems, which process language within and between lobes, are important for reading (see Figure 2). The first is the left parietotemporal system (Area A in Figure 2) that appears to be involved in word analysis—the conscious, effortful decoding of words (Shaywitz et al., 2002). This region is critical in the process of mapping letters and written words onto their sound correspondences—letter sounds and spoken words (Heim & Keil, 2004). This area is also important for comprehending written and spoken language (Joseph et al., 2001). The second system that is important for reading is the left occipitotemporal area (Area B in Figure 2). This system seems to be involved in automatic, rapid access to whole words and is a critical area for skilled, fluent reading (Shaywitz et al., 2002, 2004).

What Does Brain Imaging Research Tell Us about Dyslexia?
Structural Brain Differences

Studies of structural differences in the brains of people of all ages show differences between people with and without reading disabilities. The brain is chiefly made up of two types of material: gray matter and white matter. Gray matter is what we see when we look at a brain and is mostly composed of nerve cells. Its primary function is processing information. White matter is found within the deeper parts of the brain, and is composed of connective fibers covered in myelin, the coating designed to facilitate communication between nerves. White matter is primarily responsible for information transfer around the brain. Booth and Burman (2001) found that people with dyslexia have less gray matter in the left parietotemporal area (Area A in Figure 2) than nondyslexic individuals. Having less gray matter in this region of the brain could lead to problems processing the sound structure of language (phonological awareness). Many people with dyslexia also have less white matter in this same area than average readers, which is important because more white matter is correlated with increased reading skill (Deutsch, Dougherty, Bammer, Siok, Gabrieli, & Wandell, 2005). Having less white matter could lessen the ability or efficiency of the regions of the brain to communicate with one another.

Other structural analyses of the brains of people with and without RD have found differences in hemispherical asymmetry. Specifically, most brains of right-handed, nondyslexic people are asymmetrical with the left hemisphere being larger than the same area on the right. In contrast, Heim and Keil (2004) found that right-handed people with dyslexia show a pattern of symmetry (right equals left) or asymmetry in the other direction (right larger than left). The exact cause of these size differences is the subject of ongoing research, but they seem to be implicated in the reading and spelling problems of people with dyslexia.

Functional Brain Differences

We lack space here for a detailed explanation of imaging techniques. For excellent descriptions of several techniques, readers are directed to Papanicolaou, Pugh, Simos, and Mencl (2004) and Richards (2001). One commonly used method for imaging brain function is functional magnetic resonance imaging (fMRI), a noninvasive, relatively new method that measures physiological signs of neural activation using a strong magnet to pinpoint blood flow. This technique is called "functional" because participants perform tasks while in (or under) the magnet, allowing measurement of the functioning brain rather than the activity of the brain at rest.

Several studies using functional imaging techniques that compared the brain activation patterns of readers with and without dyslexia show potentially important patterns of differences. We might expect that readers with RD would show underactivation in areas where they are weaker and overactivation in other areas in order to compensate, and that is exactly what many researchers have found (e.g., Shaywitz et al., 1998).

This type of functional imaging research has just begun to be used with children. This is in part because of the challenges involved in imaging children, including the absolute need for the participant's head to remain motionless during the scanning. We will present the largest, best-specified study as an example of these new findings with children. Shaywitz et al. (2002) studied 144 right-handed children with and without RD on a variety of in- and out-of-magnet tasks. They compared brain activation between the two groups of children on tasks designed to tap several component processes of reading: identifying the names or sounds of letters, sounding out nonsense words, and sounding out and comparing meanings of real words. The nonimpaired readers had more activation in all of the areas known to be important for reading than the children with dyslexia.

Shaywitz et al. (2002) also found that the children who were good decoders had more activation in the areas important for reading in the left hemisphere and less in the right hemisphere than the children with RD. They suggested that for children with RD, disruption in the rear reading systems in the left hemisphere that are critical for skilled, fluent reading (Area B in Figure 2) leads the children to try and compensate by using other, less efficient systems (Area A in Figure 2 and systems in the right hemisphere). This finding could explain the common experience in school that even as children with dyslexia develop into accurate readers, their reading in grade-level text is often still slow and labored without any fluency (e.g., Torgesen, Rashotte, & Alexander, 2001).

In summary, the brain of a person with dyslexia has a different distribution of metabolic activation than the brain of a person without reading problems when accomplishing the same language task. There is a failure of the left hemisphere rear brain systems to function properly during reading. Furthermore, many people with dyslexia often show greater activation in the lower frontal areas of the brain. This leads to the conclusion that neural systems in frontal regions may compensate for the disruption in the posterior area (Shaywitz et al., 2003). This information often leads educators to wonder whether brain imaging can be used as a diagnostic tool to identify children with reading disabilities in school.

Can We Screen Everyone Who Has Reading Difficulties?

Not yet. It is an appealing vision of putting a child we are concerned about in an fMRI machine to quickly and accurately identify his or her problem, but research has not taken us that far. There are several reasons why a clinical or school-based use of imaging techniques to identify children with dyslexia is not currently feasible. One is the enormous cost of fMRI machines, the computers, and the software needed to run them. Another part of the cost is the staff that is needed to run and interpret the results. Also, in order for this technology to be used for diagnosis, it needs to be accurate for individuals. Currently, results are reliable and reported for groups of participants, but not necessarily for individuals within each group (Richards, 2001; Shaywitz et al., 2002). The number of children who would be identified as being average when they really have a problem (false negatives) or as having a problem when they are average (false positives) would need to be significantly lower for imaging techniques to be used for diagnosis of individual children.

Can Dyslexia Be Cured?

In a word, no. Dyslexia is a lifelong condition that affects people into old age. However, that does not mean that instruction cannot remediate some of the difficulties people with dyslexia have with written language. A large body of evidence shows what types of instruction struggling readers need to be successful (e.g., National Institute of Child Health and Human Development, 2000; Snow et al., 1998; Torgesen, 2000). Now researchers can also "look" inside the brains of children before and after an intensive intervention and see for the first time the effects of the intervention on the brain activity of children with RD. The following are two such studies.

Aylward et al. (2003) imaged 10 children with dyslexia and 11 average readers before and after a 28-hour intervention that only the students with dyslexia received. They compared the two groups of students on out-of-magnet reading tests as well as the level of activation during tasks of identifying letter sounds. They found that while the control children showed no differences between the two imagings, the students who received the treatment showed a significant increase in activation in the areas important for reading and language during the phonological task. Before the intervention, the children with RD showed significant underactivation in these areas as compared to the control children, and after the treatment their profiles were very similar. These results must be viewed with caution because of several limitations. One limitation is the lack of specificity about the intervention that was provided, another is the small sample size, and the last is the lack of an experimental control group (i.e., a group of children with RD who did not receive the treatment). Without an experimental control group, we cannot be certain that the intervention caused the changes found in the brain activation because of so many other possible explanations.

Table 2 Summary of Intervention Used in Brain Imaging Study of Students with RD

Duration	The individual tutoring intervention occurred daily for 50 minutes from September to June, which yielded an average of 126 sessions or 105 tutoring hours per student.
Instruction	Each session consisted of a framework of five steps that the tutors followed with each student. This framework was not scripted, but was individualized based on the student's progress.
	Step 1: Brief and quick-paced review of sound-symbol relationships from previous lessons and introduction of new correspondences.
	Step 2: Word work practice of phonemic segmentation and blending with letter cards or tiles, which occurred in a very systematic and explicit fashion.
	Step 3: Fluency building with sight words and phonetically regular words made up of previously taught sound-symbol correspondences.
	Step 4: Oral reading practice in phonetically controlled text, uncontrolled trade books, and nonfiction texts.
	Step 5: Writing words with previously taught patterns from dictation.
Content	The intervention consisted of six levels that began with simple closed syllable words (e.g., *cat*) and ended with multisyllabic words consisting of all six syllable types.

For a complete description of the instructional intervention, see Blachman et al. (2004).

Shaywitz et al. (2004) addressed these limitations in their investigation of brain activation changes before and after an intervention. They studied 78 second and third graders with reading disabilities who were randomly assigned to three groups: the experimental intervention, school-based remedial programs, or control. A summary of the instructional intervention is provided in Table 2 and a full and detailed description of the intervention and out-of-magnet reading assessments can be found in Blachman et al. (2004).

Before the intervention, all groups looked similar in their brain activity, but immediately after the intervention the experimental and control groups had increased activation in the left hemispheric regions important for reading. One year after intervention, the experimental group showed increased activity in the occipitotemporal region important for automatic, fluent reading (Area B in Figure 2), while at both time points the level of compensatory activation in the right hemisphere decreased. Shaywitz et al. (2002) concluded, "These findings indicate that . . . the use of an evidence-based phonologic reading intervention facilitates the development of those fast-paced neural systems that underlie skilled reading" (p. 931).

Important Considerations to Keep in Mind about the Brain Research

While research advances have allowed us to look more closely within the brain for the first time and revealed important information about how and where we think during reading, there are important considerations that must be remembered. One is that with the exception of the research by B.E. Shaywitz, S. Shaywitz, and their colleagues, the sample sizes in each study are very small. The evidence from these small studies is converging into results that are reliable, but the results may change as more and more participants are included in the research base. This is especially true with children where both the number of studies and the sample sizes are quite small.

Second, we must consider the type of task being used in the magnet. Because of the requirement that the person's head not move during the imaging, researchers are not able to study people actually reading aloud. Instead, they give tasks that require the person to read silently and then make a decision that he or she indicates with a push button (e.g., Do the letters *t* and *v* rhyme? Do *leat* and *jete* rhyme?). Because the researchers have worked carefully on these tasks and have specified the particular process that is being measured, we can trust their conclusions about what the activation levels mean; however, the tasks are quite removed from natural classroom reading and should not be interpreted as if they were the same. The area of brain research is developing rapidly; technological advances are being made that will address these issues as time goes on.

Recommendations for Teachers

What does all of this information mean for school personnel and their students? Once teachers understand the underlying processes and causes of reading disabilities, they can use this information as they work with students and their families. The following are specific recommendations based on the neurological research:

- Adequate assessment of language processing is important in determining why students struggle to learn to read. Dyslexia, or reading disability, is a disorder of the language processing systems in the brain. Specific information about exactly what sorts of weaknesses are present is needed in order to determine the appropriate instruction to meet each student's needs.

Table 3   Informational Resources about Dyslexia for Parents and Teachers

Organization	Contact Information	Description
The Council for Exceptional Children, Division for Learning Disabilities	1110 North Glebe Rd., Suite 300, Arlington, VA 22201-5704, USA Phone: 1-888-CEC-SPED URL:www.teachingld.org	The Division for Learning Disabilities (DLD) is a division of the Council for Exceptional Children (CEC), an international professional organization dedicated to improving educational outcomes for individuals with exceptionalities and students with disabilities. DLD works on behalf of students with learning disabilities and the professionals who serve them.
The International Dyslexia Association	Chester Building, Suite 382, 8600 LaSalle Road, Baltimore, MD 21286-2044, USA Phone: 1-410-296-0232 URL:www.interdys.org	The International Dyslexia Association (IDA) is a scientific and educational organization dedicated to the study and treatment of dyslexia. IDA focuses its resources in four major areas: information and referral services, research, advocacy, and direct services to professionals in the field of learning disabilities.
Learning Disabilities Association of America	4156 Library Road, Pittsburgh, PA 15234-1349, USA Phone: 1-412-341-1515 URL:www.ldaamerica.orq	The Learning Disabilities Association of America (LDA) is an organization founded by parents of children with learning disabilities. The LDA works to provide education, encourage research into learning disabilities, create a climate of public awareness, and provide advocacy information and training.
LD OnLine	WETA Public Television 2775 Quincy Street Arlington, VA 22206, USA URL:www.ldonline.org	LD OnLine is an educational service of public television station WETA in association with the Coordinated Campaign for Learning Disabilities. It features thousands of articles on learning and reading disabilities, monthly columns by experts, a free question-and-answer service, and a directory of professionals and services.
National Center for Learning Disabilities	381 Park Avenue S., Suite 1401, New York, NY 10016, USA Phone: 1-888-575-7373 URL:www.ncld.org	The National Center for Learning Disabilities (NCLD) is an organization devoted to working with individuals with LD, their families, educators, and researchers. NCLD provides essential information, promotes research and programs to foster effective learning, and advocates for policies to protect and strengthen educational rights and opportunities.

- Imaging research confirms that simple tasks can more reliably be interpreted as "red flags" suggesting that a young child may be at risk for dyslexia. It is vital to begin using screening and progress monitoring procedures early on to measure children's understanding of sounds in speech, letter sounds in words, and fluent word recognition. Using such assessment in an ongoing way throughout a child's school career can help teachers know what skills to teach and whether a child is developing these skills.

- Explicit, intense, systematic instruction in the sound structure of language (phonemic awareness) and in how sounds relate to letters (phonics) is needed for readers with dyslexia. Imaging research confirmed that instruction in the alphabetic principle caused distinct differences in brain activation patterns in the students with RD (Shaywitz et al., 2004). Keep in mind

that the intervention was explicit, intense, long term, and specifically focused on phonological processing, phonics, and fluency.

- The roles of motivation and fear of failing are important when discussing reading problems. Students do not struggle simply because they are not trying hard enough. They may have a brain difference that requires them to be taught in a more intense fashion than their peers. Without intense intervention, low motivation may develop as students try to avoid a difficult and painful task.

- School personnel can use their knowledge of the neurological characteristics and basis of dyslexia to help their students understand their strengths and weaknesses around reading and language. Understanding a possible reason why they find something difficult that no one else seems to struggle with may help relieve some of the mystery and negative feelings that many people with a disability feel. Sharing our knowledge of brain research may demystify dyslexia and help students and their parents realize that language processing is only one of many talents that they have and that they are not "stupid," they simply process language differently than their peers.

Recommendations for Parents

The identification of a child with dyslexia is a difficult time for parents and teachers. We suggest that teachers can help parents learn more about their child's difficulty in the following ways:

- Teachers can share information about the student's specific areas of weakness and strength and help parents realize the underlying causes of their child's difficulty. This conversation can also include information about how to help their child use areas of strength to support areas of weakness.
- It is critical to help parents get clear about what dyslexia is and is not. Sharing the common misconceptions and the correct information found in Table 1 with parents may help clear up any confusion that may exist.
- Early intervention with intense, explicit instruction is critical for helping students avoid the lifelong consequences of poor reading. Engaging parents early in the process of identifying what programs and services are best for their child will ensure greater levels of success and cooperation between home and school.
- There are many organizations devoted to supporting individuals with RD and their families. Accessing the knowledge, support, and advocacy of these organizations is critical for many families. A list of several large organizations to share with parents can be found in Table 3.
- Finally, teachers can often best help families by simply listening to the parents and their concerns for their children. Understanding a disability label and what that means for the future of their child is a very emotional process for parents and many times teachers can help by providing a sympathetic ear as well as information.

Imaging research has demonstrated that the brains of people with dyslexia show different, less efficient, patterns of processing (including under and overactivation) during tasks involving sounds in speech and letter sounds in words. Understanding this has the potential to increase the confidence teachers feel when designing and carrying out instruction for their students with dyslexia.

References

Adams, M.J. (1990). *Beginning to read: Thinking and learning about print.* Cambridge, MA: MIT Press.

American Optometric Association. (2004). *The use of tinted lenses and colored overlays for the treatment of dyslexia and other related reading and learning disorders.* St. Louis, MO: Author. Retrieved on June 12, 2005, from www.aoa.org/documents/TintedLenses.pdf

Aylward, E.H., Richards, T.L., Berninger, V.W., Nagy, W.E., Field, K.M., Grimme, A.C., et al. (2003). Instructional treatment associated with changes in brain activation in children with dyslexia. *Neurology, 61,* 212–219.

Blachman, B.A., Schatschneider, C., Fletcher, J.M., Francis, D.J., Clonan, S.M., Shaywitz, et al. (2004). Effects of intensive reading remediation for second and third graders and a 1-year follow-up. *Journal of Educational Psychology, 96,* 444–461.

Booth, J.R., & Burman, D.D. (2001). Development and disorders of neurocognitive systems for oral language and reading. *Learning Disability Quarterly, 24,* 205–215.

Catts, H.W., & Kamhi, A.G. (2005). *Language and reading disabilities* (2nd ed.). Boston: Pearson.

Deutsch, G.K., Dougherty, R.F., Bammer, R., Siok, W.T., Gabrieli, J.D., & Wandell, B. (2005). Children's reading performance is correlated with white matter structure measured by diffusion tensor imaging. *Cortex, 41,* 354–363.

Francis, D.J., Shaywitz, S.E., Stuebing, K.K., Shaywitz, B.A., & Fletcher, J.M. (1996). Developmental lag versus deficit models of reading disability: A longitudinal, individual growth curves analysis. *Journal of Educational Psychology, 88,* 3–17.

Heim, S., & Keil, A. (2004). Large-scale neural correlates of developmental dyslexia. *European Child & Adolescent Psychiatry, 13,* 125–140.

Iovino, I., Fletcher, J.M., Breitmeyer, B.G., & Foorman, B.R. (1998). Colored overlays for visual perceptual deficits in children with reading disability and attention deficit/hyperactivity disorder: Are they differentially effective? *Journal of Clinical & Experimental Neuropsychology, 20,* 791–806.

Joseph, J., Noble, K., & Eden, G. (2001). The neurobiological basis of reading. *Journal of Learning Disabilities, 34,* 566–579.

Lyon, G.R., Shaywitz, S.E., & Shaywitz, B.A. (2003). Defining dyslexia, comorbidity, teachers' knowledge of language and reading. *Annals of Dyslexia, 53,* 1–14.

Morris, R.D., Stuebing, K.K., Fletcher, J.M., Shaywitz, S.E., Shankweiler, D.P., Katz, L., et el. (1998). Subtypes of reading disability: Variability around a phonological core. *Journal of Educational Psychology, 90,* 347–373.

National Institute of Child Health and Human Development. (2000). *Report of the National Reading Panel. Teaching children to read: An evidence-based assessment of the scientific research literature on reading and its implications for reading instruction* (NIH Publication No. 00–4769). Washington, DC: U.S. Government Printing Office.

Papanicolaou, A.C., Pugh, K.R., Simos, P.G., & Mencl, W.E. (2004) Functional brain imaging: An introduction to concepts and applications. In P. McCardle & V. Chhabra (Eds.), *The voice of evidence in reading research.* Baltimore: Paul H. Brooks.

Rayner, K., Foorman, B.R., Perfetti, C.A., Pesetsky, D., & Seidenberg, M.S. (2001). How psychological science informs the teaching of reading. *Psychological Science in the Public Interest, 2*(2), 31–74.

Richards, T.L. (2001). Functional magnetic resonance imaging and spectroscopic imaging of the brain: Application of the fMRI and fMRS to reading disabilities and education. *Learning Disability Quarterly, 24,* 189–203.

Shaywitz, B.A., Shaywitz, S.E., Pugh, K.R., Mencl, W.E., Fulbright, R.K., Skudlarksi, P., et al. (2002). Disruption of posterior brain systems for reading in children with developmental dyslexia. *Biological Psychiatry, 52,* 101–110.

Shaywitz, S.E. (1996). Dyslexia. *Scientific American, 275*(5), 98–104.

Shaywitz, S.E., Fletcher, J.M., Holahan, J.M., Shneider, A.E., Marchione, K.E., Stuebing, K.K., et al. (1999). Persistence of dyslexia: The Connecticut Longitudinal Study at adolescence. *Pediatrics, 104,* 1351–1359.

Shaywitz, B.A., Shaywitz, S.E., Blachman, B.A., Pugh, K.R., Fulbright, R.K., Skudlarski, P., et al. (2004). Development of left occipitotemporal systems for skilled reading in children after a phonologically-based intervention. *Biological Psychiatry, 55,* 926–933.

Shaywitz, S.E., Shaywitz, B.A., Fletcher, J.M., & Escobar, M.D. (1990). Prevalence of reading disability in boys and girls: Results of the Connecticut Longitudinal Study. *Journal of the American Medical Association, 264,* 998–1002.

Shaywitz, S.E., Shaywitz, B.A., Fulbright, R.K., Skudlarski, P., Mencl, W.E., Constable, R.T., et al. (2003). Neural systems for compensation and persistence: Young adult outcome of childhood reading disability. *Biological Psychiatry, 54,* 25–33.

Shaywitz, S.E., Shaywitz, B.A., Pugh, K.R., Fulbright, R.K., Constable, R.T., Mencl, W.E., et al. (1998). Functional disruption in the organization of the brain for reading in dyslexia. *Proceedings of the National Academy of Sciences, 95,* 2636–2641.

Snow, C.E., Burns, M.S., & Griffin, P. (Eds.). (1998). *Preventing reading difficulties in young children.* Washington, DC: National Academy Press.

Torgesen, J.K. (2000). Individual differences in response to early interventions in reading: The lingering problem of treatment resisters. *Learning Disabilities Research & Practice, 15,* 55–64.

Torgesen, J.K. (2002). The prevention of reading difficulties. *Journal of School Psychology, 40,* 7–26.

Torgesen, J.K., Rashotte, C.A., & Alexander, A. (2001). Principles of fluency instruction in reading: Relationships with established empirical outcomes. In M. Wolf (Ed.), *Dyslexia, fluency, and the brain.* Timonium, MD: York.

Wagner, R.K., & Torgesen, J.K. (1987). The nature of phonological processing and its causal role in the acquisition of reading skills. *Psychological Bulletin, 101,* 192–212.

Ziegler, J.C., & Goswami, U. (2005). Reading acquisition, developmental dyslexia, and skilled reading across languages: A psycholinguistic grain size theory. *Psychological Bulletin, 131,* 3–29.

HUDSON teaches at the University of Washington (Box 353600, Seattle, WA 98195, USA). E-mail rhudson@u.washington.edu. **HIGH** teaches in the Taylor County School District, Perry, Florida. **AL OTAIBA** teaches at the Florida Center for Reading Research and Florida State University in Tallahassee.

Author Note—The authors thank the many teachers whose valuable comments on previous versions of this manuscript have greatly improved its quality. In particular, we appreciate the helpful comments of Sondra Stauffer, Jason Maas, Jenny Levy, Jennifer Beach, and Carol Connor and students in the Language and Literacy Assessment course at Florida State University.

Build Organizational Skills in Students with Learning Disabilities

RITA F. FINSTEIN, FEI YAO YANG, AND RÁCHELE JONES

Organization is an essential skill for all of us. For the student who has a learning disability (LD), development of expertise may require direct instruction and guidance (Borich, 2000). The true talent of the student with LD can be masked by his inability to produce work that reflects his abilities. A student who cannot find his paper but assures you that it is finished, the one who brings a math paper that appears to be a mass of unintelligible gibberish, or the student who hands you her English paper in a crumpled wad, may simply be telling you that he or she needs help with organizational skills. Lack of organizational skills can influence the work quality, the satisfaction of turning a paper in on time, and the self-worth of any student, but it is especially significant for students with LD. This student may not turn in his science assignment because he misplaced it or forgot that he had it to do, did not take it home, and thus did not have it to turn in on time.

Good organizational skills useful throughout life can be learned through small, integrated steps practiced in and out of school. Teachers, parents, and others can foster acquisition of organizational skills. They can encourage students with LD to:

1. Believe That They Can Do What Is Asked

As the student with LD shows small increments of progress, teachers need to praise and praise often. Positive attitudes are contagious and help in learning any skill. True praise builds confidence in students with disabilities. It is not possible to say often enough "Good job. I like the way you followed the three math steps" or "Well done," when the teacher hands back the spelling test or "I like the way you are planning your day," when the student remembers to go to tutoring.

2. Work Cooperatively with Parents

Teachers should model a good relationship between home and school. A strong partnership helps the student with LD (Bryan & Burstein, 2004). Teachers can show parents how to monitor homework and to help their child follow a work schedule at home. Teachers can open communication between the parents and themselves with phone conferences and correspondence.

3. Post Needed Information on a Bulletin Board

At home, parents can help their child be organized by using a bulletin board, refrigerator door, or other convenient location to post "To Do" lists. A large metal clip can be used to collect school notices and messages that need to be returned to school. This provides a convenient place that the child will always know where to put school correspondence (Practicing Organizational Skills at Home, 2005). The parent should use guided practice, and with time, the student will be more independent in making "To Do" lists.

4. Use Checklists to Track Activities

Checklists are used frequently for school-age students. Checklists provide a way for the student to check off each task as it is finished, for example, bringing required materials to each class and returning materials to their proper place. In addition, checklists also empowers the student to feel a sense of accomplishment and self-confidence, as the marked-through or crossed-out items means that he has finished those responsibilities.

5. Make and Update a Calendar

A calendar can give an overview to an entire day, week, or school year. It helps break large tasks into sizeable, workable units. Use of different colors for various activities helps highlight the importance of due dates for projects, assignments, and exams. In addition, the calendar helps the student with LD to meet deadlines. Calendars useful for home and school can be a tool to assist students in completing tasks on time and in managing time effectively. Parents can check the calendar at home, and the teacher can monitor it at school.

6. Follow a Daily Agenda

Used with the calendar, the daily agenda breaks tasks listed on the calendar into steps for completion. The availability of commercially purchased daily agendas that provide a place to list tasks to be done or considered each day helps the student with LD meet her deadlines as marked on the calendar.

7. Use an Organizer/Planner

Organizers/planners in various formats—oral cues, charts, and diagrams (which distinguished them from the daily agenda)—are used to sketch out specific daily activities, such as homework or steps of a task or project. Parents and teachers can model the use of an organizer/planner, and with guided practice, students with LD will (a) learn the concept of preview and overview and (b) understand priorities of activities and when and how to complete the activity. They will also discover that free time can be scheduled within the daily time restraints.

8. Pair with a General Education Student

One of the most powerful influences on a student's learning is peer pressure. Teams can be formed, with one general education student who is proficient in organization skills paired with the student who needs help with such skills. The general education student acts as a role model for his partner in these teams. The organized student can mentor his buddy in organizational skills, establish appropriate attitudes for classes, and give hints on how to study for tests. The peer–buddy relationship not only fosters cooperative learning but also contributes to the success or failure of performance in school in many ways (Borich, 2000).

9. Carry Scripts/How-To Cards

Mobile remainders help students stay focused throughout the day. Students with LD can use these cards to prompt them about specific steps and remind them to complete a task. These cards are convenient to pull out of their notebook or pocket as necessary.

10. Post Reminders

Reminders provide a fast and visual communication to track task completion and can be stuck to one's notebook, inside one's locker, and so on. Students can check the reminder to know specifically what is expected. If Jim needs to be reminded of the steps to do his math problems, these can be posted inside his math book, and as he uses that book, the visual reminder is right there for him to reference. If Mary needs help remembering the "i before e" rule, the reminder is stuck on her spelling list and is visible when she begins to study.

11. Keep Everything Where It Belongs

The adage "a place for everything, and everything in its place," is true. All students misplace or lose an assignment, a book, a note to take home or return to school. These events seem to be daily happenings for the student with LD. She needs an assigned place for books, supplies, and notes traveling to and from school.

The student in elementary school with his own desk needs to put books in a specific order and a specific spot on or near his desk. To always know that the math book is directly above the language book is not only comforting but reliable. Covering each book with a different colored cover or having book titles on the spine of each book helps to identify each text with ease.

Secondary school brings use of a locker, which may exacerbate organizational challenges. The locker should have a designated place for anything that really needed and should not house unneeded articles. Textbooks can be arranged according to the class period in which they are used and should be always stored in that order. At the beginning of the year or semester, the student may have to use a posted note inside the door of his locker to remind him of this arrangement. Books should be arranged so that the spine side is out with the subject name clearly written on each spine.

At home, the student with LD needs an established place to put his books upon returning home. If he always puts his book bag in his room next to his desk, he will not have to wonder where it is. If sharpened pencils are in the well on his desk, he will always find them there. He benefits from a specific time and place to do his schoolwork, establishing a routine. It will soon become a habit if the student does his homework at 7 P.M. every evening in his room for an hour.

12. Determine What to Carry

The student who is not in a self-contained classroom and travels from room to room during the day sometimes needs help to know what and how much to take from her locker and when and how often to visit it. A counselor may be able to arrange a schedule of classes that helps with organization. For example, the counselor can arrange classes that are back to back to be on the same floor, or at least in the same part of the building, instead of having the student be on the first floor and then the third floor the next hour or in room 101, which is on the southeast end of the building, during third period, and room 163, which is on the northwest end of the building, for fourth period. However, if convenient scheduling is not possible, the student will benefit from carrying the books for first and second period with her when she leaves her locker instead of having to come back after first period to get that book for second period. This can be adjusted, depending how many books need to be carried at one time, but the object is to stress that the student should not have to return to her locker between every class.

Another situation finds the student trying to carry all that he needs for the entire day with him to every class. The student should carry only what he needs and not load himself down with books and materials he does not need to carry. This may mean he carries materials for just two classes, or it can mean that he carry more. The student may carry only the books and supplies he needs for the morning classes as he leaves for first period. At lunch he can return to his locker, put away the morning materials, and get all that is needed for the afternoon. It depends on the student's schedule. Teachers can stress the importance of this through role play, discussion, relating personal incidents, or asking students about their experiences. Essentials needed for every class should be carried at all times. This will include at least two pencils, a pen, notebook paper, and some means of storing assignments. If there are other items needed for a specific class, they can be added at the morning or afternoon stop to the locker.

An important stop at the locker is the one right before leaving school. The student with LD should check her schedule, planner, or "To Do" list—whatever she is using to document what it is she has to do—and pull from the locker those books and materials she needs to complete her homework at home. This will help eliminate not completing assignments because the materials needed to do the assignments were left at school.

13. Know Teacher Routines

Students with LD need to know the established routines for each teacher they have and follow them. Teachers at the beginning of a term hand out class requirements and expectations; the student should keep these in a notebook for reference. A good plan of action upon entering a classroom is to check to see if pencils are sharpened, look at the board to see if there is an introductory assignment to do, sit in the assigned seat, and have all books accessible for use.

14. Carry an Efficient and Orderly Notebook

A notebook with dividers separating space for each subject is a vital organizational tool. After each subject divider, a folder for assignments completed and a folder for assignments still to do not only remind the student what he must do but also secure a place for the work. Everything in the notebook should be secured either within the rings or in folders to avoid losing them if the notebook is dropped. A calendar or schedule at the front of the notebook to record daily assignments keeps the student aware of what he has done and what he still needs to do.

15. Wear a Rubber Band Bracelet

To encourage time on task and completion of work, a younger child can wear a rubber band around the wrist of her writing hand until her assignment is completed and then move the rubber band to the other wrist. The objective of this switch from the hand with which the work is done to the other, nonwriting hand,

is that it supplies a visible sign that whatever it was that had to be finished is now done.

16. Date and Title Assignments

Students can be helped in organizing their papers by dating and titling every assignment. This not only helps in keeping work in order but also gives a time frame for what needs to be studied for a test. If the test is to be over notes from February 11 to February 20, a paper dated January 30 would not be one that needs to be studied.

17. Engage in Guided Practice

Sessions to teach organizational strategies have been successful in social studies in Chicago (Fatata-Hall, 1998). Students with LD improved their grades by participating in classes that teach them good organization strategies. Teachers modeled steps and procedures, and students helped each other to improve their skills. Barry and Moore (2004) record success in giving students time to practice the steps to good organization. In another study, direct instruction in organizational strategies, such as time management, prioritizing, and study skills, increased student ability and awareness in organizing time, activities, and school work (Anday-Porter, Henne, & Horan, 2000).

18. Communicate with Teachers When Assignments Seem Overwhelming

The student should let teachers know that some assignments may be beyond her level. Lack of organizational skills is compounded when the student is also struggling with something beyond her abilities.

19. Engage in Mentoring Programs

Mentor programs are effective in assisting students with LD achieve at higher levels (Shevits, Weinfeld, Jewler, & Barnes-Robinson, 2003). A student struggling with organizational skills is teamed with an adult strong in these skills. The adult can model good skills and guide the struggling student to improve his organizational competence.

20. Have an Individualized Education Program (IEP) That Addresses Organizational Skills

The IEP lists short- and long-term goals for students. The student with LD who needs assistance in organization needs written goals to address these needs. For example, a short-term goal might be for the student to use a "To Do" list to monitor completion of math assignments for a 2-week period, with a long-term goal to complete all math assignments in the semester through use of a "To Do" list to monitor daily assignments.

References

Anday-Porter, S., Henne, K., & Horan, S. (2000). *Improving student organizational skills through the use of organizational skills in the curriculum.* Retrieved February 9, 2005, from ERIC Document Reproduction Service No. ED355616.

Barry, L., & Moore, W. E., IV. (2004). Students with specific learning disabilities can pass state competency exams: Systematic strategy instruction makes a difference. *Preventing School Failure, 48*(3), 10–15.

Borich, G. D. (2000). *Effective teaching methods* (4th ed.). Upper Saddle River, NJ: Prentice Hall.

Bryan, T., & Burstein, K. (2004). Improving homework completion and academic performance: Lessons from special education. *Theory into Practice, 43*(3), 213–219.

Fatata-Hall, K. (1998). *Acquisition and application of study skills and test taking strategies with eighth grade learning disabled failing social studies.* Retrieved February 9, 2005, from ERIC Document Reproduction Service No. S0029064.

Practicing organizational skills at home. (n.d.). Retrieved February 9, 2005, from http://www.hellofriend.org/parents/organizational.html.

Shevits, B., Weinfeld, R., Jewler, S., & Barnes-Robinson, L. (2003). Mentoring empowers gifted/learning disabled students to soar! *Roeper Review, 26*(1), 37–40.

All three authors are doctoral students and graduate or research assistants in special education, have completed all course work, and are working on their dissertations, each concentrating on a different aspect of autism spectrum disorders and its impact. **RITA F. FINSTEIN,** MA, retired after 33 years of teaching in the public schools to pursue a doctorate. She has certification in special education, English, math, history, and early childhood and is a language retraining (for dyslexia) therapist. **FEI YAO YANG,** MEd, a Chinese student from Taiwan, graduated from Chianan Medical Junior College with a chemistry degree. Upon coming to the United States, she received a master's degree in generic special education from the University of Central Oklahoma. Her plan is to return to Taiwan to teach special education at the university level. **RÁCHELE JONES,** MA, has been studying Asperger syndrome for more than 4 years, since the diagnosis of her eldest son and, subsequently, other family members with Asperger syndrome. Currently, her primary focus is on communication issues within Asperger syndrome and how these issues affect learning. Address: Rita F. Finstein, Texas Tech University, Box 2071, Lubbock, TX 79409-1071; e-mail: ritafin@cox.net.

From *Intervention in School and Clinic,* by Rita Finstein, Fei Yao Yang, and Rachele Jones, Vol. 42, No. 3, January 2007, pp. 174–178. Copyright © 2007 by Pro-Ed, Inc. Reprinted by permission via Rightslink.

Inclusion by Design
Engineering Inclusive Practices in Secondary Schools

Ms. Johnson is a special education teacher at Sunshine Middle School. Her assignment includes a total of six classes and one planning period. For three periods out of the day, she teaches a learning strategy course for students with mild disabilities (e.g., learning disabilities), and for the other three periods of the day, she works with the science and social study teachers assisting them in two ways: (a) consulting with teachers to discuss specific students and strategies to assist those students in the classroom and (b) offering in-class support for students who need more extensive support to succeed in the general education environment. For example, Ms. Johnson works with Mr. Smith, the seventh grade social studies teacher. In the beginning, Mr. Smith always took the teacher role and Ms. Johnson always took the helper role. But recently they experimented with a change in roles as both become more comfortable with offering assistance and leading the lesson. Both teachers agree that the key to the success of Ms. Johnson's periodic visits to the classroom to aid students' education will not run smoothly without deliberate planning and continued communication. It seems that inclusion can work, but it must be intentionally designed. This article describes the design process an engineer might use when designing a new project in order to help teachers understand the importance of intentional design for inclusive education.

CHARLES DUKES AND PAMELA LAMAR-DUKES

If teachers think like engineers, it is possible to design inclusive education. By utilizing the basic components of the design process, the parameters of an inclusive education program can be defined. This conceptual design can then be combined with subsystems and mechanisms that reliably assist teachers to move from merely embracing inclusive philosophy to the implementation of inclusive practices. This differentiation between philosophy and practice is especially salient on the secondary level where inclusive practices are often discussed in a positive light but may not be implemented with any real enthusiasm (Keefe & Moore, 2004). Before discussing the merits of the engineering metaphor, inclusive education on the secondary level is briefly examined.

> **If teachers think like engineers, it is possible to design inclusive education.**

Inclusive Education in Secondary Schools

Accountability for all students to make academic and social gains has become increasingly important. Both political and social pressures influenced the development of school programs intended to meet the needs of all students in spite of ability. Even in light of a mature literature base on inclusive education (see Ryndak & Fisher, 2006, for a review of inclusive education),

many questions remain about inclusive education as a service delivery model on the secondary level. However, there is no evidence to suggest that inclusive service delivery models can be effectively superimposed onto existing school programs without direct intervention from administrators and without a fundamental change to the way teachers deliver educational services to students (DiPaola, Tschannen-Moran, & Walther-Thomas, 2004). There is a clear difference between inclusive philosophy and inclusive practice (Artiles, Kozleski, Dorn, & Christensen, 2008). Although it is essential for teachers to understand the rules and regulations of Federal legislation (i.e., Individuals With Disabilities Education Improvement Act, IDEA, 2004), it is also critical to understand the spirit of the Federal legislation which serves as the basis for creating and maintaining inclusive practices (e.g., expanding the principle of least restrictive environment to include access to the general education curriculum).

There is no single method by which to practice inclusive education, but the underlying belief that all professionals are responsible to promote the academic and social development of all students is key (Dukes & Lamar-Dukes, 2006). Inclusive philosophy is not intended to be used as a guiding principle for curriculum selection or instructional methods, but instead to provide a frame for some of the basic notions about the *who* (students receiving services) and the *where* (location where students receive services) of inclusive education. Thus, it follows that a definition of inclusive education is the process by which educators provide appropriate supports and services to students with disabilities in the least restrictive environment, namely the general education classroom (Idol, 2006). For the purposes in this article, the mechanisms by which these supports and services are formulated are referred to as *inclusive practices*. Based on the structure of elementary and secondary schools, inclusive practices must be developed and implemented differently. Secondary schools present a unique challenge for a teacher, which means that service delivery must vary in response to the differing school structure.

Unique Features of Inclusive Education in Secondary Schools

One of the most contentious issues surrounding inclusive education is the modification or changing of the general curriculum. This issue is especially poignant in secondary schools where there is a general tendency for teachers to be more narrowly focused on content within academic areas. This rigid focus is only one of several potential barriers that may actually impede inclusive education on the secondary level. For example, the need for basic literacy in the areas of reading, writing, computation, and science creates rigorous academic demands for students (Michael & Trezek, 2006). It is possible that this structure impedes the promotion of inclusive education as the frequency and duration of contact between students and educators is different, making remedial or direct instruction a difficult venture (Weiss & Lloyd, 2002). These unique aspects of secondary education require that teachers take special care to understand the nature of inclusive education and the necessary changes to their work lives (Wasburn-Moss, 2005).

In order to cultivate inclusive practices in secondary schools, special education teachers must expand their focus beyond individual student needs, and general educators must release themselves of an exclusive focus on academic content. The collaborative effort of all educators around the tenets of effective instruction can serve as a solid foundation for inclusive education to take hold. By framing inclusive education as a way in which to make instruction more effective for all students, it is possible that general educators will find the investment in change worthwhile. In fact, one of the key factors contributing to the sustainability of school reform is teachers' acceptance of the reform and how closely aligned the reform efforts are with teachers' current beliefs and teaching styles (Sindelar, Shearer, Yendol-Hoppey, & Liebert, 2006). Thus, it is essential that the instructional demands of secondary schools are placed front and center when designing inclusive service delivery methods. Instruction stands out as the critical component of effective services for low-achieving students and students with disabilities (Gravois, Rosenfield, & Vail, 1999).

The challenges associated with inclusive education can be detailed with relative ease. It is not difficult to locate a long line of teachers who may report the difficulties they face. This is not to suggest that there are not a number of teachers who have faced these challenges and come out on top. But clearly there are many examples of unsuccessful inclusive education programs. If inclusive education is framed as a design problem, it is possible to use engineering as a metaphor to enhance our understanding of how exactly to design a viable program on the secondary level. But before laying out the design specifications to create an inclusive education program, the way engineers think and how the engineering thought process can help teachers is described.

Engineering Used as an Organizing Principle

Often, just mention of the word engineering brings about feelings of intimidation, at least for those outside the engineering field. This is unfortunate because the basic idea behind engineering is the science and art of design (Petroski, 1992). If engineering is framed as a means to generate the solution to a particular problem, then perhaps it is not so out of reach. In fact, the basic principles of design already have an enormous influence on the way educators think (see Rose, Meyer, Strangman, & Rappolt, 2002, for a review of universal design). Therefore, applying engineering principles is not an intellectual stretch for teachers, but rather a helpful metaphor that can greatly enhance teachers' thinking when faced with some of the most challenging design problems. In order to really benefit from the use of engineering as a helpful metaphor, it is necessary to introduce some of the ways in which engineers think as well as the basic components of the design process.

How Engineers Think

Engineering design is a complex process made up of a wide variety of activities to meet a need (Oakley, 1990). In other words, engineers design products or processes to meet the needs of people; they design solutions to problems. Design is often complicated when a process requires that several different distinct systems must function as one, which is the case for inclusive education. Depending on the circumstances, engineers ask themselves one of two different questions no matter the task: (a) What can I make to improve this process? or (b) How can I make this process better? We all enjoy the outcomes resulting from this line of thinking, such as extensive freeway systems or light bulbs that last 5 years, and we continue to benefit from the way engineers think in order to solve problems.

But how do engineers approach problems in the first place? First, engineers define the problem at hand. Although the solution to any one problem varies from the next, generally the solution is either a new product or process or the enhancement of an already existing product or process. Second, engineers approach the problem by thinking about conceptual design and design execution. The former is used to help clarify the parameters of the problem and the latter is used to clarify the procedures by which the concept is executed or implemented. Third, engineers dedicate some of their thinking to developing procedures that are implemented using various methodologies. These methodologies include a collection of general approaches that are open, iterative, and flexible (Oakley, 1990). In summary, engineers clearly define problems; conceptualize the problem; think about executing the solution; and use a general, flexible approach to implement the solution. This description clarifies the way engineers think, but how do they go about actually designing the products or processes that so beautifully meet some of our everyday needs? This is done by using the design process which is discussed next.

Identify the problem or need:

- What are my goals for inclusion?
- What barriers might hinder my inclusive design?
- Who or what may help facilitate my inclusive design?
- Where is this design supposed to happen (in which classroom)?
- Who is this design supposed to help?
- When is this design taking place (scheduling)?

Identify the purpose or function of the system:

- How will my inclusive design help my students?
- How will my inclusive design help other teachers?
- How will I help my students achieve academically?
- How will I help teachers develop the skills necessary to facilitate inclusion?
- How will I address resistance from teachers, administration, or students?
- How will I ensure that I meet my goals?
- How will I rebound if I experience a setback?

Develop design concepts and specifications:

- What things must I have in place for this design to be a success?
- Who must be on board with this plan?
- What assistance is needed (person, technology, or materials)?
- What professional development is required?
- Will students need to be trained to utilize service delivery?
- How can I minimize the stigma attached to service delivery?

Build, test, and evaluate the system:

- How is my design working?
- Are students learning intended concepts?
- Are teachers able to effectively teach all students?
- Are we reaching the goals set for our inclusive design?
- Are there unexpected aspects that may need adjusting?

Figure 1 Step-by-step inclusive design.

The Fundamentals of the Design Process

At its core, engineering is built on the design process. Its steps are (a) indentifying the problem or need; (b) identifying the purpose or function of the system; (c) developing design concepts and specifications; and (d) building, testing, and evaluating the system (Savage, 2006). There are other ways in which to describe the design process, but this description provides an adequate foundation from which to understand the design of inclusive education programs. The design process provides a wonderful metaphor from which to gain a deeper understanding of how direct efforts to engineer or design inclusive practices is necessary to ensure the academic and social success of students with disabilities. Figure 1 provides a presentation of the steps described and a set of guiding questions that further clarify how to use the design process for inclusive education. But how does the design process apply to inclusive education?

Using the Design Process for Inclusive Education

Step one calls for the identification of the problem or need. Although the inclusion of students with disabilities is clearly not a problem, it is an issue that requires a great deal of work from many different people. When thinking about the issues involved in designing an inclusive education program, it is important to define the parameters of the issue. The design process begins by identifying all of the issues that may help or hinder the final process that is used. A common parameter that many engineers consider is called *design space*. This is simply the space or environment where the product is used. For teachers, schools serve as the primary design space, but we must go beyond considerations of the physical structure and consider other factors. Scheduling in secondary schools also deserves special attention, and designing an inclusive service delivery model requires consideration of the surface design space (physical structure) and deep design space (scheduling). After giving careful consideration to identifying the issues and parameters of the intended design, step two requires identifying the purpose or function of the system. Engineers have a very unique way of thinking about the products and processes that they develop. They are always interested in how the product or process will work, but they are also concerned about the conditions under which the product or process may fail. In essence, engineers think about how the product or process is used and then imagine the greatest trauma that may befall their creation. They then attempt to make the product or process strong enough to withstand this hypothesized trauma. In regard to inclusive education, failure is best thought of as a collapse or breakdown of the inclusive service delivery model. This may be evident in teachers refusing to teach students with disabilities, teachers lacking the skill necessary to teach students with disabilities, or it may result in large segments of students with disabilities failing to meet adequate yearly progress. If the service delivery model fails to meet one of the intended goals, then it is possible that the entire system may be deemed as a failure. Inclusive service delivery models should be structured with failsafe mechanisms to withstand at least some of these traumas to the system and remain intact. The third step is developing design concepts and specifications. Engineers conceptualize the design of the product or process. This conceptualized schematic is then used to design the necessary steps to execute the design. Essentially, engineers develop the basic concept (these are *what* questions) and then develop the procedures to execute the design (these are *how* questions). When designing inclusive education, the initial concept is simple; all students, regardless of ability, need to receive effective instruction. This is not to suggest that executing inclusive education is simple, but the basic concept is simple and this is one of the most important aspects of thinking like an engineer. Ask simple questions that require simple answers and the desired product or process develops. The final step in the design process requires engineers to build, test, and evaluate their product or system. For educators, this is highly familiar as implementation of a new initiative is a common part of the educational process. This is the design process as practiced by engineers, but completely accessible to educators to help design inclusive education.

Armed with knowledge about the way engineers think and the steps in the design process, it is easier to understand some of the difficulties teachers face in secondary schools when attempting to design inclusive service delivery models. Now that the foundation for thinking like an engineer is laid, it is time to move on to the design specifications of inclusive education. The next section discusses how conceptual design moves to design execution.

Design Specifications for the Subsystems of Inclusive Education

Engineers must always be acutely aware of the big picture when approaching a new project. Every aspect of the product or process must be kept in mind during the conceptual design phase as the product or process is not intended to function in a vacuum, but rather in a highly specific context. Engineers know that it is often ineffective to think about only one design. It is more effective to think about a collection of designs that operate together to form a whole that ultimately meets the need. Inclusive education is not any different, and in fact inclusive education calls for a complex mix of subsystems to meet the needs of all students (see Lamar-Dukes & Dukes, 2005, for a description of teacher supports). The next section briefly reviews the design process and discusses the progression from concept to execution, providing details about the subsystems and the procedures necessary to make inclusive education work.

Design Process: From Design to Execution

When thinking about the need presented by inclusive education, it is important to ask if we can satisfy this need with a new product or process or can use an existing product or process. There are a number of ways in which to answer this question, but for this example, we will use a new process. Consider what contributes to this new process and what might detract or even cause this process to completely fail. For example, some teachers have positive perceptions of inclusive education (Reeves, 2006), and this may help direct the selection of specific procedures when it is time to actually implement the inclusive education program. But, on the other side of the issue, accommodation and/or modification of classroom-based material or high-stakes testing can dismantle any secondary school's inclusive education program. These two examples show how important it is that the design team (i.e., teachers, administrators, and others responsible for designing the program) generate as many good concepts as possible to address all potential issues.

Next, develop the specifications or procedures by which the designed process is implemented. When developing procedures, it is possible to approach the design from a number of different ways. For our purposes here, mechanisms (e.g., support networks) used to facilitate the implementation of the inclusive education subsystems is emphasized. There are a number of subsystems that must be in place for inclusive education, but it is understood that these subsystems not only require some unique features but also require a teacher-driven mechanism that supports the operation of these subsystems.

Support Networks

Support networks are an essential component of secondary inclusive schooling. They are an organizational component that involves coordination of teams and individuals who support each other and are motivated by a committed school administration (Boscardin, 2005; Scheffel, Kallam, Smith, & Hoernicke, 1996). Teacher collaboration is not guaranteed by virtue of physical proximity or administrative mandate. The creation of inclusive education practices at the secondary level requires specific attention to the creation of teacher teams that have the space, time, and knowledge to function as a team. For teachers to make inclusive practices work in schools, professional collaboration is crucial. The following 10 subsystems set the stage for the work necessary to design optimal conditions for inclusive practices based on consistent and effective collaboration between general and special education teachers. Each subsystem is followed by a brief illustration of how it might manifest in a secondary school using Ms. Johnson and Mr. Smith, the social studies teacher, as an example.

Belief and vision. The phrase *all means all* is quite often used in relation to inclusive education and characterizes a belief about who receives an education. Although the debate and confusion about inclusive practices persists, there is a call for the responsible inclusion of students with disabilities in classrooms where general education teachers are well supported (Heward, 2006). The promotion of a specific vision for inclusive practices initially involves attempts to change the surface design space as the landscape of the school should promote messages about achievement for all students. Teachers need to understand the nuances of both inclusive philosophy and practices, and it is necessary for educators and support staff to collaboratively formulate a vision statement.

> *Ms. Johnson believes that all students have the potential to be served in a general education classroom, and she helps Mr. Smith include a student with moderate disabilities into his classroom. Mr. Smith is willing to work with the student, especially after Ms. Johnson shares her beliefs and views on the importance and benefits of inclusion not only for this child, but for all the students in Mr. Smith's class.*

Time. Teachers need time to work collaboratively and/or consult with each other to accomplish the task of implementing inclusive practices. Time to collaborate allows several professionals to be available and have access to each other. Secondary schools present surface design spaces as well as deep design spaces that must be uncovered. In this case, time, class schedules, and teacher schedules must be thoroughly investigated so that the educational support team understands the implications of various service delivery models. For example, special education teachers who split their time across a number of different classrooms must have enough time to actually deliver meaningful services to particular teachers and students. It is possible that some general education teachers receive subpar support because special education teachers simply do not have enough time to deliver the appropriate service.

Ms. Johnson knows that she needs to devote time to plan lessons and actually deliver those lessons in the general education classroom with Mr. Smith. After reviewing their schedules and preferences, they come up with times that they can sit down together and plan and evaluate instruction. They also decide times when Ms. Johnson can be in the classroom to help deliver instruction, and they develop a schedule for when they are both available for parent or student conferences.

Classroom (work) space. Consideration of work space may sound trivial, but a number of teachers in secondary schools are forced to share classroom space. Like belief and vision, space is a surface design problem related to the whole structure of the school, and require broad considerations of how classroom space is used over the school day. Teachers are professionals who need space to operate and conduct their interactions professionally. Teachers working in support roles need access to an open physical space throughout the school day to develop educational supports or perhaps conduct meetings with other teachers or parents.

Mr. Smith knows that Ms. Johnson provides support to students on a regular basis in his classroom. He set aside space for her in the classroom so that she can work with small groups of students or work with students one-on-one. After consulting with Ms. Johnson on items that she may find useful in her day-to-day operations, Mr. Smith ensures that those items are available to her and that she has storage space.

Documentation. The fundamental conventions of teaching include designing, implementing, and evaluating teaching and learning. The instructional plan includes objectives, activities, and one or more evaluation methods to verify student learning. Inclusive education requires the detailing of many more aspects of the learning process. In inclusive classrooms, teachers are also responsible for documenting how and when educational services are delivered. Part of this documentation process begins with the individualized education program (IEP) and expands to include progress data.

The IEP provides goals, objectives, effects of disability on learning, and appropriate accommodations unique to the student in question. This document serves as the starting point for teacher collaboration in inclusive classrooms. The next step is turning the IEP into a living document by converting the supports detailed in the IEP into a classroom reality. Clearly, this is one of the most critical considerations for inclusive practices, as documentation of services is one sure way of indicating the effectiveness of the service delivery model. Thus, documentation is one of the most appropriate areas where the educational team should hypothesize about potential failures. Questions that may drive these considerations might include (a) What might impede teachers from documenting service delivery in the classrooms? or (b) What is the most appropriate manner in which to indicate the success of the inclusive model (e.g., teacher performance, student performance, or perhaps some combination of both)? These and other questions can help the educational support team think about the limits of the service delivery model and ensure that the initial design of the system takes into account many of these considerations.

Ms. Johnson knows that she must be able to utilize documentation effectively to plan and evaluate service delivery and instruction. Along with Mr. Smith, she identifies those classroom events they need to track based on the IEP. Together they identify which goals or benchmarks to document based on student needs and curricular requirements. Then they decide which documentation instruments are used and how to collect documentation. They both understand that documenting service delivery assists them in planning future instruction and evaluating the effectiveness of their efforts.

Conflict resolution. Experienced teachers are familiar with the ups and downs of working with others. In inclusive schools, the dynamics of professional relationships change as many teachers work together in nontraditional ways and take on challenges traditionally left to special education teachers. As stated previously, simply sharing physical space does not constitute collaboration and there are no guarantees that teachers will exit their teacher education programs with knowledge or actual experience in collaboration. This lays much of the responsibility for creating an atmosphere where collaboration can take hold and thrive on the core team of teachers responsible for engineering inclusive practices. The team may have to assist other personnel in learning about the nature of collaboration and some of the common pitfalls associated with collaborative work. Outside of the informal conversations that take place naturally, there is a need for formal discussions and training in conflict resolution. It is possible to incorporate conflict resolution in the greater professional development program. In cooperation with school administrators, the educational support team can plan and develop effective processes to manage a wide range of possible conflicts among teachers (e.g., differences in classroom management techniques).

Mr. Smith and Ms. Johnson know that conflicts are bound to arise when working together, so they attended a staff development session detailing ways to work together. In this session, they were instructed to begin their partnership by identifying their non-negotiables in the classroom, discuss their plans on how to communicate with each other, discuss their plans on how to handle disagreements if they should arise, determine the overall workload, and assign responsibility for each activity. Mr. Smith and Ms. Johnson set aside time to discuss these issues and their partnership prior to starting their working relationship.

Initial and ongoing professional development. The traditional formats for professional development generally involve single sessions where participants are expected to *sit and get* the material (McLeskey & Waldron, 2002). This format does not allow teachers to place inclusive education at the front and center as a schoolwide focus. Although some of the barriers present in secondary schools are difficult to alter (e.g., special educators' content knowledge), there are others that are highly amendable to professional development (e.g., collaborative practices).

Mr. Smith and Ms. Johnson attended initial training on collaboration before the school year began. At the beginning of the year, they made a wish list of other professional development activities they thought would make their partnership run smoothly. They also participated on a planning team to identify other professional development activities for themselves and others at their school to ease student transition. Mr. Smith requested that Ms. Johnson assist him, through coaching, to obtain certain skills that may help him become a more effective teacher.

Fluid and open lines of communication. One of the most critical aspects of general education is the referral process to special education. General education teachers must evaluate students and make difficult decisions about typical progress versus stifled progress different enough to constitute a learning deficit in need of formal evaluation (Vaughn, Bos, & Schumm, 2003). Secondary teachers do not generally make initial referrals, but are faced with students who may not make sufficient strides in academic progress. Communication is absolutely critical to teachers when trying to understand why students are not making progress at the secondary level. The main issue here for teachers is the need for sufficient contact with special and general education teachers, providing everyone with the information necessary to make informed decisions. In order to communicate effectively, teachers' documentation and data collected about services delivered in the classrooms is shared, and educational support teams are responsible for facilitating communication among teachers involved in collaborative work.

One of the most critical aspects of general education is the referral process to special education.

Mr. Smith is concerned about a student in his class who has not been identified as needing special education services. He collects some data concerning the student such as test scores, attendance, and writing samples so that Ms. Johnson and he can discuss the student's needs. After discussion with Mr. Smith, Ms. Johnson suggests that they bring the student's needs up in the next school support team meeting along with the data that they have collected thus far.

Standards of practice. The topography of inclusive education is different for different schools, but the guiding principles remain the same. In a similar vein, teachers often implement instructional methods in slightly different ways based on experience, personal beliefs, and other factors. In spite of individual differences, teachers should still adhere to the principles of effective instruction (see Mastropieri & Scruggs, 2002, for a review of effective instruction). Educational support teams are charged with creating a set of industry or school standards that dictate the use of empirically supported instructional methods and educational supports.

While sitting in the teachers' lounge, Mr. Johnson is approached by Mr. Taft who has a student with disabilities included in his class. Mr. Taft explains that because he is teaching English, he is not able to do some of the things that Mr. Johnson does in his class. Mr. Johnson talks a little more with Mr. Taft to make sure that Mr. Taft understands that although the subjects are different, they both should be guided by the same principles of effective instruction. They discuss how Mr. Taft can ensure that these principles are incorporated in his lessons.

Data collection and review. The horror stories about collecting and interpreting data have been exchanged among teachers for years, and the litany of reasons given for not collecting data is commonplace in many secondary schools. However, there is a need to encourage the collection and interpretation of data detailing inclusive education efforts. Data that are collected on student productivity and progress can most effectively validate instructional practice. This data can be monitored on a continuous basis and help answer crucial questions about the effectiveness of educational services.

Many teachers use the term *best practices,* to call attention to a collection of instructional methods that are seemingly effective. Collecting and reviewing data is one of the most direct and sound ways in which to identify best practices. Educational support teams should encourage the collection and review of data using formal methods of analysis (Moxley, 2007), which allow teachers to make informed decisions about student progress. The educational support team assists teachers in data management so that teachers (a) understand the importance of ongoing data collection, (b) understand the function of assessment instruments and procedures, (c) have ready access to the data, and (d) are able to easily interpret student progress data in all formats including visual displays such as tables and graphs.

Mr. Smith and Ms. Johnson are nearing the end of the first 9-week session of the school year and want to determine the effectiveness of the inclusive program thus far. They decide to look at a number of different pieces of data to help them formulate their decision. They look at students' grades, service delivery documentation to identify patterns such as the frequency of service delivery, and students' knowledge and skill development that require more support. They also reflect on the integration of service delivery into the general flow of the classroom. Ms. Johnson depicts students' progress in graphs to help better track student progress.

Program evaluation. In its traditional form, program evaluation involves decisions regarding whether the special education program should be terminated, continued, or modified (Friend & Bursuck, 2006). This requires a combination of several measures of which teachers must take note. Some of the more common measures include the academic and social progress of students with disabilities, but there are other measures of interest as well. The number of children actually included in content area courses and the type and frequency of activities in which students take part are two measures that provide information about the inclusive education program. The educational support team should pay close attention to some fundamental measures that help determine whether the current program should be continued, discontinued, or modified.

> *At the end of the semester, Mr. Smith and Ms. Johnson reviewed the semester data to determine program effectiveness and whether the program should be continued, discontinued, or changed. Based on the data that they collected, Mr. Smith concluded that the students benefit from having Ms. Johnson in the class to provide additional instruction and support. Together, they decide that it may be a good idea to expand the inclusive program to other classes and subjects in the future.*

A Final Thought

Inclusive practices designed for secondary schools present a unique challenge. If framed as a design problem that can be addressed with some basic engineering principles, it is possible for educational support teams to utilize building blocks to engineer effective, inclusive practices.

References

Artiles, A. J., Kozleski, E. B., Dorn, S., & Christensen, C. (2008). Learning in inclusive education research: Re-mediating theory and methods with a transformative agenda. *Review of Research in Education, 32,* 65–107.

Boscardin, M. L. (2005). The administrative role in transforming secondary schools to support inclusive evidence-based practices. *American Secondary Education, 33*(3), 21–32.

DiPaola, M., Tschannen-Moran, M., & Walther-Thomas, C. (2004). School principals and special education: Creating the context for academic success. *Focus on Exceptional Children, 37*(1), 1–10.

Dukes, C., & Lamar-Dukes, P. (2006). Special education: An integral part of small high schools. *High School Journal, 89*(3), 1–9.

Friend, M., & Bursuck, W. D. (2006). *Including students with special needs: A practical guide for classroom teachers* (4th ed.). Boston: Allyn and Bacon.

Gravois, T. A., Rosenfield, S., & Vail, L. (1999). Achieving effective and inclusive school settings: A guide for professional development. In S. I. Pfeiffer & L. A. Reddy (Eds.), *Inclusion practices with special needs students: Theory, research, and application* (pp. 145–170). New York: The Haworth Press.

Heward, W. L. (2006). *Exceptional children: An introduction to special education* (8th ed.). Upper Saddle River, NJ: Pearson.

Idol, L. (2006). Toward inclusion of special education students in general education: A program evaluation of eight schools. *Remedial and Special Education, 27*(2), 77–94.

Keefe, E. B., & Moore, V. (2004). The challenge of co-teaching in inclusive classrooms at the high school level: What the teachers told us. *American Secondary Education, 32*(3), 77–88.

Lamar-Dukes, P., & Dukes, C. (2005). Twenty ways to consider the roles and responsibilities of the inclusion support teacher. *Intervention in School and Clinic, 41*(1), 55–59.

Mastropieri, M., & Scruggs, T. (2002). *The inclusive classroom: Strategies for effective instruction.* Upper Saddle River, NJ: Pearson Merrill Prentice Hall.

McLeskey, J., & Waldron, N. L. (2002). Professional development and inclusive schools: Reflections on effective practice. *The Teacher Educator, 37*(3), 159–172.

Michael, M. G., & Trezek, B. J. (2006). Universal design and multiple literacies: Creating access and ownership for students with disabilities. *Theory Into Practice, 45*(4), 311–318.

Moxley, R. A. (2007). Graphing in the classroom for improving instruction: From lesson plans to research. *Education and Treatment of Children, 30*(2), 111–126.

Oakley, M. (1990). *Design management: A handbook of issues and methods.* Oxford, UK: Blackwell Reference.

Petroski, H. (1992). *To engineer is human: The role of failure in successful design.* New York, NY: Vintage Books.

Reeves, J. R. (2006). Secondary teacher attitudes toward including English-Language Learners in mainstream classrooms. *The Journal of Educational Research, 99*(3), 131–142.

Rose, D. H., Meyer, A., & Strangman, N., & Rappolt, G. (2002). *Teaching every student in the digital age: Universal design for learning.* Alexandria, VA: Association for Supervision and Curriculum Development.

Ryndak, D. L., & Fisher, D. (Eds.) (2006). *The foundation of inclusive education.* Baltimore: TASH.

Savage, R. N. (2006). The role of design in materials science and engineering. *International Journal of Engineering Education, 22*(5), 917–924.

Scheffel, D. L., Kallam, M., Smith, K. N., & Hoernicke, P. A. (1996). *Inclusion: What it is and how it works best.* Fort Hays, KS: Fort Hays State University. (ERIC Document Reproduction Service No. ED412663)

Sindelar, P., Shearer, D. K., Yendol-Hoppey, D., & Liebert, T. W. (2006). The sustainability of inclusive school reform. *Exceptional Children, 72,* 317–331.

Vaughn, S., Bos, C, & Schumm, J. S. (2003). *Teaching exceptional, diverse, and at-risk students in the general education classroom* (3rd ed.). Boston: Allyn and Bacon.

Wasburn-Moss, L. (2005). Preparing special educators for secondary positions. *Action in Teacher Education, 27*(3), 26–39.

Weiss, M. P., & Llyod, J. W. (2002). Congruence between roles and actions of secondary special educators in co-taught and special education settings. *The Journal of Special Education, 36*(2), 58–68.

CHARLES DUKES (CEC FL Federation), Assistant Professor, Department of Exceptional Student Education, Florida Atlantic University, Boca Raton. **PAMELA LAMAR-DUKES** (CEC DC Federation), Outreach Project Director, TASH, Washington, DC.

Address correspondence to Charles Dukes, Florida Atlantic University, Department of Exceptional Student Education, 777 Glades Road, Boca Raton, FL 33431 (e-mail: cdukes@fau.edu).

UNIT 4

Intellectual Disabilities/ Autistic Spectrum Disorders

Unit Selections

Key Points to Consider

- What are research-based strategies that insure that students with developmental disabilities achieve in general education classrooms?

- How can teachers promote acceptance and friendships for students with autistic spectrum disorders in the general education classroom?

- Which method of education for students with autism is more effective; ABA or TEACCH?

- Should teachers use their preferred method or should parents be allowed to choose?

Student Website
www.mhcls.com

Internet References

Appleseed
http://www.appleseednetwork.org

Arc of the United States
http://www.thearc.org

Disability-Related Sources on the Web
http://www.arcarizona.org

Gentle Teaching
http://www.gentleteaching.nl

In our efforts to be more "politically correct" and to not inflict pain, we now avoid labels such as "mentally retarded." We always put the individual first and add the condition of disability second (when and if it is necessary). Students and adults who have cognitive skills falling two standard deviations below the norm for their age are now considered intellectually developmentally disabled. Children who have sustained brain damage through traumatic brain injury, even if they score two standard deviations below the intellectual norm for age, are traumatically brain injured, not developmentally disabled or intellectually impaired. Children and adults with autism or autistic spectrum disorders (such as Asperger's syndrome) are subsumed under a separate disability category by the U.S. Individuals with Disabilities Education Improvement Act (IDEIA). Three out of four individuals with classic autism score two standard deviations below the IQ mean. Nevertheless, intellectual developmental disorders, traumatic brain injuries, and autistic spectrum disorders are each recognized as separate disability categories by IDEIA.

© Imagestate Media (John Foxx)/Imagestate

Children with significantly subnormal intelligence were once classified as "educable," "trainable," or "custodial" for purposes of placement. These terms are strongly discouraged today. Even severely developmentally disabled children are educable and can benefit from some schooling. They must leave where they are, to be where we hope they can be. The current preferred categorical terms for children who are developmentally challenged are "intermittent," "limited," "extensive," and "pervasive." These terms refer to how much support the individuals need to function and to succeed as much as possible.

IDEIA mandates free and appropriate public school education for every child, regardless of mentation. While the legal windows on education are from ages 6 to 16 in the United States, individuals with developmental disabilities are entitled to a free and appropriate education from age of assessment (birth, early childhood) to age 21. This encompasses parent-child education programs and preschool programs early in life and transitional services into the community and world of work after the public school education is completed.

The IDEIA mandates free and appropriate education (FAPE) in the least restrictive environment (LRE) with nondiscriminatory, multidisciplinary assessment, annually updated individualized education programs (IEPs), parental participation, and due process. All these rights are given to children with intellectual disabilities. Inclusion is not mandated, only the LRE.

The inclusion of children with disabilities in regular education classes has been controversial (see Unit 1) throughout the time span since 1975. Some school systems have succeeded brilliantly in integrating students with intellectual developmental disabilities into their regular classes. Other schools have fought the law every step of the way. There have been few negative consequences for school systems or whole state education departments who have resisted placing intellectually disabled students in regular classrooms. Therefore, some parents still invoke due process and bring formal complaint procedures against schools to get their children out of full-time special classes or special schools.

A child with an intellectual developmental disability (intellectual impairment) who is in the mildest "intermittent" classification needs support at school at times when special needs arise and at times of life transitions. This terminology is generally used for children whose disabilities do not create an obvious and continual problem. These children have slower mentation but also have many abilities.

The next level of support, classified as "limited," is usually used for children whose disabilities create daily limitations on their abilities but who can achieve a degree of self-sufficiency after an appropriate education in the least restrictive environment. Limited refers to the period of time from diagnosis until adulthood (age 21). The "extensive" support classification extends the support throughout the lifespan for individuals whose developmental disabilities prohibit them from living independently. The "pervasive" support classification is used infrequently. It is only for those individuals whose disabilities prevent them from most activities of self-help. Pervasive support is intensive and life-sustaining in nature.

The majority of children with developmental disabilities (intellectual impairments) can be placed in the intermittent support classification. To casual observers, they often do not appear to have any disabilities. However, their ability to process, store, and retrieve information is limited. In the past, this group of children was given IQ measurements between two and three standard deviations below the mean (usually an IQ below 70 but above 55). Intelligence testing is an inexact science with problems of both validity and reliability. The current definition of developmental disability endorsed by the American Association on Mental Deficiency (AAMD) does not include any IQ scoring results other than to use the phrase "subaverage intellectual functioning." It emphasizes the problems that individuals with developmental disabilities have with adaptive skills such as communication, self-care, home living, social skills, community use, self-direction, health and safety, functional academics, leisure, and work.

The causes of developmental disabilities and autistic spectrum disorders are unclear. About one-half of all individuals are suspected of having sustained some brain damage prenatally, neonatally, or in childhood. Among the better-known factors that contribute to brain tissue damage are early birth or low birth weight, anoxia, malnutrition, drugs, viruses, radiation, trauma, and tumors.

The first selection chosen for this unit on developmental disabilities, Sally E. and Bennett A. Shaywitz, in summarizing their recent research findings, suggest that advances in medicine, combined with reading research, can virtually eliminate reading disabilities.

In the second article of this section, Edwin Darden, a lawyer, presents the concerns of educating children with autistic spectrum disorders most appropriately. Two methods, ABA and TEACCH, each have supporters. Should teachers use the method they prefer or use the method the parents request? More parents are requesting due process hearings to assure that their children with autism have the most meaningful education. This can be very expensive for school systems when parents prevail.

Reading Disability and the Brain

SALLY E. SHAYWITZ AND BENNETT A. SHAYWITZ

The past decade has witnessed extraordinary progress in our understanding of the nature of reading and reading difficulties. Never before have rigorous science (including neuroscience) and classroom instruction in reading been so closely linked. For the first time, educators can turn to well-designed, scientific studies to determine the most effective ways to teach reading to beginning readers, including those with reading disability (National Reading Panel, 2000).

What does the evidence tell us? Several lines of investigation have found that reading originates in and relies on the brain systems used for spoken language. In addition, accumulating evidence sheds light on the nature of reading disability, including its definition, prevalence, longitudinal course, and probable causes. Although the work is relatively new, we have already made great progress in identifying the neural systems used for reading, identifying a disruption in these systems in struggling readers, and understanding the neural mechanisms associated with the development of fluent reading.

Reading and Spoken Language

Spoken language is instinctive—built into our genes and hardwired in our brains. Learning to read requires us to take advantage of what nature has provided: a biological module for language.

For the object of the reader's attention (print) to gain entry into the language module, a truly extraordinary transformation must occur. The reader must convert the print on the page into a linguistic code: the phonetic code, the only code recognized and accepted by the language system. Unless the reader-to-be can convert the printed characters on the page into the phonetic code, these letters remain just a bunch of lines and circles, totally devoid of meaning. The written symbols have no inherent meaning of their own but stand, rather, as surrogates for the sounds of speech.

To break the code, the first step beginning readers must take involves spoken language. Readers must develop *phonemic awareness*. They must discover that the words they hear come apart into smaller pieces of sound.

On the basis of highly reliable scientific evidence, investigators in the field have now reached a strong consensus: Reading reflects language, and reading disability reflects a deficit within the language system. Results from large and well-studied populations with reading disability confirm that in young school-age children and in adolescents, a weakness in accessing the sounds of spoken language represents the most robust and specific correlate of reading disability. Such findings form the foundation for the most successful, evidence-based interventions designed to improve reading (National Reading Panel, 2000).

Understanding Reading Disability

Reading disability, or *developmental dyslexia*, is characterized by an unexpected difficulty in reading in children and adults who otherwise possess the intelligence, motivation, and education necessary for developing accurate and fluent reading. Dyslexia is the most common and most carefully studied of the learning disabilities, affecting 80 percent of all individuals identified as learning disabled and an estimated 5–17 percent of all children and adults in the United States.

Incidence and Distribution of Dyslexia

Recent epidemiological data indicate that like hypertension and obesity, reading ability occurs along a continuum. Reading disability falls on the left side of the bell-shaped curve representing the normal distribution of reading ability.

Dyslexia runs in families: One-fourth to one-half of all children who have a parent with dyslexia also have the disorder, and if dyslexia affects one child in the family, it is likely to affect half of his or her siblings. Recent studies have identified a number of genes involved in dyslexia.

Good evidence, based on surveys of randomly selected populations of children, now indicates that dyslexia affects boys and girls equally. Apparently, the long-held belief that only boys suffer from dyslexia reflected bias in school-identified samples: The more disruptive behavior of boys results in their being referred for evaluation more often, whereas girls who struggle to read are more likely to sit quietly in their seats and thus be overlooked.

Longitudinal studies indicate that dyslexia is a persistent, chronic condition rather than a transient "developmental lag." Children do not outgrow reading difficulties. The evidence-based interventions now available, however, can result in improved reading in virtually all children.

Neurobiological Origins of Dyslexia

For more than a century, physicians and scientists have suspected that dyslexia has neurobiological origins. Until recently, however, they had no way to examine the brain systems that we use while reading. Within the last decade, the dream of scientists, educators, and struggling readers has come true: New advances in technology enable us to view the working brain as it attempts to read.

Perhaps the most convincing evidence for a neurobiological basis of dyslexia comes from the rapidly accumulating and converging data from functional brain imaging investigations. The process of functional brain imaging is quite simple. When we ask an individual to perform a discrete cognitive task, that task places processing demands on specific neural systems in the brain. Through such techniques as functional magnetic resonance imaging (fMRI), we can measure the changes that take place in neural activity in particular brain regions as the brain meets those demands. Because fMRI uses no ionizing radiation and requires no injections, it is noninvasive and safe. We can use it to examine children or adults on multiple occasions.

Using functional brain imaging, scientists around the world have discovered not only the brain basis of reading but also a glitch in the neural circuitry for reading in children and adults who struggle to read. Our studies and those of other investigators have identified three regions involved in reading, all located on the left side of the brain. In the front of the brain, Broca's area (technically the inferior frontal gyrus) is involved in articulation and word analysis. Two areas located in the back of the brain are involved in word analysis (the parieto-temporal region) and in fluent reading (the occipito-temporal region, also referred to as the word form area).

Studies of dyslexic readers document an underactivation of the two systems in the back of the brain together with an over-activation of Broca's area in the front of the brain. The struggling readers appear to be turning to the frontal region, which is responsible for articulating spoken words, to compensate for the fault in the systems in the back of the brain.

Researchers have observed this neurobiological signature of dyslexic readers across cultures and across different languages. The observation of this same pattern in both children and adults supports the view that reading difficulties, including the neural disruption, do not go away with maturity. To prevent failure for students with reading disability, we must identify the disability early and provide effective reading programs to address the students' needs.

The Importance of Fluency

In addition to identifying the neural systems used for reading, research has now revealed which systems the brain uses in two important phases in the acquisition of literacy.

Beginning reading—breaking the code by slowly, analytically sounding out words—calls on areas in the front of the brain (Broca's area) and in the back of the brain (the parieto-temporal region).

But an equally important phase in reading is fluency—rapid, automatic reading that does not require attention or effort. A fluent reader looks at a printed word and instantly knows all the important information about that word. Fluent reading develops as the reader builds brain connections that eventually represent an exact replica of the word—a replica that has integrated the word's pronunciation, spelling, and meaning.

Fluency occurs step-by-step. After systematically learning letters and their sounds, children go on to apply this knowledge to sound out words slowly and analytically. For example, for the word "back," a child may initially represent the word by its initial and final consonants: "b—k." As the child progresses, he begins to fill in the interior vowels, first making some errors—reading "back" as "bock" or "beak," for example—and eventually sounding out the word correctly. Part of the process of becoming a skilled reader is forming successively more detailed and complete representations of familiar words.

After the child has read the word "back" correctly over and over again, his brain has built and reinforced an exact model of the word. He now reads that word fluently—accurately, rapidly, and effortlessly. Fluency pulls us into reading. A student who reads fluently reads for pleasure and for information; a student who is not fluent will probably avoid reading.

In a study involving 144 children, we identified the brain region that makes it possible for skilled readers to read automatically. We found that the more proficiently a child reads, the more he or she activated the occipito-temporal region (or word form area) in the back of the brain. Other investigators have observed that this brain region responds to words that are presented rapidly. Once a word is represented in the word form area, the reader recognizes that word instantly and effortlessly. This word form system appears to predominate when a reader has become fluent. As a result of this finding, we now know that development of the word form area in the left side of the brain is a key component in becoming a skilled, fluent reader.

Helping Struggling Readers Become More Fluent

Our study of 144 children also revealed that struggling readers compensate as they get older, developing alternate reading systems in the front of the brain and in the *right* side of the brain—a functioning system, but, alas, not an automatic one. These readers do not develop the critical left-side word form region necessary for rapid, automatic reading. Instead, they call on the alternate secondary pathways. This strategy enables them to read, but much more slowly and with greater effort than their classmates.

This research evidence of a disruption in the normal reading pathways provides a neurobiological target for reading interventions. In a new study, we hypothesized that an evidence-based, phonologically mediated reading intervention would help dyslexic readers develop the fast-paced word form systems serving skilled reading, thus improving their reading accuracy and fluency. Under the supervision of Syracuse University professor Benita Blachman, we provided 2nd and 3rd grade struggling readers daily with 50 minutes of individual tutoring that was systematic and explicit, focusing on helping the students understand the *alphabetic principle,* or how letters and combinations of letters represent the sounds of speech.

Students received eight months (105 hours) of intervention during the school year in addition to their regular classroom reading instruction. The experimental intervention replaced any additional reading help that the students might have received in school. Certified teachers who had taken part in an intensive training program provided the tutoring.

Immediately after the yearlong intervention, students in the experiment made significant gains in reading fluency and demonstrated increased activation in left hemisphere regions, including the inferior frontal gyrus and the parieto-temporal region. One year after the experimental intervention ended, these students were reading accurately and fluently and were activating all three left-side brain regions used by good readers. A control group of struggling readers receiving school-based, primarily nonphonological reading instruction had not activated these reading systems.

These data demonstrate that an intensive, evidence-based reading intervention brings about significant and durable changes in brain organization so that struggling readers' brain activation patterns come to resemble those of typical readers. If we provide intervention at an early age, then we can improve reading fluency and facilitate the development of the neural systems that underlie skilled reading.

Evidence-Based Effective Reading Instruction

In addition to new neurological research on the nature of reading, educators can draw on a body of rigorous, well-designed, scientific studies to guide reading instruction. In 1998, the U.S. Congress mandated the National Reading Panel to develop rigorous scientific criteria for evaluating reading research, apply these criteria to existing reading research, identify the most effective teaching methods, and then make findings accessible for parents and teachers. As a member of the Panel, I can attest to its diligence. After two years of work, the Panel issued its report (2000).

The major findings of the report indicate that in order to read, all children must be taught alphabetics, comprising phonemic awareness and phonics; reading fluency; vocabulary; and strategies for reading comprehension. These elements must be taught systematically, comprehensively, and explicitly; it is inadequate to present the foundational skills of phonemic awareness and phonics incidentally, casually, or fragmentally. Children do not learn how letters represent sounds by osmosis; we must teach them this skill explicitly. Once a child has mastered these foundational skills, he or she must be taught how to read words fluently.

Good evidence now indicates that we can teach reading fluency by means of repeated oral reading with feedback and guidance. Using these methods, we can teach almost every child to read. It is crucial to align all components of a program with one another—for example, to provide so-called decodable booklets that give the student practice in the specific letter-sound linkages we are teaching. The use of decodable booklets enables the repeated practice necessary to build the automatic systems in the word form region that lead to fluent reading.

Neuroscience and Reading Research Agree

We are now in an era of evidence-based education. Objective scientific evidence—provided by brain imaging studies and by the National Reading Panel's rigorous scientific review of the literature—has replaced reliance on philosophy or opinion.

In considering a reading program, educators should ask several key questions:

- Is there scientific evidence that the program is effective?
- Was the program or its methodology reviewed by the National Reading Panel?
- In reading instruction, are phonemic awareness and phonics taught systematically and explicitly?
- How are students taught to approach an unfamiliar word? Do they feel empowered to try to analyze and sound out an unknown word first rather than guess the word from the pictures or context?
- Does the program also include plenty of opportunities for students to practice reading, develop fluency, build vocabulary, develop reading comprehension strategies, write, and listen to and discuss stories?

Children are only 7 or 8 years old once in their lifetime. We cannot risk teaching students with unproven programs. We now have the scientific knowledge to ensure that almost every child can become a successful reader. Awareness of the new scientific knowledge about reading should encourage educators to insist that reading programs used in their schools reflect what we know about the science of reading and about effective reading instruction.

As seen in *Educational Leadership*, March 2004, based on the book *Overcoming Dyslexia* by Sally E. Shaywitz (Knopf, 2003). Grateful acknowledgement is made to Sally Shaywitz, c/o Writers' Representatives LLC (to whom all inquiries should be directed for permission to reprint).

Autism, the Law, and You

School districts are facing more IDEA cases as a growing number of students are diagnosed. What policies and procedures should you have in place?

EDWIN C. DARDEN

Autism. The very word sends chills down the spine of school attorneys and tempts board members and superintendents to think about their waning bank accounts.

That description is not meant to be rude or disrespectful. Sadly, throughout the United States, the special education needs of autistic children are a frequent source of conflict. In nearly all cases, the federal Individuals with Disabilities Education Act (IDEA) applies and imposes certain obligations on school districts.

IDEA requires a special team—including in-school experts—to collaborate with parents to devise a learning plan tailored to the unique needs of a particular autistic child. Drafting an individualized education program (IEP) can be as traumatic as a no-holds-barred wrestling match—and with no rounds and no time limit, school districts cannot be saved by the bell.

So, both sides battle on, using every law, policy, and procedure at their disposal.

What Is Autism?

Autism is a brain disorder that affects the ability of children to learn and respond properly to social cues. It alters both verbal and nonverbal communication and is characterized by repetitive activities and resistance to change in daily routines. While autism cannot be cured, researchers have discovered that intensive early education can spark significant improvements.

Two Hollywood versions of autism occupy the public mind. The first is from a 1979 made-for-TV movie called "Son-Rise: A Miracle of Love." The enduring image is an autistic boy named Raun who could not form complete sentences and spent hours spinning a dinner plate on a tile floor and oddly waving his hands in the air.

The other vision is from the 1988 film "Rain Man." As the autistic Raymond Babbitt, Dustin Hoffman demonstrates a savant-style gift for numbers and has a humanizing effect on his self-absorbed brother, played by Tom Cruise.

Raun was taught by his parents at home; Raymond was institutionalized. Today, both Raun and the school-aged "Rain Man" would likely be taught in public schools.

In the past 10 years, the number of children diagnosed with autism has exploded. Autism now affects about one in every 150 children in the nation. It is four times more prevalent in boys than girls.

Autism falls within the category of Pervasive Development Disorders (PDDs), and is termed a "spectrum disorder"—meaning symptoms can range from mild to severe.

While the universally agreed-upon goal is independence, the battles begin over how to get there and what method of in-school instruction will be most effective.

Philosophies Equal Dilemma

A primary source of strain between school districts and parents comes when choosing between the two leading ways of teaching autistic children. They are: Treatment and Education of Autistic and Related Communication-Handicapped Children (TEACCH) versus Applied Behavioral Analysis (ABA). Experts disagree as to which one is most effective and under what circumstances.

TEACCH and ABA both emphasize family involvement and predictable routines, for example. But they differ significantly in that TEACCH involves group instruction, structured teaching, and independent time. ABA emphasizes extensive one-on-one time, collecting information and using objective measures of the desired behaviors, and monitoring the results to ensure skill acquisition. ABA treatment can potentially require 30 to 40 hours of personal attention per week and cost as much as $60,000 per year for a single child.

A core question: What does a free appropriate education under IDEA require? Should the method of teaching (TEACCH or ABA) be specified in the IEP? Or, should the method be left flexible? An IEP is the equivalent of a contract, and if the instruction method is named, it is mandatory. An open-ended approach leaves discretion to school officials. Often, the inclusion or exclusion of method in the IEP is what leads to formal appeals and acrimony.

Superintendents, board members, and school officials are faced with a difficult challenge. As public officials they must weigh the needs of all populations: special education, gifted education, general education, and kids struggling academically. If they maximize the education of autistic children, for example, they run the risk of short-changing other children.

The Legal Outlook

IDEA does not require school districts to provide the maximum education possible to autistic children—or any others in special education. Parents are not entitled to dictate to school districts that they provide the crème de la crème of educational services when a less expensive method will suffice. The education has to be meaningful, must be personalized to the needs of the child, and provide "some educational benefit."

The U.S. Supreme Court this past term dealt indirectly with autism when it ruled that parents are not required to hire a lawyer when going to court. At issue was the education of an autistic child. The court said parents have "independent enforceable rights," that entitle them to pursue a grievance in the interest of their child.

One federal court case that contains a variety of lessons involves Stefan Jaynes, who was diagnosed with autism at 2 years old. Under IDEA, Stefan's parents sought and received an IEP in 1994, but the Newport News, Va., school district, according to the record, failed to implement the IEP and placed him in a regular preschool program. The district also did not involve parents in developing the initial IEP.

When Brian and Julianna Jaynes realized that Stefan was regressing, they withdrew him from the public school program and began an ABA regimen at home with tutors working one-on-one with the boy for several hours a day.

A due process hearing resulted in a victory for the parents. The hearing officer also granted them reimbursement for the ABA program. The case, *Stefan Jaynes v. Newport News Public School District,* went before a Virginia state review officer. From there it was appealed by the school system to the federal district court and finally the federal Court of Appeals. The outcome remained the same, with the administrative officer and both courts ruling in favor of the parents.

The case is binding only in Maryland, North Carolina, South Carolina, Virginia, and West Virginia, but several general lessons can be learned. Among them: the need to respond in a timely way when presented with a child who needs special education; to assure the classroom placement is appropriate and leads to learning; to involve parents and obtain specific consent to the IEP where possible; and the potentially high financial cost when IDEA procedures are not followed to the letter.

Policy Questions to Consider

- Is your staff well versed in the TEACCH and ABA methods of educating autistic youngsters and have they developed a preference based on their experience of success?
- Do you listen closely when in-school or outside experts suggest techniques that might help a particular child learn?
- Are you familiar with court rulings in your jurisdiction that might affect your obligations or give you options?
- Has your in-house legal office or outside counsel developed an expertise in special education law?
- Are your building personnel trained to work creatively within constraints to resolve differences of opinion before they escalate?
- Autism can be an isolating condition. Are your autistic children mainstreamed in regular classrooms or educated separately?
- With autism being identified primarily in preschool years, are you in touch with agencies in your area so you can be prepared for the future?

Solving Things Peaceably

For school districts, the key is the IEP meeting. Building representatives should be skilled in seeking solutions that are sensible, keeping in mind the twin goals of educating each autistic child to the fullest, while doing the same for other children in the district.

Districts need to be careful, however, about setting a precedent. Parents know which jurisdictions are viewed as "pushovers" and which are automatic "no" districts on special education. A firm middle ground allows for a fair hearing about the needs of children, but does not sacrifice other students outside of special education.

The debate about autism is not about to end soon. Thus, for school officials the key is to be reasonable, but for safekeeping, to seek legal help at each step along the way.

EDWIN C. DARDEN (EDarden@appleseednetwork.org), an *ASBJ* contributing editor, is an attorney and the director of education policy for Appleseed, a national organization focusing on K–12 education law, education policy, and social justice.

From *American School Board Journal,* September 2007, pp. 60–61. Copyright © 2007 by National School Board Association. Reprinted by permission.

UNIT 5

Emotional and Behavioral Disorders

Unit Selections

Key Points to Consider

- Can teachers recognize depression in their students? What interventions are appropriate for depression?

- Why do female students with EBDs drop out of school? What educational methods can help them?

- What instructional methods and disciplinary procedures facilitate obedience in students with EBDs?

- How can chronic and intense behavioral difficulties be ameliorated in the classroom to allow learning to take place?

Student Website

www.mhcls.com

Internet Reference

Pacer Center: Emotional Behavioral Disorders
   http://www.pacer.org/ebd/

The definition of a student with emotional behavioral disorder (EBD) usually conjures up visions of the violence perpetrated by a few students who have vented their frustrations by taking weapons to school. One of the hot topics in special education today is whether or not students with emotional and behavioral disorders are too dangerous to be included in regular education classes. The statistics show that students with EBDs are as likely to be the victims of violence or bullying by nondisabled classmates as to be the troublemakers. The definition of EBDs broadly includes all emotionally disordered students with subjective feelings such as sadness, fear, anger, guilt, or anxiety that give rise to altered behaviors that are outside the range of normal.

Should children with chronic and severe anger, already convicted of problem behaviors such as violent acts or threats of violence, be re-enrolled in inclusive regular education classes with individualized education plans (IEPs)? Although teachers, other pupils, and school staff may be greatly inconvenienced by the presence of one or more behaviorally disordered students in every classroom, the law is clear. The school must "show cause" if a child with EBD is to be permanently moved from the regular classroom to a more restrictive environment.

The 1994 Gun-Free Schools Act in the United States requires a one-year expulsion of a student who brings a firearm to school. The Individuals with Disabilities Education Act (IDEA) in its 1997 reauthorization made a compromise for students with EBDs or other conditions of disability. If bringing a gun to school is related to their disability (for example, as the result of being teased or bullied), they are exempt from the Gun-Free Schools Act legislation. They can be expelled, but only for 10 days while the school determines their degree of danger to others. If they are judged to really be dangerous, they can temporarily be given an alternate educational placement for 45 days, subject to reassessment. Their IEPs should not be rewritten to place them in a permanent restrictive setting unless their acts were clearly unrelated to their disabilities (hard to prove). This double standard is very controversial. Students without disabilities can be expelled with no educational provisions for one full year.

The dilemma about inclusive classroom placements for aggressive and disruptive students with EBDs is unsolved. Many teachers cite behavior management problems as their biggest concern, or occasionally, as their reason for leaving the teaching profession.

For educational purposes, children with behavior disorders are usually divided into two main behavioral classifications: (1) withdrawn, shy, or anxious behaviors and (2) aggressive, acting-out behaviors. The debate about what constitutes a behavior disorder, or an emotional disorder, is not fully resolved. *The Diagnostic and Statistical Manual of Mental Disorders,* 4th edition, revised text, sees serious behavioral disorders as a category first diagnosed in infancy, childhood,

© Imagestate Media (John Foxx)/Imagestate

or adolescence. Among the disorders of childhood are eating disorders, tic disorders, elimination disorders, separation anxiety disorders, reactive attachment disorders, oppositional defiant disorder, and conduct disorder.

An alliance of educators and psychologists proposed that IDEA remove the term "serious emotional disturbances" and instead focus on behaviors that adversely affect educational performance. Behavior—usually considered a sign of emotional disorder, such as anxiety, depression, or failure of attachment—can be seen as disordered if it interferes with academic, social, vocational, and personal accomplishment. So, also, can eating, elimination, or tic disorders and any other responses outside the range of "acceptable" for school or other settings. Such a focus on behavior can link the individualized educational plan curriculum activities to children's behavioral response styles.

Inclusive education does not translate into acceptance of disordered behaviors in the regular education classroom. Two rules of thumb for the behavior of all children, however capable or incapable, are that they conform to minimum standards of acceptable conduct and that disruptive behaviors be subject to fair and consistent disciplinary action. In order to ensure more orderly, well-regulated classroom environments, many schools are instituting conflict management courses.

What causes students to act out with hostile, aggressive behaviors directed against school personnel or other students? An easy, often-cited reason is that they are barraged with images of violence on the news, in music, on videos, on television programs, and in movies. It is too facile: Media barrage is aimed at everyone, yet only a few decide that they want to become violent and harm others. Aggressive, bullying children commonly come from homes where they see real violence, anger, and insults. They often feel disconnected, rejected, and afraid. They do not know how to communicate their distress. They may appear to be narcissistic, even as they seek attention in negative, hurtful ways. They usually have fairly easy access to weapons, alcohol, and other substances of abuse. They usually do not know any techniques of conflict management other than acting out.

In the first article, the authors suggest using a proactive approach in dealing with challenging issues as they work to guide the behavior of all young children.

R. Marc Crundwell and Kim Killu address the problem of teaching students with symptoms of depression. First, depression must be recognized. Second, an environment which supports them must be established. Mental health professionals can help. With identification and accommodations, students who are withdrawn, anxious, and depressed can have better outcomes.

The next article posits that many discipline problems could be eliminated by whole school initiatives that create and sustain an environment that addresses positive social and emotional development as well as academics.

Education for incarcerated adolescents is a right guaranteed by IDEA until age 21 when they are diagnosed with EBDs. Signe Nelson and Lynn Olcott present data on what educational methods work for adolescent women in jail, and what methods failed them before their incarcerations.

In the last article, "Classroom Problems That Don't Go Away," Laverne Warner and Sharon Lynch present suggestions for ameliorating and/or preventing conflicts and anti-social acts within the regular education curriculum by teaching alternative behaviors.

Heading Off Disruptive Behavior

How early intervention can reduce defiant behavior—and win back teaching time.

HILL M. WALKER, ELIZABETH RAMSEY, AND FRANK M. GRESHAM

More and more children from troubled, chaotic homes are bringing well-developed patterns of antisocial behavior to school. Especially as these students get older, they wreak havoc on schools. Their aggressive, disruptive, and defiant behavior wastes teaching time, disrupts the learning of all students, threatens safety, overwhelms teachers—and ruins their own chances for successful schooling and a successful life.

In a poll of AFT teachers, 17 percent said they lost four or more hours of teaching time per week thanks to disruptive student behavior; another 19 percent said they lost two or three hours. In urban areas, fully 21 percent said they lost four or more hours per week. And in urban secondary schools, the percentage is 24. It's hard to see how academic achievement can rise significantly in the face of so much lost teaching time, not to mention the anxiety that is produced by the constant disruption (and by the implied safety threat), which must also take a toll on learning.

But it need not be this way in the future. Most of the disruption is caused by no more than a few students per class[1]—students who are, clinically speaking, "antisocial." Provided intervention begins when these children are young, preferably before they reach age 8, the knowledge, tools, and programs exist that would enable schools to head off most of this bad behavior—or at least greatly reduce its frequency. Schools are not the source of children's behavior problems, and they can't completely solve them on their own. But the research is becoming clear: Schools can do a lot to minimize bad behavior—and in so doing, they help not only the antisocial children, they greatly advance their central goal of educating children.

In recent decades, antisocial behavior has been the subject of intense study by researchers in various disciplines including biology, sociology, social work, psychiatry, corrections, education, and psychology. Great progress has been made in understanding and developing solutions for defiant, disruptive, and aggressive behavior (see Burns, 2002). The field of psychology, in particular, with its increasingly robust theories of "social learning" and "cognition," has developed a powerful empirical literature that can assist school personnel in coping with, and ultimately preventing, a good deal of problematic behavior. Longitudinal and retrospective studies conducted in the United States, Australia, New Zealand, Canada, and various western European countries have yielded knowledge on the long-term outcomes of children who adopt antisocial behavior, especially those who arrive at school with it well developed (see Reid et al., 2002). Most importantly, a strong knowledge base has been assembled on interventions that can head off this behavior or prevent it from hardening (Loeber and Farrington, 2001).

To date, however, this invaluable knowledge base has been infused into educational practice in an extremely limited fashion. A major goal of this article (and of our much larger book) is to communicate and adapt this knowledge base for effective use by educators in coping with the rising tide of antisocial students populating today's schools. In our book, you'll find fuller explanations of the causes of antisocial behavior, of particular forms of antisocial behavior like bullying, and of effective—and ineffective—interventions for schools. And all of this draws on a combination of the latest research and the classic research studies that have stood the test of time.

In this article, we look first at the source of antisocial behavior itself and ask: Why is it so toxic when it arrives in school? Second, we look at the evidence suggesting that early intervention is rare in schools. Third, we look at a range of practices that research indicates should be incorporated into school and classroom practice. Fourth, in the accompanying sidebars we give examples of how these practices have been combined in different ways to create effective programs.

I. Where Does Antisocial Behavior Come from and What Does That Mean for Schools?

Much to the dismay of many classroom teachers who deal with antisocial students, behavior-management practices that work so well with typical students do not work in managing antisocial behavior. In fact, teachers find that their tried and true behavior-management practices often make the behavior of antisocial students much worse. As a general rule, educators do not have a thorough understanding of the origins and developmental course of such behavior and are not well trained to deal with moderate to severe levels of antisocial behavior. The older these students become and the further along the educational track they progress, the more serious their problems become and the more difficult they are to manage.

How can it be that behavior-management practices somehow work differently for students with antisocial behavior patterns? Why do they react differently? Do they learn differently? Do they require interventions based on a completely different set of learning principles? As we shall see, the principles by which they acquire and exercise their behavioral pattern are quite typical and predictable.

One of the most powerful principles used to explain how behavior is learned is known as the Matching Law (Herrnstein, 1974). In his original formulation, Herrnstein (1961) stated that the rate of any given behavior matches the rate of reinforcement for that behavior. For example, if aggressive behavior is reinforced once every three times it occurs (e.g., by a parent giving in to a temper tantrum) and prosocial behavior is reinforced once every 15 times it occurs (e.g., by a parent praising a polite request), then the Matching Law would predict that, on average, aggressive behavior will be chosen five times more frequently than prosocial behavior. Research has consistently shown that behavior does, in fact, closely follow the Matching Law (Snyder, 2002). Therefore, how parents (and later, teachers) react to aggressive, defiant, and other bad behavior is extremely important. The Matching Law applies to all children; it indicates that antisocial behavior is learned—and, at least at a young enough age, can be unlearned. (As we will see in the section that reviews effective intervention techniques, many interventions—like maintaining at least a 4 to 1 ratio of praising versus reprimanding—have grown out of the Matching Law.)

First Comes the Family . . .

Antisocial behavior is widely believed to result from a mix of constitutional (i.e., genetic and neurobiological) and environmental (i.e., family and community) factors (Reid et al., 2002). In the vast majority of cases, the environmental factors are the primary causes—but in a small percentage of cases, there is an underlying, primarily constitutional, cause (for example, autism, a difficult temperament, attention deficit/hyperactivity disorder [ADHD], or a learning disorder). Not surprisingly, constitutional and environmental causes often overlap and even exacerbate each other, such as when parents are pushed to their limits by a child with a difficult temperament or when a child with ADHD lives in a chaotic environment.

Patterson and his colleagues (Patterson et al., 1992) have described in detail the main environmental causes of antisocial behavior. Their model starts by noting the social and personal factors that put great stress on family life (e.g., poverty, divorce, drug and alcohol problems, and physical abuse). These stressors disrupt normal parenting practices, making family life chaotic, unpredictable, and hostile. These disrupted parenting

practices, in turn, lead family members to interact with each other in negative, aggressive ways and to attempt to control each others' behavior through coercive means such as excessive yelling, threats, intimidation, and physical force. In this environment, children learn that the way to get what they want is through what psychologists term "coercive" behavior: For parents, coercion means threatening, yelling, intimidating, and even hitting to force children to behave. (Patterson [1982] conducted a sequential analysis showing that parental use of such coercive strategies to suppress hostile and aggressive behavior actually increased the likelihood of such behavior in the future by 50 percent.)

For children, coercive tactics include disobeying, whining, yelling, throwing tantrums, threatening parents, and even hitting—all in order to avoid doing what the parents want. In homes where such coercive behavior is common, children become well-acquainted with how hostile behavior escalates—and with which of their behaviors ultimately secure adult surrender. This is the fertile ground in which antisocial behavior is bred. The negative effects tend to flow across generations much like inherited traits.[2]

By the time they are old enough for school, children who have developed an antisocial profile (due to either constitutional or environmental factors) have a limited repertoire of cooperative behavior skills, a predilection to use coercive tactics to control and manipulate others, and a well-developed capacity for emotional outbursts and confrontation.

. . . Then Comes School

For many young children, making the transition from home to school is fraught with difficulty. Upon school entry, children must learn to share, negotiate disagreements, deal with conflicts, and participate in competitive activities. And, they must do so in a manner that builds friendships with some peers and, at a minimum, social acceptance from others (Snyder, 2002). Children with antisocial behavior patterns have enormous difficulty accomplishing these social tasks. In fact, antisocial children are more than twice as likely as regular children to initiate unprovoked verbal or physical aggression toward peers, to reciprocate peer aggression toward them, and to continue aggressive behavior once it has been initiated (Snyder, 2002).[3]

From preschool to mid-elementary school, antisocial students' behavior changes in form and increases in intensity. During the preschool years, these children often display aversive behaviors such as frequent whining and noncompliance. Later, during the elementary school years, these behaviors take the form of less frequent but higher intensity acts such as hitting, fighting, bullying, and stealing. And during adolescence, bullying and hitting may escalate into robbery, assault, lying, stealing, fraud, and burglary (Snyder and Stoolmiller, 2002).

Although the specific form of the behavior changes (e.g., from noncompliance to bullying to assault), its function remains the same: Coercion remains at the heart of the antisocial behavior. As children grow older, they learn that the more noxious and painful they can make their behavior to others, the more likely they are to accomplish their goals—whether that goal is to avoid taking out the trash or escape a set of difficult mathematics problems. An important key to preventing this escalation (and therefore avoiding years of difficult behavior) is for adults to limit the use of coercive tactics with children—and for these adults to avoid surrendering in the face of coercive tactics used by the child. This has clear implications for school and teacher practices (and, of course, for parent training, which is not the subject of this article).

Frequent and excessive noncompliance in school (or home) is an important first indicator of future antisocial behavior. A young child's noncompliance is often a "gate key" behavior that triggers a vicious cycle involving parents, peers, and teachers. Further, it serves as a port of entry into much more serious forms of antisocial behavior. By treating noncompliance effectively at the early elementary age (or preferably even earlier), it is possible to prevent the development of more destructive behavior.

Frequent and excessive noncompliance in school (or home) is an important first indicator of future antisocial behavior.

II. Early Intervention Is Rare

How many children are antisocial? How many are getting help early? To study the national incidence of antisocial behavior among children, researchers focus on two psychiatric diagnoses: oppositional defiant disorder and conduct disorder. Oppositional defiant disorder, the less serious of the two, consists of an ongoing pattern of uncooperative, angry behavior including things like deliberately trying to bother others and refusing to accept responsibility for mistakes. Conduct disorder is characterized by severe verbal and physical aggression, property destruction, and deceitful behavior that persist over time (usually one or more years). Formal surveys have generally indicated that between two and six percent of the general population of U.S. children and youth has some form of conduct disorder (Kazdin, 1993). Without someone intervening early to teach these children how to behave better, half of them will maintain the disorder into adulthood and the other half will suffer significant adjustment problems (e.g., disproportionate levels of marital discord and difficulty keeping a job) during their adult lives (Kazdin, 1993). (It is worth noting that on the way to these unpleasant outcomes, most will disrupt many classrooms and overwhelm many teachers.) When we add in oppositional defiant disorder (which often precedes and co-occurs with conduct disorder), estimates have been as high as 16 percent of the U.S. youth population (Eddy, Reid, and Curry, 2002).

In contrast, school systems typically identify (through the Individuals with Disabilities Education Act [IDEA]) slightly less than one percent of the public school population as having emotional and behavioral problems. Further, the great tendency of schools is to identify these behavioral problems quite late in a child's school career.

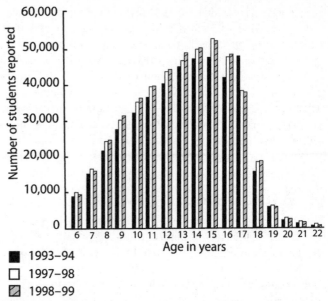

Figure 1 Students with emotional disturbance served by age, selected school years.

The figure above provides a stark example of this practice, which is more typical than not in today's public school systems. Walker, Nikiosha, Zeller, Severson, and Feil (2000) examined the number of K–12 students in the 1993–94, 1997–98, and 1998–99 school years who were certified as emotionally disturbed (the IDEA category that captures antisocial students). As the figure shows, the number of students certified as emotionally disturbed peaks around age 15 (approximately 50,000 cases) during the 1997–98 and 1998–99 school years. Similarly, the older data, from the 1993–94 school year, show the peak in referrals spread over the ages 14, 15, and 17. These results suggest that a large number of students, who were no doubt in need of supports and services for emotional disturbance in their elementary and middle school years, were not referred, evaluated, or served under special education.[4] Only in adolescence, when their behavior problems had become so intractable and difficult to accommodate, were many of these students finally identified and served. This practice of delayed referral is the polar opposite of what research clearly shows is necessary.

Our society's social, cultural, and economic problems are spilling over into our schools. They are greatly complicating schools' central task of educating students safely and effectively. But the research is clear and growing: Even though many children and youth come from and return to chaotic, coercive home environments on a daily basis, they can still acquire sufficient behavioral control to succeed in school—and to allow classmates to learn in an orderly environment.

We have substantial knowledge about how to divert at-risk children, youth, and families from destructive outcomes.[5] We believe the problem is not one of knowing what to do, but of convincing schools to effectively use research-based intervention programs over the long term.

The remainder of this article is devoted to providing educators with guidelines and programs for early intervention that greatly reduce antisocial behavior. There are no magic bullets in the material presented herein. Dealing with the antisocial student population is difficult, frustrating, and, because schools tend to intervene too late, often without identifiable rewards. However, of all those who suffer from conditions and disorders that impair school performance, these students are among those with the greatest capacity for change—particularly when they first start school.

III. What Can Schools Do?

Schools are not the source of children's antisocial behavior, and they cannot completely eliminate it. But schools do have substantial power to prevent it in some children and greatly reduce it in others.

First, and in some ways most importantly, schools can help by being academically effective. The fact is, academic achievement and good behavior reinforce each other: Experiencing some success academically is related to decreases in acting out; conversely, learning positive behaviors is related to doing better academically. Kellam and his colleagues (1994), for example, showed experimentally that gains in first-grade academic achievement, as measured by standardized achievement tests, resulted in substantially reduced levels of aggression, according to behavior ratings by their teachers. And, confirming what common sense tells us, Caprara, Barbaranelli, Pastorelli, Bandura, and Zimbardo (2000) found that positive behaviors (like cooperating, sharing, and consoling) among very young children contributed to their later academic achievement.

Aggressive first-grade boys assigned to orderly classrooms had odds of 3:1 in favor of being highly aggressive in middle school. Those assigned to chaotic classrooms had odds of 59:1 for being highly aggressive in middle school.

Second, schools can, to a large and surprising extent, affect the level of aggression in young boys just by the orderliness of their classrooms. An intriguing longitudinal study dramatically illustrates the role of this variable in the development or prevention of aggressive behavior from first grade to middle school (Kellam, Rebok, Ialongo, and Mayer, 1994). After randomly assigning students to first-grade classrooms, researchers found that nearly half of the classrooms were chaotic and the remainder were reasonably well-managed. Of the boys in the study who began schooling in the top quartile of aggressive behavior (as rated by their teachers), those assigned to orderly classrooms had odds of 3:1 in favor of being highly aggressive in middle school. However, those boys assigned to chaotic classrooms had odds of 59:1 for being highly aggressive in middle school.

This seminal finding suggests that poor classroom management by teachers in grade one is a huge, but preventable, factor in the development of antisocial behavior—and, conversely, that effective classroom management can have an enormous long-term positive effect on behavior. Thus, working closely with first-grade teachers (and, presumably, other early-grade teachers) on their behavior management can yield substantial future benefits for students and their schools by offsetting destructive outcomes.

But to some extent, this just begs the larger question: How can schools and their teachers create and sustain orderly classrooms? We summarize here the key findings and conclusions from 40 years of research. First, we present a three-tiered intervention model that matches the extent of children's behavioral problems to the power (and, therefore, cost) of the programs implemented. Second, we offer tools that can accurately and effectively identify students as young as kindergarten (and, in daycare or preschool settings, even at-risk three-year-olds can be identified) who are likely to become school behavior problems (and, later in life, delinquents and even adult criminals). Third, we review five techniques that, in combination, are at the heart of preventing antisocial behavior. Fourth, we describe specific programs with substantial and growing records of effectiveness that successfully incorporate all of the above into entirely doable, economical, and feasible school interventions. These programs can be purchased by schools from a variety of for-profit publishers and non-profit child and family services organizations. Some are inexpensive; the more expensive interventions tend to be individualized to meet the needs of highly aggressive children. All of the programs described in this article can be funded with either IDEA resources or school improvement funds. Programs for antisocial children, such as those described here, can also be funded in partnership with mental health agencies and/or through grants available through the Safe and Drug Free Schools division of the U.S. Department of Education. (See box, Funding Early Interventions.)

A. Three Levels of Intervention

Research has shown that the best way to prevent antisocial behavior is actually to start with an inexpensive school-wide intervention and then add on more intensive interventions for the most troubled kids. Building on work done by the U.S. Public Health Service, Hill Walker and his colleagues developed a model with three progressively more intensive levels of intervention to address challenging behavior within schools (Walker, Horner, Sugai, Bullis, Sprague, Bricker, and Kaufman, 1996). This model has proved to be very popular among educational researchers and has been broadly adopted by practitioners as a way to select and coordinate interventions. It is sometimes referred to in educational forums as "the Oregon Model." However, this approach is clearly a matter of public domain and is not owned by anyone. The three levels of intervention are known as "universal," "selected," and "indicated." Each is briefly described below.

"Universal" interventions are school or classroom practices that affect all students. Examples of universal interventions relevant to behavior are classwide social skills training and well-enforced school discipline codes. (Outside of education,

Funding Early Interventions

With the research reviewed here, building support for the idea of early interventions should not be difficult—but finding funds could be if you don't know where to look. One source is Title I. Schools in which at least 40 percent of the students are poor should look into using the schoolwide provision of Title I to fund universal interventions. Under Title I schoolwide, you can combine several federal, state, and local funding streams to support school improvement programs. Insofar as students are identified as emotionally disturbed, their interventions can be funded by IDEA. The federal government also provides funding to reduce behavior problems through the Safe and Drug Free Schools and Communities Act. In this case, state education agencies receive funds to make grants to local education agencies and governors receive funds to make complementary grants to community-based organizations. Schools can also partner with mental health agencies, enabling services to be covered by insurance such as Medicaid and the State Children's Health Insurance Program. Plus, most states have funding streams that could support the programs described in this article. (For more information on funding, see chapter two of *Safe, Supportive, and Successful Schools: Step by Step*, available from Sopris West for $49; order online at www.sopriswest.com/swstore/product.asp?sku=872)

the polio vaccination is an example of a "universal intervention.") It may seem odd to implement a program for all students when most teachers can easily identify children who have, or are developing, antisocial behavior. But schoolwide programs accomplish three things. First, they improve almost all students' behavior—and most students, even if they don't qualify as troublemakers, still need some practice being well-behaved. Second, universal interventions have their greatest impact among students who "are on the margins"—those students who are just beginning to be aggressive or defiant. Sometimes, systematic exposure to a universal intervention will be sufficient to tip them in the right direction. Third, the universal intervention offers a foundation that supports the antisocial students throughout the day by reinforcing what they are learning in their more intensive selected and indicated interventions; these latter interventions are more efficient and have a greater impact when they are applied in the context of a prior, well-implemented, universal intervention.

Approximately 80 to 90 percent of all students will respond successfully to a well-implemented universal intervention (Sugai et al., 2002). Once the school environment is orderly, the antisocial students pop up like corks in water. These students have "selected" themselves out as needing more powerful "selected" interventions that employ much more expensive and labor-intensive techniques. The goal with these students is to decrease the frequency of their problem behaviors, instill appropriate behaviors, and make the children more responsive

to universal interventions (Sugai et al., 2002). While selected interventions typically are based in the school, to be their most effective they often require parental involvement. Nevertheless, even when parents refuse to participate, selected interventions still have positive effects and are well worth the effort.

The vast majority of antisocial students will start behaving better after being involved in universal and selected interventions, but schools can expect that a very small percentage of antisocial students (about one to five percent of the total youth population) will not. These are the most severe cases—the most troubled children from the most chaotic homes—and they require extremely intensive, individualized, and expensive interventions. These interventions, called "indicated," are typically family focused, with participation and support from mental health, juvenile justice, and social service agencies, as well as schools. Most non-specialized schools will find that running such an intervention is beyond their capacity. It's for such students that alternative education settings are necessary.

This three-tiered intervention model offers a structure that educators can use when they are reviewing and trying to coordinate programs. It ensures that all students' needs will be met efficiently—each child is exposed to the level of intervention that his behavior shows he needs. This is a very cost-effective model for schools because interventions become much more expensive as they become more specialized.

But it all begins with effective early screening.

B. Early Screening and Identification of Potentially Antisocial Students

Many fields have well-established practices to identify problems early and allow for more effective treatments. For instance, in medicine, routine screening procedures such as prostate-specific antigen (PSA) tests to detect prostate cancer, mammograms to detect breast cancer, and Papanicolaou (Pap) tests to detect the early states of cervical cancer have been routine for years. Unfortunately, similar proactive, early identification approaches are not commonly used to identify children with, or at risk of developing, antisocial behavior.

But research shows that early identification is absolutely critical: Children who have not learned appropriate, non-coercive ways to interact socially by around 8 years of age (the end of third grade) will likely continue displaying some degree of antisocial behavior throughout their lives (Loeber and Farrington, 1998). We also know that the longer such children go without access to effective and early intervention services (particularly after the age of 8), the more resistant to change their behavior problems will be (Gresham, 1991) and the more expensive it will be to induce the change.

Yet, as discussed previously, schools offer special education services to just one percent of students, though two to 16 percent manifest some form of antisocial behavior—and virtually no special education services are provided before students become adolescents. The technology (usually simple normed checklists and observation instruments, as described below) for identifying such children is gradually becoming more accurate for children at younger and younger ages (Severson and Walker, 2002).

A particularly valuable approach to screening is known as "multiple gating" (Loeber, Dishion, and Patterson, 1984). Multiple gating is a process in which a series of progressively more precise (and expensive) assessments or "gates" are used to identify children who need help with their behavior. One such screening procedure is the Systematic Screening for Behavior Disorders (SSBD) (Walker and Severson, 1990).

This screening procedure offers a cost-effective, mass screening of all students in grades one to six in regular education classrooms. The SSBD is made up of a combination of teacher nominations (Gate 1), teacher rating scales (Gate 2), and observations of classroom and playground problem behavior (Gate 3). It was nationally standardized on 4,500 students for the Gate 2 measures and approximately 1,300 students for the Gate 3 measures. It represents a significant advance in enabling the systematic and comprehensive screening of behavioral problems among general education students (Gresham, Lane, and Lambros, 2002). The major advantage of the SSBD is first, its ease of use, and second, its common set of standards for teachers to use in evaluating students' behavior; these standards remove most of the subjectivity that is endemic to the referral process commonly used in schools (Severson and Walker, 2002). If all schools employed universal screening (and backed it up with effective early interventions), an enormous amount of defiant and destructive behavior could be prevented—and innumerable teaching hours could be preserved.

Researchers have found that teachers do tend to praise their regular students for good behavior, but they tend not to seize opportunities to praise antisocial students when they are behaving well.

C. Key Features of Effective Interventions

When dealing with well-established antisocial behavior, a combination of the following techniques is usually required in order to successfully bring about behavior change: (1) a consistently enforced schoolwide behavior code, (2) social-skills training, (3) appropriately-delivered adult praise for positive behavior, (4) reinforcement contingencies and response costs, and (5) time-out (see Wolf, 1978). Each of these techniques is briefly explained below.

Over the past three decades, an extensive body of research has developed on the effectiveness of these techniques for preventing and remediating problem behavior within the context of schools. Studies of the use of these techniques show that positive strategies (appropriate praise, social-skills training, providing free-time privileges or activities) are generally sufficient for developing and maintaining the appropriate behavior of most students. However, students with challenging behavior often also require sanctions of some type (e.g., time-out or loss of privileges) in order to successfully address their problems. Extensive research clearly shows that, to be most effective,

intervention programs or regimens incorporating these techniques should be applied across multiple settings (classrooms, hallways, playgrounds, etc.), operate for a sufficient time period for them to work, and should involve teachers and parents in school-home partnerships whenever possible.

No single technique applied in isolation will have an enduring impact. Used together, however, they are effective—especially for antisocial students age 8 or younger. Assembling these techniques into feasible and effective daily routines can be done by individual teachers in well-run schools. But it is difficult, time-consuming, and fraught with trial and error. Among the fruits of the past several decades of research on this topic is a group of carefully developed and tested programs that integrate these techniques into entirely doable programs that don't overly distract teachers from their main job: teaching. Several are briefly described in this and the following section.

1. A Well-Enforced Schoolwide Behavior Code

A schoolwide behavior code creates a positive school climate by clearly communicating and enforcing a set of behavioral standards. The code should consist of 5 to 7 rules—and it's essential to carefully define and provide examples of each rule. Ideally, school administrators, teachers, related services staff, students, and parents should all be involved in the development of the code. But writing the code is just the first step. Too often, teachers and others complain, a behavior code is established—and left to wither. To be effective, students must be instructed in what it means, have opportunities to practice following the rules, have incentives for adhering to it (as described in the third and fourth techniques), and know that violating it brings consequences.

One excellent, inexpensive program for teaching the schoolwide behavior expectations reflected in a code is called Effective Behavior Support (EBS). The principal features of EBS are that all staff (administrative, classroom, lunchroom, playground, school bus, custodial, etc.) recognize and abide by the same set of behavioral expectations for all students. The behavior expectations are explicitly taught to students and they are taught in each relevant venue. In groups of 30 to 45, students are taken to various parts of the school (e.g., the bus loading zone, cafeteria, main hallway, gym, and classrooms) to discuss specific examples of behaviors that would, and would not, meet the behavior expectations. Once they have learned the expectations, they are motivated to meet them by earning rewards and praise for their good behavior.

2. Social Skills Training

As discussed earlier, many antisocial students enter school without adequate knowledge of—or experience with—appropriate social skills. These skills must be taught, practiced, and reinforced. This is the purpose of social skills training. Skills taught include empathy, anger management, and problem solving. They are taught using standard instructional techniques and practiced so that students not only learn new skills, but also begin using them throughout the school day and at home. While the training is vital for antisocial students, all students benefit from improving their social skills—especially students "on the margin" of antisocial behavior. Social skills curricula are typically taught in one or two periods a week over the course of several months and in multiple grades.

3. Adult Praise

Adult praise (from teachers, parents, or others) is a form of focused attention that communicates approval and positive regard. It is an abundantly available, natural resource that is greatly underutilized. Researchers have found that teachers do tend to praise their regular students for good behavior, but they tend not to seize opportunities to praise antisocial students when they are behaving well (Mayer & Sulzer-Azaroff, 2002). This is indeed unfortunate because praise that is behavior specific and delivered in a positive and genuine fashion is one of our most effective tools for motivating all students and teaching them important skills. Reavis et al. (1996) note that praise should be immediate, frequent, enthusiastic, descriptive, varied, and involve eye contact. We would also suggest that the ratio of praise to criticism and reprimands be at least 4:1—and higher if possible. Although antisocial students may not immediately respond to praise because of their long history of negative interactions with the adults in their lives, when paired with other incentives (such as the type of reward system described below), the positive impact of praise will eventually increase.

4. Reinforcement Contingencies and Response Costs

Rewards and penalties of different sorts are a common feature of many classroom management strategies. Research shows that there are specific "best" ways to arrange these reinforcements to effectively motivate students to behave appropriately. These strategies are called individual reinforcement contingencies, group reinforcement contingencies, and response costs. Individual contingencies are private, one-to-one arrangements between a teacher or parent and a student in which specified, positive consequences are made available dependent ("contingent") upon the student's performance. Earning a minute of free time for every 10 or 15 math problems correctly solved, or attempted, is an example of an individual contingency.

Group contingencies are arrangements in which an entire group of individuals (e.g., a class) is treated as a single unit and the group's performance, as a whole, is evaluated to determine whether a reward is earned, such as an extra five minutes of recess. (Note: A group can fail to earn a reward, such as an extra five minutes of recess, but should not be penalized, such as by losing five minutes of the normal recess.) This strategy gets peers involved in encouraging the antisocial student to behave better. For example, if the antisocial student disrupts the class, instead of laughing at his antics, other students will encourage him to quiet down so that they can all earn the reward. To make it easier to keep track of students' behavior, reinforcement contingencies are often set up as point systems in which students must earn a certain number of points within a certain time period in order to earn a reward.

"Response costs" are a form of penalty that is added to the package of contingencies when working toward a reward is not quite enough to change students' behavior. Teachers can increase the effectiveness of contingencies by adding a response cost so that good behavior earns points and bad behavior subtracts points—making it much harder to earn a reward. (Response costs are the basis for late fees, traffic tickets, penalties in football, foul shots in basketball, and other sanctions in public life.)

5. Time-Out

Time-out is a technique of last resort in which students are removed for just five to 15 minutes from situations in which they have trouble controlling their behavior and/or their peers' attention is drawn to their inappropriate behavior. We recommend both in-classroom time-out for minor infractions and out-of-classroom time-out (the principal's office or a designated time-out room) for more serious infractions. Students should be given the option of volunteering for brief periods of time-out when they temporarily cannot control their own behavior, but teachers should *never* physically try to force students into time-out. Finally, *in-class* time-out should be used sparingly and should *not* be used with older students. Older students who need to be removed from a situation can be sent to the principal's office or another "cool-down" room instead of having an in-class time-out.

The research foundation for these techniques is quite strong and the empirical evidence of their effectiveness is both persuasive and growing. For the past 40 years, researchers in applied behavior analysis have worked closely with school staff and others in testing and demonstrating the effectiveness of these techniques within real world settings like classrooms and playgrounds. Literally hundreds of credible studies have documented the effectiveness of each of these techniques—as well as combinations of them—in remediating the problems that antisocial children and youth bring to schooling. The research has also surfaced guidelines for the effective application of the techniques in school contexts (Walker, 1995).

IV. Effective Programs for Preventing Antisocial Behavior

In spite of huge advances in our knowledge of how to prevent and treat antisocial behavior in the past decade, the Surgeon General's Report on Youth Violence indicates that less than 10 percent of services delivered in schools and communities targeting antisocial behavior patterns are evidence-based (see Satcher, 2001). As these children move through schools without effective intervention services and supports, their problems are likely to become more intractable and ever more resistant to change. This is simply not necessary. Effective, manageable programs exist.

We highlight three promising interventions—Second Step, First Step to Success, and Multisystemic Therapy—as examples of, respectively, universal, selected, and indicated interventions. The coordinated implementation of these or similar programs can make a remarkable difference in the orderliness of schools and classrooms and in the lives of antisocial youth (not to mention the victims of their aggression).

Second Step, a social skills training program for K-9 students, is described in detail. It was recently rated as the number one program for ensuring school safety by a blue ribbon panel of the U.S. Department of Education. Evaluations of Second Step have found results ranging from decreases in aggression and disruption among 109 preschool and kindergarten children from low-income, urban homes (McMahon, 2000) to less hostility and need for adult supervision among over 1,000 second- to fifth-grade students (Frey, Nolen, Van Schoiack-Edstrom, and Hirschstein, 2001).

First Step, is an intensive intervention for highly aggressive K-3 students. Experimental studies with kindergartners have found great improvments in their overall classroom behavior and academic engagement, and substantial reductions in their aggression during implementation and over many years following the end of intervention (see Walker, Kavanagh, Stiller, Golly, Severson, and Feil, 1998; Epstein and Walker, 2002). Similarly, studies involving two sets of identical twins enrolled in regular kindergarten programs found that exposure to the program produced powerful behavior changes upon introduction of the intervention that were maintained throughout the program's implementation (Golly, Sprague, Walker, Beard, and Gorham, 2000). These types of positive effects have also been replicated by other investigators. The First Step program has been included in six national reviews of effective early interventions for addressing oppositional and/or aggressive behavior in school.

Multisystemic Therapy (MST) is a family-focused intervention conducted by a trained therapist. It is aimed at the most severely at-risk youth, those who have been or are about to be incarcerated, often for violent offenses. Very often, the student has already been assigned to an alternative education setting. The therapist teaches parents the skills they need to assist their antisocial child to function more effectively across a range of social contexts. Daily contact between the student and therapist is common in the early stages of MST and reduces to several times per week as the intervention progresses. Therapists periodically talk to teachers to find out about the children's behavior, attendance, and work habits. Most importantly, teachers need to let therapists know when they perceive incremental improvements in the children's behavior—the therapists use this information to guide their work with the families. According to the Blueprints for Violence Prevention Project, MST has been found to reduce long-term rates of being re-arrested by 25 to 70 percent, to greatly improve family functioning, and to lessen mental health problems (Blueprints, 2003). (To find out if MST is available in your area, visit www.mstservices.com).

As the research clearly shows, these three programs have the potential to prevent countless acts of aggression and positively influence both school and family functioning.

Disruptive student behavior will decrease and teaching time will increase, allowing all children to learn more. Office discipline referrals will decrease, freeing up school staff to address other school needs like supporting instruction. Effective programs do require an upfront investment of time and energy, but over the school year, and certainly over the school career, they more than "pay for themselves" in terms of teaching time won back.

Effective programs require an upfront investment of time and energy, but they more than "pay for themselves" in terms of teaching time won back.

An obvious subtext in the article has been that elementary schools—and especially K-3 teachers—must bear the burden of preventing antisocial behavior. This may come as a surprise since behavior problems seem so much more severe as children age. But if there's one uncontestable finding from the past 40 years of research on antisocial children, it's this: The longer students are allowed to be aggressive, defiant, and destructive, the more difficult it is to turn them around. While high schools can, and should, do what they can to help antisocial students control themselves, elementary schools can, and should, actually help antisocial children to become socially competent.

Notes

1. In the AFT's poll, of the 43 percent of teachers who said they had students in their classes with discipline problems, more than half said the problems were caused by one to three students. Poll conducted by Peter D. Hart Research Associates, October 1995.

2. It is important to note that the kind of coercive interaction described is very different from parents' need to establish authority in order to appropriately discipline their children. This is accomplished through the clear communication of behavioral expectations, setting limits, monitoring and supervising children's behavior carefully, and providing positive attention and rewards or privileges for conforming to those expectations. It also means using such strategies as ignoring, mildly reprimanding, redirecting, and/or removing privileges when they do not. These strategies allow parents to maintain authority without relying on the coercion described above and without becoming extremely hostile or giving in to children's attempts to use coercion.

3. This unfortunate behavior pattern soon leads to peer rejection (Reid, Patterson and Snyder, 2002). When behaviorally at-risk youth are rejected and forsaken by normal, well-behaved peers, they often begin to form friendships amongst themselves. If, over several years (and particularly in adolescence), these friendships solidify in such a way that these youth identify with and feel like members of a deviant peer group, they have a 70 percent chance of a felony arrest within two years (Patterson et al., 1992).

4. Kauffman (1999) suggests that the field of education actually "prevents prevention" of behavioral disorders through well-meaning efforts to "protect" difficult children from being

labeled and stigmatized by the screening and identification process.

5. Successful model programs have been reviewed and described extensively by Catalano, Loeber, and McKinney (1999), by Loeber and Farrington (2001), and by Reid and his colleagues (2002).

References

Blueprints for Violence Prevention (2003). Multisystemic Therapy online at www.colorado.edu/cspv/blueprints/model/programs/MST.html

Burns, B. (2002). Reasons for hope for children and families: A perspective and overview. In B. Murns & K.K. Hoagwood (Eds.), *Community treatment for youth: Evidence-based interventions for severe emotional and behavioral disorders* (pp. 1–15). New York: Oxford University Press.

Caprara, G., Barbaranelli, C., Pastorelli, C., Brandura, A., & Zimbardo, P. (2000). Prosocial foundations of children's academic achievement. *Psychological Science, 11*(4), 302–306.

Catalano, R., Loeber, R., & McKinney, K. (1999). School and community interventions to prevent serious and violent offending. *Juvenile Justice Bulletin.* U.S. Department of Justice, Office of Juvenile Justice and Delinquency Prevention, Washington, D.C.

Eddy, J.M., Reid, J.B., & Curry, V. (2002). The etiology of youth antisocial behavior, delinquency and violence and a public health approach to prevention. In M.R. Shinn, H.M. Walker, & G. Stoner (Eds.), *Interventions for academic and behavior problems II: Preventive and remedial approaches,* (pp. 27–51). Bethesda, Md.: National Association for School Psychologists.

Epstein, M. & Walker, H. (2002). Special education: Best practices and First Step to Success. In B. Burns & K. Hoagwood (Eds.), *Community treatment for youth: Evidence-based intervention for severe emotional and behavioral disorders* (pp. 177–197). New York: Oxford University Press.

Frey, K.S., Nolan, S.B., Van Schoiack-Edstrom, L., and Hirschstein, M. (2001, June). "Second Step: Effects on Social Goals and Behavior." Paper presented at the annual meeting of the Society for Prevention Research, Washington, D.C.

Golly, A., Sprague, J., Walker, H.M., Beard, K., & Gorham, G. (2000). The First Step to Success program: An analysis of outcomes with identical twins across multiple baselines. *Behavioral Disorders, 25*(3), 170–182.

Gresham, F.M. (1991). Conceptualizing behavior disorders in terms of resistance to intervention. *School Psychology Review, 20,* 23–36.

Gresham, F.M., Lane, K., & Lambros, K. (2002). Children with conduct and hyperactivity attention problems: Identification, assessment and intervention. In K. Lane, F.M. Gresham, & T. O'Shaughnessy (Eds.), *Children with or at risk for emotional and behavioral disorders* (pp. 210–222). Boston: Allyn & Bacon.

Grossman, D., Neckerman, M., Koepsell, T., Ping-Yu Liu, Asher, K., Beland, K., Frey, K., & Rivara, F. (1997). Effectiveness of a violence prevention curriculum among children in elementary school: A randomized, control trial. *Journal of the American Medical Association, 277*(20), pp. 1605–1611.

Herrnstein, R. (1961). Relative and absolute strength of response as a function of frequency of reinforcement. *Journal of the Experimental Analysis of Behavior, 4,* 267–272.

Herrnstein, R. (1974). Formal properties of the matching law. *Journal of the Experimental Analysis of Behavior, 21,* 486–495.

Kauffman, J. (1999). How we prevent emotional and behavioral disorders. *Exceptional Children, 65,* 448–468.

Kazdin, A. (1993). Adolescent mental health: Prevention and treatment programs. *American Psychologist, 48,* 127–141.

Kellam, S., Rebok, G., Ialongo, N., & Mayer, L. (1994). The course and malleability of aggressive behavior from early first grade into middle school: Results of a developmental epidemiologically based prevention trial. *Journal of Child Psychology and Psychiatry, 35*(2), 259–281.

Loeber, D. & Farrington, D. (2001). *Child delinquents: Development, intervention and service needs.* Thousand Oaks, Calif.: Sage.

Loeber, R., Dishion, T., & Patterson, G. (1984). Multiple-gating: A multistage assessment procedure for identifying youths at risk for delinquency. *Journal of Research in Crime and Delinquency, 21,* 7–32.

Loeber, R. & Farrington, D. (Eds.). (1998). *Serious and violent juvenile offenders: Risk factors and successful interventions.* Thousand Oaks, Calif.: Sage.

Loeber, R. & Farrington, D.P. (2001) *Serious and violent juvenile offenders: Risk factors and successful interventions.* Thousand Oaks, Calif.: Sage.

Mayer, G.R. & Sulzer-Azanoff, B. (2002). Interventions for vandalism and aggression. In M. Shinn, H. Walker, & G. Stoner (Eds.), *Interventions for academic and behavior problems II: Preventive and remedial approaches* (pp. 853–884). Bethesda, Md.: National Association of School Psychologists.

McMahon, S.D., et al. (2000). "Violence Prevention: Program Effects on Urban Preschool and Kindergarten Children." *Applied and Preventive Psychology, 9,* 271–281.

Patterson, G. (1982). *A social learning approach, Volume 3: Coercive family process.* Eugene, Ore.: Castalia.

Patterson, G.R., Reid, J.B., & Dishion, T.J. (1992). *Antisocial boys.* Eugene, Ore.: Castalia.

Reavis, H.K., Taylor, M., Jenson, W., Morgan, D., Andrews, D., & Fisher, S. (1996). *Best practices: Behavioral and educational strategies for teachers.* Longmont, Colo.: Sopris West.

Reid, J.B., Patterson, G.R., & Snyder, J.J. (Eds.). (2002). *Antisocial behavior in children and adolescents: A developmental analysis and the Oregon Model for Intervention.* Washington, D.C.: American Psychological Association.

Satcher, D. (2001). *Youth violence: A report of the Surgeon General.* Washington, D.C.: U.S. Public Health Service, U.S. Department of Health and Human Services.

Severson, H. & Walker, H. (2002). Proactive approaches for identifying children at risk for sociobehavioral problems. In K. Lane, F.M. Gresham, & T. O'Shaughnessy (Eds.), *Interventions for children with or at-risk for emotional and behavioral disorders,* pp. 33–53. Boston: Allyn & Bacon.

Snyder, J. (2002). Reinforcement and coercion mechanisms in the development of antisocial behavior: Peer relationships. In J. Reid, G. Patterson, & L. Snyder (Eds.), *Antisocial behavior in children and adolescents: A developmental analysis and model for intervention,* pp. 101–122. Washington, D.C.: American Psychological Association.

Snyder, J. & Stoolmiller, M. (2002). Reinforcement and coercive mechanisms in the development of antisocial behavior. The family. In J. Reid, G. Patterson, & J. Snyder (Eds.), *Antisocial behavior in children and adolescents: A developmental analysis and model for intervention* (pp. 65–100). Washington, D.C.: American Psychological Association.

Sugai, G. & Horner, R., & Gresham, F. (2002) Behaviorally effective school environments. In M. Shinn, H. Walker, & G. Stoner (Eds.). *Interventions for academic and behavior problems II: Preventive and remedial approaches* (pp. 315–350). Bethesda, Md.: National Association of School Psychologists.

Walker, H.M. (1995). *The acting-out child: Coping with classroom disruption.* Langmont, Colo.: Sopris West.

Walker, H.M., Horner, R.H., Sugai, G., Bullis M., Spraque, J.R., Bricker, D. & Kaufman, M.J. (1996). Integrated approaches to preventing antisocial behavior patterns among school-age children and youth. *Journal of Emotional and Behavioral Disorders, 4,* 193–256.

Walker, H., Kavanagh, K., Stiller, B., Golly, A., Severson, H., & Feil, E. (1997). *First Step to Success: An early intervention program for antisocial kindergartners,* Longmont, Colo.: Sopris West.

Walker, H., Kavanagh, K., Stiller, B., Golly, A., Severson, H., & Feil, E. (1998). First Step: An early intervention approach for preventing school antisocial behavior. *Journal of Emotional and Behavioral Disorders, 6*(2), 66–80.

Walker, H. & Severson, H. (1990). *Systematic screening for behavioral disorders.* Longmont, Colo.: Sopris West.

Walker, H.M., Nishioka, V., Zeller, R., Severson, H., & Feil, E. (2000). Causal factors and potential solutions for the persistent under-identification of students having emotional or behavioral disorders in the context of schooling. *Assessment for Effective Intervention, 26*(1) 29–40.

Wolf, M.M. (1978). Social validity: The case for subjective measurement, or how applied behavior analysis is finding its heart. *Journal of Applied Behavior Analysis, 11,* 203–214.

HILL M. WALKER is founder and co-director of the Institute on Violence and Destructive Behavior at the University of Oregon, where he has been a professor since 1967. Walker has published hundreds of articles; in 1993 he received the Outstanding Research Award from the Council for Exceptional Children and in 2000 he became the only faculty member to receive the University of Oregon's Presidential Medal. **ELIZABETH RAMSEY** is a school counselor at Kopachuck Middle School in Gig Harbor, Wash., and a co-author of the Second Step program. **FRANK M. GRESHAM** is distinguished professor and director of the School Psychology Program at the University of California-Riverside. He is co-author of the Social Skills Rating System and co-principal investigator for Project REACH. The Division of School Psychology in the American Psychological Association selected him for the Senior Scientist Award. Together, Walker, Ramsey, and Gresham wrote Antisocial Behavior in School: Evidence-Based Practices, on which this article is based.

Understanding and Accommodating Students with Depression in the Classroom

R. MARC CRUNDWELL AND KIM KILLU

Despite advances in educational programming and intervention, educators are constantly challenged to effectively educate students who have emotional and behavioral disorders (E/BD). The behavioral excesses and deficits of these students contribute to the learning challenges they face in the classroom. Most students with E/BD academically perform at least 1 year below the standard grade level (Cullinan, 2002), and have difficulty mastering academic skills and content material. The deleterious effect on academic and social functioning can have a cumulative effect on achievement and school success. Students falling under the E/BD category are more likely to be excluded from general education settings (Heflin & Bullock, 1999) and have marginal to unsatisfactory educational performance (U.S. Department of Education, 1998). The general education environment is often unequipped to provide the resources and support necessary for the academic, behavioral, and social success of these students. There exists a critical need for research that addresses academic instruction for students with E/BD (Gunter & Denny, 1998). More importantly, there is a lack of research-based interventions available to educators for this population, especially in the areas of accommodations and modifications.

It also is important to note that students with E/BD do not comprise a homogeneous group; the category of E/BD includes a wide variety and scope of disorders, and mood disorders are one such category. "A general, pervasive mood of unhappiness or depression" is one of the defining characteristics of serious emotional disturbance, as defined within the Individuals With Disabilities Education Improvement Act (2004). The relationship between depression, the comorbid occurrence of other disorders, and academic and social deficiencies is evident. Depression and mood disorders present a significant challenge in the classroom; resulting symptoms can impact memory, recall, motivation, problem solving, task completion, physical and motor skills, and social interactions (Hammen & Rudolph, 2003; Nolen-Hoeksema, Girgus, & Seligman, 1992). Little information is available on practical instructional accommodations and modifications for use by the classroom teacher. A greater need exists to provide accommodations in the classroom to facilitate more successful classroom placements and educational performance. Educators need this information to effectively design and present instruction to those students displaying characteristics of mood disorders. This article describes the characteristics of mood disorders/depression in children and adolescents, and discusses two cases in which educators designed effective accommodations and modifications in the classroom for these two students with depression.

What Is Depression?

Depression is a mood disorder that can begin at any age and which is characterized by persistent sad or irritable mood throughout the day. Individuals with depression have decreased interest in daily activities, display decreased pleasure in previously enjoyed activities, and often have consistent feelings of worthlessness and guilt. Depression in children and adolescents usually takes the form of a major depressive disorder in which multiple and severe symptoms of depression persist nearly every day for at least 2 weeks (American Psychiatric Association, 2000). Many other children and adolescents might have a milder form of depression known as dysthymic disorder, which lasts at least 1 year and impairs functioning both at home and at school. Depression in children and adolescents does not represent a personal weakness or a character flaw, nor is it the result of poor parenting (Cash, 2003). It is more than just "feeling down," having a "bad day," or having normal reactions to a significant life event (e.g., breakup of a relationship). Children and adolescents with depression also might show changes in appetite, disturbed sleep patterns, impaired concentration, increased defiance or oppositional behavior, and withdrawal from friends or activities.

What Does Depression Look Like in the Classroom?

Research and clinical experience have indicated that depression typically manifests itself differently in children and in adolescents (Kashani, Rosenberg, & Reid, 1989). It is also important to recognize that the symptoms or characteristics of depression appear

Table 1 Common Characteristics of Childhood and Adolescent Depression

Children	Adolescents
Higher levels of irritability	Irritability (on a lesser scale)
More somatic complaints	Argumentative
Difficulty concentrating	Expresses self-esteem and self-worth issues
Forgetfulness/memory difficulties	Negative view of past, present, and future
Easily irritated by peers	Self-deprecating comments
Physical look of depression/being very sad	Attendance problems (e.g., truancy)
Difficulties with planning and organizing	Lack of interest or boredom
Heightened sensitivity to criticism	Reduced pleasure in previously enjoyed activities
Less likely to engage in peer interactions	Late for school
Less occurrence of task completion	Rejected by peers
Less alert and attentive	Substance abuse
Exhibiting separation issues regarding parents	Increased risk-taking behavior/impulsivity
Reluctance to attend school	
Attendance issues (missed days due to illness)	
Poor work performance/lack of follow-up	

to be impacted by developmental differences between children and adolescents. Table 1 provides a summary of symptoms often seen in children and adolescents with depression.

It is important to recognize that students with depression might not ask for help or assistance. This is a result of their own feelings and their belief that no one cares about them, or is due to their negative worldview and a belief that there is nothing that can be done to help them (Cash, 2003). Younger students with depression often do not have the language skills or self-awareness to recognize and report their depressed state. Middle school and high school students often lack self-awareness of their depressed mood.

Why School Personnel Should Know about Depression

Schools and school personnel can play important roles in the early identification, intervention, and prevention of depression in children and adolescents. Cash (2003) indicates that schools can assist students with depression by ensuring that five key areas are addressed.

Destigmatizing Depression

Schools can serve an important role by destigmatizing depression and providing information about the disorder. School personnel, students, and parents can be educated on the signs of depression and the risks associated with depression, and can assist in making the disorder easier to identify. This includes helping students differentiate between having normal feelings of sadness and being depressed.

Identifying Depression

Schools can train staff members, students, and parents on appropriate interventions so that early identification and intervention can be undertaken appropriately on behalf of students with depression. Early identification of students with depression can lead to intervention by those parties trained to deal with early-stage depression, which can lead to more positive outcomes for these students.

Early identification of students with depression can lead to more positive outcomes for these students.

Monitoring Students at Risk for Depression

Schools can ensure close monitoring of at-risk students, especially during periods of high stress for the individual (e.g., suicide of another student) or for the school as a whole (e.g., exam time).

Creating a Supportive Environment for Students with Depression

Schools can take steps to create a caring and supportive environment that reduces alienation for students with depression.

Using Mental Health Officials to Assist Students with Depression

Schools can use the expertise of mental health professionals such as school psychologists, social workers, and counselors to assist in designing and implementing training for all groups. Such professionals also can aid in providing interventions. This can also be helpful for teachers in developing appropriate accommodations within the classroom and in the school. Schools can also utilize these professionals to assist students and families to access outside treatment agencies that can provide support to these students and their families.

What Teachers Need to Know

Depression experienced in childhood and adolescence has been associated with serious impairments in academic, cognitive, and interpersonal functioning within the school setting (Hammen & Rudolph, 2003; Nolen-Hoeksema et al., 1992). Numerous studies have reported significant negative correlations between ratings of academic competence and depression (Leon, Rendali, & Garber, 1980; Slotkin, Forehand, Fauber, McCombs, & Long, 1988). Studies examining the relationship between depression and academic grades generally have revealed significant negative correlations between scores on the Children's Depression Inventory, a measure of childhood depression, and academic grades (Forehand, Brody, Long, &

Fauber, 1988). Further, adolescents with higher depression scores are less likely to graduate from high school (Kandel & Davies, 1986).

Research also has shown a strong link between childhood depression and dysfunctional patterns of attitudes about the self, styles of cognitive appraisal, and interpretations of events and outcomes. Children and adolescents suffering from depression often give up quickly on tasks perceived as daunting, refuse to attempt academic tasks as they feel they are too difficult, and quickly doubt their ability to independently complete academic tasks or engage in problem-solving activities. These children also are far more likely to view events, activities, and their experiences more negatively.

Comorbidity of depression with other disorders often results in teachers being confused about whether depression is occurring, and consequently missing signs of depression in students. Depression in children and adolescents often is comorbid with anxiety disorders (Brady & Kendall, 1992), attention deficit hyperactivity disorder, oppositional defiant disorder, and conduct disorder (Fleming & Offord, 1990). Substance abuse also often is found to co-exist with depression, with high levels of substance abuse found in depressed adolescents (Armstrong & Costello, 2002; Yorbik, Birmaher, Axelson, Williamson, & Ry an, 2004). Additionally, suicidal ideation is common in children and adolescents with depression (Kashani & Carlson, 1987; Mitchell, McCauley, Burke, & Moss, 1988; Ryan et al., 1987). Suicide attempts are also an area of concern for students with depression (Mitchell et al., 1987). For children and adolescents, these comorbid conditions also must be addressed when providing treatment for depression.

Depression can impact significantly on the academic and social functioning of both children and adolescents, and comorbidity issues are substantial; therefore, it is important that teachers understand the disorder and its characteristics. Having knowledge about the disorder increases the ability to identify children and adolescents who could have depression and to make appropriate referrals, participate in assessment activities related to diagnosis, and to be active in interventions to assist these individuals within the school setting. Teachers who are knowledgeable about depression in children and adolescents are more able to provide effective accommodations and modifications to their academic programs, as well as support these students socially within the classroom.

Accommodations for Students with Depression

Depression impacts many areas that affect a student's success in school, including the student's memory, speech, thought, emotions, personality, planning, anxiety, frustration, social interactions, academic achievement, and physical and motor activity. As a result, students with depression can require a variety of accommodations within the classroom and school, as well as multiple instructional strategies to increase their success and academic achievement. Although school staff must find ways to assist children and adolescents with depression in the school and classroom, there currently are no evidence-based depression-specific school interventions

for the disorder from which school personnel can draw (Lofthouse & Fristad, 2006). No research-supported interventions are available, but school personnel have access to a number of strategies that can benefit these children and adolescents in the classroom and in the school. These strategies often also are useful for working with other children who are experiencing difficulties.

Depression impacts many areas that affect a student's success in school, including the student's memory, speech, thought, emotions, personality, planning, anxiety, frustration, social interactions, academic achievement, and physical and motor activity.

The following case studies provide a discussion of the strategies that were used to assist these students, while focusing on the profile of depression for each student. It is worth noting that, in some cases, students with more severe symptoms than those described in the case studies below might require home instruction, a self-contained program, day treatment, or even hospitalization. The interventions presented in the following case studies are idiosyncratic; treatment is designed to meet the individual needs of the student. Figure 1, however, lists common approaches to depression which could prove useful within the educational setting. Many of these strategies also are evident within the cases presented.

Case Study 1

Winston is an 11-year-old boy in Mrs. Steen's sixth-grade general education classroom. For the past several months, Mrs. Steen has noticed a steady decline in Winston's overall academic performance, degree and frequency of social interactions, and ability to follow classroom rules and routines. She reports that he is more irritable with her and his peers, he isolates himself, and he chooses not to interact with his peers, despite their repeated attempts to interact with him. Winston often arrives late for his classes, spends a great deal of time looking for materials to be used in class, and has a difficult time getting started on independent work. He seems to have a low level of energy, difficulty focusing and attending, and is not alert to his surroundings. He becomes easily frustrated when presented with tasks that formerly were fairly easy for him to accomplish. Winston used to enjoy eating lunch with his peers, and he now prefers to eat alone; he rarely finishes his lunch. During group activities, he asks Mrs. Steen if he can work alone.

Mrs. Steen is concerned about the changes she has seen in Winston. She has consulted with her school's prereferral intervention team and with Winston's parents. The parents were relieved that Mrs. Steen had approached them, as they noted similar issues. The school psychologist recommended that Winston's parents have him evaluated by his pediatrician, and they provided the pediatrician with a list of concerns. Winston's pediatrician made a referral to a psychologist who diagnosed Winston as being depressed.

Develop clear expectations and guidelines

Provide frequent feedback

Teach goal setting and monitoring

Teach problem-solving skills

Assist student in developing, organizing, and planning his or her day across a variety of domains (e.g., academic, social, personal, familial)

Modify/accommodate work demands based upon the student's performance levels/stamina (e.g., more time, frequent breaks, opportunities for physical movement)

Develop a primary contact to assist with coordinating academic responsibilities and intervention

Strategically increase opportunities for social interactions

Monitor for suicidal ideations and develop a "no-harm contract" if necessary

Develop a home-school communication system that addresses academic, social, emotional, and adaptive-behavior skills

Promote frequent communication among all team members or staff who work directly with the student

Monitor student compliance with medication regimen, and the medication side effects and effectiveness

Regularly monitor student performance and make appropriate modifications to the intervention plan when necessary

Figure 1 Common strategies/interventions for students with depression.

The school's treatment team met with the psychologist to collaborate on developing individualized school-based accommodations to help improve Winston's academic, social, and behavioral functioning. The team members, psychologists, parents, and Winston met to discuss possible options and important areas in which to develop accommodations. The following accommodations were viewed as important starting points. All parties agreed on the importance of continued collaboration, monitoring, and evaluation of Winston's performance in the targeted areas of academic, social, and behavioral functioning.

Mrs. Steen met with Winston at the beginning of each week to assist him in developing, reviewing, and evaluating specific goals for his academic, social, and behavioral functioning. They set goals for work completion, work submission, frequency of social interactions, and number of minutes of physical activity. The rationale for this was that these areas targeted the major symptoms of his depression. Secondly, the team members thought that it was important for Winston to take an active role in setting goals and engaging in the intervention process.

All of Winston's teachers met to develop clear guidelines and expectations for him. Mrs. Steen served as the liaison between Winston and his other teachers. She reviewed the guidelines and expectations with him each week, and provided Winston with a positive and proactive framework through which he could address his goals in the academic, social, and behavioral domains.

Every day, Mrs. Steen assisted Winston in coordinating his course work with his other teachers and developing a checklist to self-manage his in-class assignments, projects, and homework. This was important because children with depression often have difficulty with organization, engagement, and task completion.

Because of difficulties with organizing and fluctuating mood, the team felt that it was important to be proactive and recognize that children with depression require more monitoring and feedback. As a result, Winston checked in with Mrs. Steen before lunch and at the end of each day and they reviewed his daily progress.

Mrs. Steen, as well as Winston's other teachers, periodically asked him whether he needed a break from the classroom. The team felt that doing so would help avoid having Winston in an environment that he perceived as aversive. He could leave the room, take a short break, and return to the classroom to complete his work. Children with depression have mood and energy fluctuations throughout the day; therefore, the team members decided it was best to proactively address this issue.

On a task-by-task basis, each teacher assisted Winston with developing and managing a timeline that was based on his mood and energy levels. This enabled teachers to shorten or modify class work and assignments to meet Winston's needs.

Due to Winston's difficulty focusing on and initiating independent work, each teacher provided Winston with a study sheet before exams and each teacher reviewed his or her study guide with Winston prior to the exam. During exams, Winston was provided with opportunities for intermittent breaks and was allowed to walk around the building for a short period before returning to the exam.

To maintain Winston's friendships and foster an accepting environment, class time included cooperative group activities, and participants were carefully selected by the teacher to increase the likelihood of positive interactions. Winston also was given opportunities for—and guidance with—orchestrating fun and rewarding activities with his peers.

Due to Winston's fluctuating energy level, the team decided on a task-by-task basis that Winston may be provided with photocopies of class notes and audiotapes of lectures. Teachers monitored Winston's energy levels and peak performance times, and structured their instruction and interactions with Winston to maximize learning time.

Winston, his parents, and the team members met regularly to evaluate and monitor his progress and made modifications to his accommodations, as necessary, based upon his needs and performance.

As a result of the accommodations, school personnel and Winston's parents noted measurable improvements in his academic performance, social interactions, and behavioral functioning. Over the course of several months, Winston increased his work completion and submission rate, and engaged in more interactions with his peers. Winston himself reported an appreciable improvement in his mood and energy level. School staff and Winston's parents agreed to continue to collaborate regarding maintaining the interventions put in place for him and to continue to closely monitor his progress. For school staff, key components of the intervention were thought to be the high level of collaboration and family involvement, and the inclusion of Winston as an active participant in the design, intervention, and evaluation process.

Case Study 2

Brenda is a 16-year-old high school junior whose family immigrated to the United States from the Middle East 5 years ago. Since her arrival in the United States, Brenda has been a bright student, maintaining a 3.6 GPA in her course work despite the language barrier. Within the past year, however, Brenda has been displaying behaviors symptomatic of severe depression. Her grades and work completion levels have decreased dramatically, she has lost interest in most daily activities, she cries often, and she has a difficult time concentrating. Brenda's pediatrician recently has prescribed antidepressants for her. Brenda has responded positively to the medication, but also has experienced some side effects, including increased thirst, more frequent need to go to the bathroom, and feeling some rebound effects when the medication is wearing off. Since her family's immigration, it appears as if Brenda has had a difficult time adjusting to the social aspects of life in the United States. She has established a few relationships with her peers, yet these relationships appear to be more superficial. Brenda does not interact with these peers outside of school through visits, outings, e-mails, instant messages, or phone calls. When asked about these relationships, Brenda states that she feels like an outcast because of her perceived cultural differences. She has befriended a few teachers, one of whom is her bilingual teacher. Speaking in their native tongue, she often shares her thoughts and feelings on what is going on in her life. Brenda has also shared her thoughts on some events of family turmoil and feelings of severe anxiety with the bilingual teacher, and has stated that she has often thought of death as a "way out." Most notable is her recent weight loss. Brenda reports being frequently criticized by family members for her weight. Her food consumption at school can consist of french fries and a diet soda, and this has occurred for the past 6 months. At home, her parents report that she eats little dinner and expresses having very little appetite. Contrary to prior social interactions, she appears to be very childlike in her interactions with others, acting more like a young girl than a young woman. For example, she whines often, is extremely shy, and can be irritable and argumentative. At school, teachers have overheard other students comment that they don't like Brenda because she is always in a bad mood. Brenda has three other siblings and reports that the entire family ignores her and does not care about her.

A meeting was held with the director of special education, the vice principal, the guidance counselor, the bilingual teacher, the parents, and Brenda to discuss the concerns of all parties. During the course of the meeting, the guidance counselor took the lead in discussing Brenda's needs and the role that the school could provide in designing accommodations for her in the classroom. The following is a summary of the conclusions felt to be the most reasonable and effective for Brenda.

Brenda already had established a rapport with the bilingual teacher, so they briefly met once a day to "touch base" on the effectiveness of the interventions proposed. Prior to this, Brenda, the guidance counselor, and the bilingual teacher sat down and established goals and ways to monitor and evaluate them, and set clear expectations and guidelines for Brenda. Students with depression

can be disengaged and lack awareness of what they are experiencing; therefore, the team thought it important for Brenda to have an actual role in the development of her accommodations.

Due to Brenda's previous comments about thoughts of death, Brenda signed a "no-suicide contract" which can also be referred to as a "no-harm contract" (Weiss, 2001). No-suicide contracts are an agreement in which a promise is elicited from an individual that if they experience suicidal ideas or impulses they will inform a health-care professional, family member, teacher, or friend rather than engage in self-injurious behavior. In her contract Brenda promised to seek out the bilingual teacher. Brenda understood that the agreement meant that the teacher would initiate contact with the guidance counselor to follow through on an appropriate response.

Brenda and the guidance counselor met once per week to review Brenda's progress toward the goals established. The guidance counselor assisted Brenda as she worked to accomplish her goals, and gave her strategies to maintain her progress. The counselor also set up a meeting with Brenda and her other teachers to address the problems she is currently facing, and to evaluate Brenda's need for accommodations for examinations and larger projects. Biweekly meetings including Brenda and her teacher for each subject area were scheduled, so that the teachers could review Brenda's progress and provide feedback.

The guidance counselor helped to develop a home-school communication/tracking system that facilitated better communication between the school and Brenda's family. Both sides noted daily progress toward goals and provided qualitative feedback on Brenda's mood and her social interactions. The need for familial involvement in Brenda's success was imperative. To maximize the effectiveness of the interventions proposed, it was critical that the school have an understanding of the family's perspective.

> **To maximize the effectiveness of the interventions proposed, it was critical that the school have an understanding of the family's perspective.**

Students with depression have difficulty with organization, goal development, and follow-through. To address this facet of Brenda's needs, during their daily meetings the bilingual teacher taught Brenda how to utilize a daily planner. They checked the planner daily, and the teacher helped her learn to use it effectively. This was a functional skill that Brenda could apply in other domains of her life.

Once a month, Brenda and her parents had a meeting with the director of special education, the vice principal, the guidance counselor, and the bilingual teacher. All of Brenda's other teachers were invited and were welcomed to attend as well and each month a few did, in fact, attend. The meeting involved a discussion of Brenda's progress, a review of her successes and accomplishments, and a determination of whether alterations or new accommodations were required. Continued collaboration with the family and between all school personnel was essential in maintaining the integrity of the accommodations. In addition, all members involved had collected data on the effectiveness of the accommodations, and the regularly scheduled meetings served as opportunities to receive feedback and to make any decisions on how to proceed.

Brenda enrolled in an after-school program that focused on direct instruction of social skills. The program focused on group interventions with the guidance counselor and on individual sessions with the school social worker. To support the development of her social skills, Brenda's parents also enrolled her in a local cultural center so that Brenda could participate in its adolescent social-activity group. Because students with depression have a tendency to withdraw from social interactions and to view interactions with others more negatively, it was important to provide direct intervention in this area combined with increased opportunities to use these skills. It was expected that Brenda would view social interactions more positively and that her willingness to engage in them would increase.

Brenda's teachers were encouraged to utilize more collaborative learning activities so that Brenda was given opportunities to choose group membership. The teachers closely monitored her performance in and contribution to the group to ensure that Brenda was participating as well as to provide social support as required. Group activities allow for interactions with peers in a safe environment and can result in more engaged and active learning. Group learning activities offer many benefits for students, including sharing cognitive responsibilities and the reduction of stress which often is associated with more independent learning activities and demands (Perkins, 1993). These activities can be helpful in addressing the impact of depression on academic functioning.

Brenda was given access to recorded class lectures to allow her to review them and make personal notes to help her learn material. Brenda's teachers also worked with her to develop effective learning and study strategies to increase her independent use of them and to improve her performance in all academic areas. These included both general learning strategies and domain-specific strategies. General learning strategies are those that have broad applicability across various academic domains and include note-taking, outlines, conceptual mapping, and mnemonic strategies. Domain-specific strategies, in contrast, are those strategies that are specific to a domain or a task. Students who effectively use strategies are more successful overall (Alexander & Judy, 1988). To assist Brenda in the classroom, teachers also increased their level of prompting and feedback. They also worked with Brenda to divide tasks into smaller, more manageable components.

The guidance counselor worked with Brenda to closely match her with a tutor in the school's peer tutoring program. Due to the academic decline that Brenda was experiencing, the team thought it essential that Brenda receive academic intervention before she got too far behind in her studies. The use of a tutoring program also provided another social venue for Brenda to interact with her peers.

Brenda experienced some side effects from the medication she has been taking for her depression, and accommodations were discussed and implemented by her teachers. As a result of her increased thirst, Brenda was provided with unlimited access to water and juice. She was allowed to keep a water bottle on her desk. Brenda was also given a permanent hall pass so that she could leave the room and easily address her increased need to use the restroom. In addition, she was assigned a seat close to the door to decrease any disruption of the classroom. To address rebound effects, Brenda was provided with more opportunities to move around the classroom and engage in activities that were gentle and calming. The school and Brenda's physician also explored Brenda's in-school medication schedules and attempted to make appropriate adjustments.

During the course of the school year, it was noted that Brenda made slow but steady progress in the areas of academic work completion and performance and in her social interactions. Over time, the school personnel developed the trust of the family, which assisted in overcoming cultural and language barriers. Brenda also reported increased feelings of support from her family, school personnel, and peers. Outside of the school setting, Brenda began interacting with a few other girls from the school.

The no-suicide contract was in place for the entire school year; however, it was not acted upon at any time. From the school's perspective, the high level of collaboration between school staff was extremely important—especially the roles of the guidance counselor and bilingual teacher, who both took on significant lead roles. Also important from both the school's and family's perspective was the high level of ongoing monitoring of Brenda's progress and the ability to address her needs through modifications and accommodations.

Final Thoughts

Depression in children and adolescents has increased in frequency, and schools face the challenge of meeting the needs of these students. Students with depression often are unable to perform within the classroom at a level commensurate with their abilities, and frequently also struggle with social interactions. As a result, it is important that teachers become increasingly aware of the impact that depression has upon children and adolescents. Teachers who have such awareness can become key personnel who play integral roles in identifying and assessing children at risk, as well as in developing and implementing interventions to assist these children. Depression can impact across a variety of domains; therefore, many students require a combination of individualized instructional strategies and accommodations to increase both their success within the classroom and their academic achievement. Because depression can present differently across individual children and adolescents, it is important to select instructional strategies and accommodations that match the needs of the student. Children and adolescents taking prescribed medication for their depression also can require special instructional strategies and accommodations to address specific side effects of the medication.

References

Alexander, P. A., & Judy, J. E. (1988). The interaction of domain-specific and strategic knowledge in academic performance. *Review of Educational Research, 58,* 375–404.

American Psychiatric Association. (2000). *Diagnostic and statistical manual of mental disorders* (4th text rev. ed.). Washington, DC: American Psychiatric Publishing.

Armstrong, T. D., & Costello, E. J. (2002). Community studies on adolescent substance use, abuse, or dependence and psychiatric comorbidity. *Journal of Consulting and Clinical Psychology, 70,* 1224–1239.

Brady, E. U., & Kendall, P. C. (1992). Comorbidity of anxiety and depression in children and adolescents. *Psychological Bulletin, 111,* 244–255.

Cash, R. E. (2003). When it hurts to be a teenager. *Principal Leadership Magazine, 4*(2), 11–15.

Cullinan, D. (2002). *Students with emotional and behavioral disorders: An introduction for teachers and other helping professionals.* Upper Saddle River, NJ: Merrill/Prentice Hall.

Fleming, J. E., & Offord, D. R. (1990). Epidemiology of childhood depressive disorders: A critical review. *Journal of the American Academy of Child and Adolescent Psychiatry, 29,* 571–580.

Forehand, R., Brody, G. H., Long, N., & Fauber, R. (1988). The interactive influence of adolescent and maternal depression on adolescent social and cognitive functioning. *Cognitive Therapy and Research, 12,* 341–350.

Gunter, P. L., & Denny, R. K. (1998). Trends, issues, and research needs regarding academic instruction of students with emotional and behavioral disorders. *Behavioral Disorders, 24,* 44–50.

Hammen, C., & Rudolph, K. D. (2003). Childhood depression. In E. Mash & R. Barkley (Eds.) *Childhood psychopathology* (pp. 153–195). New York: Guilford Press.

Heflin, L. J., & Bullock, L. M. (1999). Inclusion of students with emotional/behavioral disorders: A survey of teachers in general and special education. *Preventing School Failure, 43,* 103–111.

Kandel, D. B., & Davies, M. (1986). Adult sequelae of adolescent depressive symptoms. *Archives of General Psychiatry, 43,* 255–262.

Kashani, J. H., & Carlson, G. A. (1987). Seriously depressed preschoolers. *American Journal of Psychiatry, 144,* 348–350.

Kashani, J. H., Rosenberg, T., & Reid, J. (1989). Developmental perspectives in child and adolescent depressive symptoms in a community sample. *American Journal of Psychiatry, 146,* 871–875.

Leon, G. R., Rendall, P. C., & Garber, J. (1980). Depression in children: Parent, teacher, and child perspectives. *Journal of Abnormal Child Psychology, 82,* 221–235.

Lofthouse, N., & Fristad, M. A. (2006). Bipolar disorders. In G. G. Bear & K. M. Minke (Eds.), *Children's needs III: Development, prevention, and intervention* (pp. 211–224). Washington, DC: National Association of School Psychologists.

Mitchell, J., McCauley, E., Burke, P. M., & Moss, S. J. (1988). Phenomenology of depression in children and adolescents. *Journal of the American Academy of Child and Adolescent Psychiatry, 27,* 12–20.

Nolen-Hoeksema, S., Girgus, J. S., & Seligman, M. E. P. (1992). Predictors and consequences of childhood depressive symptoms: A 5-year longitudinal study. *Journal of Abnormal Psychology, 101,* 405–422.

Perkins, D. N. (1993). Person plus: A distributed view of thinking and learning. In G. Salomon (Ed.), *Distributed cognition: Psychological and educational considerations* (pp. 88–110). Cambridge, England: Cambridge University Press.

Ryan, N. D., Puig-Antich, J., Ambrosini, P., Rabinovich, H., Robinson, D., Nelson, B., Iyengar, S., & Twomey, J. (1987). The clinical picture of major depression in children and adolescents. *Archives of General Psychiatry, 44,* 854–861.

Slotkin, J., Forehand, R., Fauber, R., McCombs, A., & Long, N. (1988). Parent-completed and adolescent-completed CDIs: Relationship to adolescent social and cognitive functioning. *Journal of Abnormal Child Psychology, 16*(2), 207–217.

U.S. Department of Education. (1998). *Twenty-first annual report to Congress on the implementation of the Individuals with Disabilities Education Act.* Washington, DC: U.S. Department of Education.

Weiss, A. (2001). The no-suicide contract: Possibilities and pitfalls. *American Journal of Psychotherapy, 55*(3), 414–420.

Yorbik, O., Birmaher, B., Axelson, D., Williamson, D. E., & Ryan, N. D. (2004). Clinical characteristics of depressive symptoms in children and adolescents with major depressive disorder. *Journal of Clinical Psychiatry, 65,* 1654–1659.

R. Marc Crundwell (CEC MI Federation), School Psychologist, Psychological Services Department, Greater Essex County District School Board, Windsor, Ontario, Canada. **Kim Killu** (CEC MI Federation), Associate Professor, School of Education, University of Michigan–Dearborn.

Address correspondence to R. Marc Crundwell, Greater Essex County District School Board, Psychological Services Department, 451 Park Street West, P.O. Box 210, Windsor, ONT, Canada N9A 6K1 (e-mail: rmcrund@uwindsor.ca).

From *Teaching Exceptional Children,* September/October 2007, pp. 48–54. Copyright © 2007 by Council for Exceptional Children. Reprinted by permission via Copyright Clearance Center.

Rethinking How Schools Address Student Misbehavior and Disengagement

HOWARD S. ADELMAN AND LINDA TAYLOR

The essence of good classroom teaching is the ability to create an environment that first can mobilize the learner to pursue the curriculum and then can maintain that mobilization, while effectively facilitating learning. The process, of course, is meant not only to teach academics, but to turn out good citizens. While many terms are used, this societal aim requires that a fundamental focus of school improvement be on facilitating positive social and emotional development/learning.

Behavior problems clearly get in the way of all this. Misbehavior disrupts. In some forms, such as bullying and intimidating others, it is hurtful. And, observing such behavior may disinhibit others. Because of this, discipline and classroom management are daily topics at every school.

Concern about responding to behavior problems and promoting social and emotional learning are related and are embedded into the six arenas we frame to encompass the content of student/learning supports. How these concerns are addressed is critical to the type of school and classroom climate that emerges and to student engagement and re-engagement in classroom learning. As such, they need to be fully integrated into school improvement efforts.

Disengaged Students, Misbehavior, and Social Control

After an extensive review of the literature, Fredricks, Blumenfeld, and Paris conclude: *Engagement is associated with positive academic outcomes, including achievement and persistence in school; and it is higher in classrooms with supportive teachers and peers, challenging and authentic tasks, opportunities for choice, and sufficient structure.* Conversely, for many students, disengagement is associated with behavior and learning problems and eventual dropout. The degree of concern about student engagement varies depending on school population.

In general, teachers focus on content to be taught and knowledge and skills to be acquired—with a mild amount of attention given to the process of engaging students. All this works fine in schools where most students come each day ready and able to deal with what the teacher is ready and able to teach. Indeed, teachers are fortunate when they have a classroom where the majority of students show up and are receptive to the planned lessons. In schools that are the greatest focus of public criticism, this certainly is not the case.

What most of us realize, at least at some level, is that teachers in such settings are confronted with an entirely different teaching situation. Among the various supports they absolutely must have are ways to re-engage students who have become disengaged and often resistant to broad-band (non-personalized) teaching approaches. To the dismay of most teachers, however, strategies for re-engaging students in *learning* rarely are a prominent part of pre- or in-service preparation and seldom are the focus of interventions pursued by professionals whose role is to support teachers and students. As a result, they learn more about *socialization* and *social control* as classroom management strategies than about how to engage and re-engage students in classroom learning, which is the key to enhancing and sustaining good behavior.

Reacting to Misbehavior

When a student misbehaves, a natural reaction is to want that youngster to experience and other students to see the consequences of misbehaving. One hope is that public awareness of consequences will deter subsequent problems. As a result, a considerable amount of time at schools is devoted to discipline and classroom management.

An often stated assumption is that stopping a student's misbehavior will make her or him amenable to teaching. In a few cases, this may be so. However, the assumption ignores all the research that has led to understanding *psychological reactance* and the need for individuals to maintain and restore a sense of self-determination. Moreover, it belies two painful realities: the number of students who continue to manifest poor academic achievement and the staggering dropout rate in too many schools.

Unfortunately, in their efforts to deal with deviant and devious behavior and to create safe environments, too many schools overly on negative consequences and plan only for social control. Such practices model behavior that can foster rather than counter the development of negative values and often produce other forms of undesired behavior. Moreover, the tactics often make schools look and feel more like prisons than community treasures.

In schools, short of suspending a student, punishment essentially takes the form of a decision to do something that the student does not want done. In addition, a demand for future compliance usually is made, along with threats of harsher punishment if compliance is not forthcoming. The discipline may be administered in ways that suggest the student is seen as an undesirable person. As students get older, suspension increasingly comes into play. Indeed, suspension remains one of the most common disciplinary responses for the transgressions of secondary students.

As with many emergency procedures, the benefits of using punishment may be offset by many negative consequences. These include increased negative attitudes toward school and school personnel. These attitudes often lead to more behavior problems, anti-social acts, and various mental health problems. Because disciplinary procedures also are associated with dropping out of school, it is not surprising that some concerned professionals refer to extreme disciplinary practices as "pushout" strategies.

In general, specific discipline practices should be developed with the aim of leaving no child behind. That is, *stopping misbehavior must be accomplished in ways that maximize the likelihood that the teacher can engage/re-engage the student in instruction and positive learning.*

The growing emphasis on positive approaches to reducing misbehavior and enhancing support for positive behavior in and out-of-the-classroom is a step in the right direction. So is the emphasis in school guidelines stressing that discipline should be reasonable, fair, and non-denigrating (e.g., should be experienced by recipients as legitimate reactions that neither denigrate one's sense of worth nor reduce one's sense of autonomy).

Moreover, in recognizing that the application of consequences is an insufficient step in preventing future misbehavior, there is growing awareness that school improvements that engage and re-engage students reduce behavior (and learning) problems significantly. That is why school improvement efforts need to delineate:

- efforts to prevent and anticipate misbehavior
- actions to be taken during misbehavior that do minimal harm to engagement in classroom learning
- steps to be taken afterwards that include a focus on enhancing engagement. . . .

Focusing on Underlying Motivation to Address Concerns about Engagement

Moving beyond socialization, social control, and behavior modification and with an emphasis on engagement, there is a need to address the roots of misbehavior, especially underlying motivational bases. Consider students who spend most of the day trying to avoid all or part of the instructional program. An *intrinsic* motivational interpretation of the avoidance behavior of many of these youngsters is that it reflects their perception that school is not a place where they experience a sense of competence, autonomy, and or relatedness to others. Over time, these perceptions develop into strong motivational dispositions and related patterns of misbehavior.

Misbehavior Can Reflect Proactive (Approach) or Reactive (Avoidance) Motivation

Noncooperative, disruptive, and aggressive behavior patterns that are *proactive* tend to be rewarding and satisfying to an individual because the behavior itself is exciting or because the behavior leads to desired outcomes (e.g., peer recognition, feelings of competence or autonomy). Intentional negative behavior stemming from such approach motivation can be viewed as pursuit of deviance.

Misbehavior in the classroom may also be *reactive,* stemming from avoidance motivation. This behavior can be viewed as protective reactions. Students with learning problems can be seen as motivated to avoid and to protest against being forced into situations in which they cannot cope effectively. For such students, many teaching situations are perceived in this way. Under such circumstances, individuals can be expected to react by trying to protect themselves from the unpleasant thoughts and feelings that the situations stimulate (e.g., feelings of incompetence, loss of autonomy, negative relationships). In effect, the misbehavior reflects efforts to cope and defend against aversive experiences. The actions may be direct or indirect and include defiance, physical and psychological withdrawal, and diversionary tactics.

Interventions for Reactive and Proactive Behavior Problems Begin with Major Program Changes

From a motivational perspective, the aims are to (a) prevent and overcome negative attitudes toward school and learning, (b) enhance motivational readiness for learning and overcoming problems, (c) maintain intrinsic motivation throughout learning and problem solving, and (d) nurture the type of continuing motivation that results in students engaging in activities away from school that foster maintenance, generalization, and expansion of learning and problem solving. Failure to attend to motivational concerns in a comprehensive, normative way results in approaching passive and often hostile students with practices that instigate and exacerbate problems.

After making broad programmatic changes to the degree feasible, intervention with a misbehaving student involves remedial steps directed at underlying factors. For instance, with intrinsic motivation in mind, the following assessment questions arise:

- Is the misbehavior unintentional or intentional?
- If it is intentional, is it reactive or proactive?

- If the misbehavior is reactive, is it a reaction to threats to self-determination, competence, or relatedness?
- If it is proactive, are there other interests that might successfully compete with satisfaction derived from deviant behavior?

In general, intrinsic motivation theory suggests that corrective interventions for those misbehaving reactively requires steps designed to reduce reactance and enhance positive motivation for participation. For youngsters highly motivated to pursue deviance (e.g., those who proactively engage in criminal acts), even more is needed. Intervention might focus on helping these youngsters identify and follow through on a range of valued, socially appropriate alternatives to deviant activity. Such alternatives must be capable of producing greater feelings of self-determination, competence, and relatedness than usually result from the youngster's deviant actions. To these ends, motivational analyses of the problem can point to corrective steps for implementation by teachers, clinicians, parents, or students themselves.

Promoting Social and Emotional Learning

One facet of addressing misbehavior proactively is the focus on promoting healthy social and emotional development. This emphasis meshes well with a school's goals related to enhancing students' personal and social well being. And, it is essential to creating an atmosphere of "caring," "cooperative learning," and a "sense of community" (including greater home involvement).

In some form or another, every school has goals that emphasize a desire to enhance students' personal and social functioning. Such goals reflect an understanding that social and emotional growth plays an important role in

- enhancing the daily smooth functioning of schools and the emergence of a safe, caring, and supportive school climate.
- facilitating students' holistic development.
- enabling student motivation and capability for academic learning.
- optimizing life beyond schooling.

An agenda for promoting social and emotional learning encourages family-centered orientation. It stresses practices that increase positive engagement in learning at school and that enhance personal responsibility (social and moral), integrity, self-regulation (self-discipline), a work ethic, diverse talents, and positive feelings about self and others.

It should be stressed at this point that, for most individuals, learning social skills and emotional regulation are part of normal development and socialization. Thus, social and emotional learning is not primarily a formal training process. This can be true even for some individuals who are seen as having behavior and emotional problems. (While poor social skills are identified as a symptom and contributing factor in a wide range of educational, psychosocial, and mental health problems, it is important to remember that symptoms are correlates.)

What Is Social and Emotional Learning?

As formulated by the Collaborative for Academic, Social, and Emotional Learning (CASEL), social and emotional learning (SEL) "is a process for helping children and even adults develop the fundamental skills for life effectiveness. SEL teaches the skills we all need to handle ourselves, our relationships, and our work, effectively and ethically. These skills include recognizing and managing our emotions, developing caring and concern for others, establishing positive relationships, making responsible decisions, and handling challenging situations constructively and ethically. They are the skills that allow children to calm themselves when angry, make friends, resolve conflicts respectfully, and make ethical and safe choices."

CASEL also views SEL as "providing a framework for school improvement. Teaching SEL skills helps create and maintain safe, caring learning environments. The most beneficial programs provide sequential and developmentally appropriate instruction in SEL skills. They are implemented in a coordinated manner, school-wide, from preschool through high school. Lessons are reinforced in the classroom, during out-of-school activities, and at home. Educators receive ongoing professional development in SEL. And families and schools work together to promote children's social, emotional, and academic success."

Because of the scope of SEL programming, the work is conceived as multi-year. The process stresses adult modeling and coaching and student practice to solidify learning related to social and emotional awareness of self and others, self-management, responsible decision making, and relationship skills.

Natural Opportunities to Promote Social and Emotional Learning

Sometimes the agenda for promoting social and emotional learning takes the form of a special curriculum (e.g., social skills training, character education, assets development) or is incorporated into the regular curricula. However, classroom and school-wide practices can and need to do much more to (a) capitalize on *natural* opportunities at schools to promote social and emotional development and (b) minimize transactions that interfere with positive growth in these areas. Natural opportunities are one of the most authentic examples of "teachable moments."

An appreciation of what needs more attention can be garnered readily by looking at the school day and school year through the lens of goals for personal and social functioning. Is instruction carried out in ways that strengthen or hinder development of interpersonal skills and connections and student understanding of self and others? Is cooperative learning and sharing promoted? Is counterproductive competition minimized? Are interpersonal conflicts mainly suppressed or are they used as learning opportunities? Are roles provided for all students to be positive helpers throughout the school and community?

The Center's website offers specific examples of natural opportunities and how to respond to them in ways that promote personal and social growth . . .

The Promise of Promoting Social and Emotional Learning

Programs to improve social skills and interpersonal problem solving are described as having promise both for prevention and correction. However, reviewers tend to be cautiously optimistic because so many studies have found the range of skills acquired are quite limited and so is the generalizability and maintenance of outcomes. This is the case for training of specific skills (e.g., what to say and do in a specific situation), general strategies (e.g., how to generate a wider range of interpersonal problem-solving options), as well as efforts to develop cognitive-affective orientations, such as empathy training. Reviews of social skills training over several decades conclude that individual studies show effectiveness, but outcome studies often have shown lack of generalizability and social validity. However, the focus has been mainly on social skills training for students with emotional and behavior disorders.

Recent analyses by researchers involved with the Collaborative for Academic, Social, and Emotional Learning (CASEL) suggest that "students who receive SEL programming academically outperform their peers, compared to those who do not receive SEL. Those students also get better grades and graduate at higher rates. Effective SEL programming drives academic learning, and it also drives social outcomes such as positive peer relationships, caring and empathy, and social engagement. Social and emotional instruction also leads to reductions in problem behavior such as drug use, violence, and delinquency."

Promotion of Mental Health

Promotion of mental health encompasses efforts to enhance knowledge, skills, and attitudes in order to foster social and emotional development, a healthy lifestyle, and personal well-being. Promoting healthy development, well-being, and a value-based life are important ends unto themselves and overlap primary, secondary, and tertiary interventions to prevent mental health and psychosocial problems.

Interventions to promote mental health encompass not only strengthening individuals, but also enhancing nurturing and supportive conditions at school, at home, and in the neighborhood. All this includes a particular emphasis on increasing opportunities for personal development and empowerment by promoting conditions that foster and strengthen positive attitudes and behaviors (e.g., enhancing motivation and capability to pursue positive goals, resist negative influences, and overcome barriers). It also includes efforts to maintain and enhance physical health and safety and *inoculate* against problems (e.g.,

providing positive and negative information, skill instruction, and fostering attitudes that build resistance and resilience).

While schools alone are not responsible for this, they do play a significant role, albeit sometimes not a positive one, in social and emotional development. School improvement plans need to encompass ways the school will (1) *directly facilitate* social and emotional (as well as physical) development and (2) *minimize threats* to positive development (see references at end of this article). In doing so, appreciation of differences in levels of development and developmental demands at different ages is fundamental, and personalized implementation to account for individual differences is essential.

From a mental health perspective, helpful guidelines are found in research clarifying normal trends for school-age youngsters' efforts to feel *competent, self-determining,* and *connected with significant others.* And, measurement of such feelings can provide indicators of the impact of a school on mental health. Positive findings can be expected to correlate with school engagement and academic progress. Negative findings can be expected to correlate with student anxiety, fear, anger, alienation, a sense of losing control, a sense of hopelessness and powerlessness. In turn, these negative thoughts, feelings, and attitudes can lead to externalizing (aggressive, "acting out") or internalizing (withdrawal, self-punishing, delusional) behaviors.

Clearly, promoting mental health has payoffs both academically and for reducing problems at schools. Therefore, it seems evident that an enhanced commitment to mental health promotion must be a key facet of the renewed emphasis on the whole child by education leaders.

Concluding Comments

Responding to behavior problems and promoting social and emotional development and learning can and should be done in the context of a comprehensive system designed to address barriers to learning and (re)engage students in classroom learning. In this respect, the developmental trend in thinking about how to respond to misbehavior must be toward practices that embrace an expanded view of engagement and human motivation and that includes a focus on social and emotional learning.

Relatedly, motivational research and theory are guiding the development of interventions designed to enhance student's motivation and counter disengagement. And, there is growing appreciation of the power of intrinsic motivation.

Now, it is time for school improvement decision makers and planners to fully address these matters.

Young Women in Jail Describe Their Educational Lives

SIGNE NELSON AND LYNN OLCOTT

During 2007 and 2008, 21 female inmates in the women's pod at the Onondaga County (New York) Justice Center participated in an ongoing survey designed to gather information about the educational experiences and goals of young people in jail. These young women were all students in the Incarcerated Education Program, a joint program of the Onondaga County Justice Center and the Syracuse City School District in Syracuse.

The young women ranged from 16 to 20 years of age, meeting the New York State definition of a minor. The group was racially mixed with 57 percent indicating themselves to be African American; 24 percent indicating Hispanic, Native American, or mixed races; and 19 percent indicating white.

Two-thirds of all participants stated they had problems with school attendance in the past, and 62 percent said they had already stopped going to school at the time of the survey. The young women cited a variety of causal factors for leaving school, but many also indicated their future plans to continue their education. Of the 21 participants, 70 percent said they planned to enter or continue with some kind of education or training when their legal circumstances allow.

Introduction

The factors causing young people to leave school are complex. Alarmingly, early school-leaving behavior and the lack of a secondary school credential may often coincide with criminal behavior (Drapela 2005).

Educators in the Incarcerated Education Program have extensive experience with the early school-leaving behavior of youth who become involved with the criminal justice system. In 2007, these educators developed a survey to look deeper into the educational lives of the student-inmates enrolled in GED classes at the justice center. Periodically throughout 2007 and 2008 student-inmates in the Syracuse City School District program at the Onondaga County Justice Center were offered the opportunity to participate in the study.

The Onondaga County Justice Center is a modern, nine-story building in downtown Syracuse. The sheriff's department operates this direct-supervision, nonsentenced facility. During a 10-month period in 2006–2007, 644 minors were processed

through the facility's booking department; 71 of the minors were young women with neither a high school diploma nor a GED diploma. (Data from STAC, System to Track for the Account of Children, used in New York State.)

The Literature

Several studies have identified a connection between leaving high school without a diploma and subsequent deviant behavior. An analysis of nearly 40 years of research on early school-leaving behavior confirmed that the consequences of dropping out of high school, including illegal behavior, are rooted in individual attitudes, behaviors, and life events. Generally, these attitudes and events are identifiable in a young person's life, *before* the young person ceases attending school (Drapela 2005).

Most people in jails and prisons are men. According to the Correctional Association of New York (2007), women compose only about 4.5 percent of the prison population in the state. Women compose about 10 percent of the population incarcerated at the Onondaga County Justice Center. In recent years, several research questions have been explored pertaining to incarcerated women and their educational experiences and attitudes.

In a correctional center in Nebraska, a study was conducted with 31 female participants ages 15 to 18. A modified Likert scale was used to explore the participants' perceptions of the role of teachers in addressing violence in relation to learning and other educational issues. The study focused on the opinions of incarcerated young women concerning communication, learning, and violence. Students were asked to comment on their personal learning styles as well. Several young women indicated they sometimes did not ask questions in school classrooms because they feared making the teacher angry. They sometimes gave up trying to follow their teachers' presentations because the pace was too fast (Sanger et al. 2007).

In a detention center in Colorado, five women aged 20 to 46 were interviewed and asked about their educational histories. The open-ended interviews yielded several themes. Some women in the study recalled positive academic experiences in their early school years prior to a single, life-changing event that interfered with their ability to continue their middle or high school studies (Mageehon 2003).

Additional information about the learning styles of incarcerated females is available from a study of 63 women inmates in Idaho. Most participants preferred instructional methods that included hands-on methods and opportunities for the practical application of the skills being learned. As public school students, the women had often been expected to learn information through reading and demonstrate mastery through writing. Most of the women in the study were kinesthetic learners. The researchers noted that emphasis on learning through reading and writing is not the most effective strategy for teaching kinesthetic learners (Wilson et al 1997). [Editor's note: Kinesthetic learners learn best by moving their bodies, activating their large or small muscles as they learn. These are the hands-on learners or the "doers" who actually concentrate better and learn more easily when movement is involved.]

Methods

The survey instrument used at the justice center consists of 18 questions, both open ended and close ended in format. Students are encouraged to write detailed responses. The survey covers a variety of topics including family literacy experiences and individual learning modes. In addition, the survey elicits the participants' general views on the topic of young people leaving school before completion of the twelfth grade.

The results presented in this article compose a subset of data from an ongoing study. Inmate participation is voluntary and participants are informed their individual responses remain anonymous even though the aggregated survey results will be shared with educators, law enforcement professionals, and the general public.

The Participants

As noted earlier, the 21 young women providing responses ranged in age from 16 to 20 years old and were racially mixed. Some of the women were mothers having a total of six children who ranged in age between one month and six years old.

Participants were asked if they had already stopped going to school before being incarcerated and if so, at what grade level. Sixty-two percent said they had already left school. Thirty-eight percent considered themselves still enrolled. Forty-three percent of participants who said they had already left school reported that they had stopped going at some point before the end of ninth grade. The average number of incarcerations per participant was four, including detention in juvenile facilities.

Survey Results

Asked if school attendance had been a problem in the past, two-thirds of participants indicated that it had. Some of the responses were quite telling. A 19-year-old woman who had left school in the ninth grade wrote that it was hard to go to school every day because she did *"not have a nice wardrobe"* and that *"better clothes and shoes and school supplies"* would have helped her to continue in school. Her first arrest had been at 14 years old.

Over the years, teachers in the Incarcerated Education Program have noted a pattern of youth being arrested and rearrested and of these young people giving different living addresses each time they were arrested. Anecdotal data suggests that many of these young people are essentially homeless. Participants were asked with whom they were living when they left school or became incarcerated. Ten were living with their mothers. Four were living with a grandmother or other female relative. One student wrote that she didn't really remember. One student had been living on her own. Two were living in group homes. Two students declined to answer. Only one of the young women was living with both parents.

Asked why they had stopped going to school, most of the young women cited multiple reasons. Only 9.5 percent cited academic problems as the causal factor, though students in the Incarcerated Education Program do have academic difficulties. An additional 9.5 percent said they had been expelled from school. Incarceration was cited as the cause of departure from school by 14 percent of students. A combination of drugs, alcohol, the wrong friends, and the influence of the streets collectively caused 43 percent of the study group to stop going to school. Twenty-four percent cited family issues and related problems as their reason for leaving school.

The survey form allowed space for participants to share comments and advice they might have for other young people at risk of dropping out of school. These comments included:

- A 20-year-old who had left school at age 14, the same year her child was born, said simply that to drop out was, *" . . . not worth it. . . ."*
- An 18-year-old advised, *" . . . don't do drugs . . .listen to people who care. . . ."* She wrote that the school environment, family, and social issues were the reasons she had left school in the tenth grade.
- A 17-year-old offered, *" . . . keep your head up. . . ."* She had been living in a group home at the time of her arrest.
- Another 17-year-old, with many juvenile incarcerations, said, *"without your education you can't do nothing."* She noted that a deterrent to school for her had been that she *"didn't have inof credits."*
- A 19-year-old mother of two attributed her attendance problems and eventual departure from school at 14 years old to *"gettin' high."* She counseled, *" . . . don't drop out . . . it's not a good thing."*

Learning Experiences

Participants were asked if someone read to them when they were children and if so, who that person was. Seventy-one percent of respondents said, "Yes." Usually they said mothers or other female relatives had read to them. One student recalled being read to, but only by her teacher. The students shared a spectrum of popular titles with Dr. Seuss books being recalled the most often. Participants were also asked to refer back to childhood and list activities their families did together. The young women described an array of activities, including sports, camping, and family trips.

As part of the survey, each young woman was asked to look back and identify what she felt had been her best school experience. Twenty-nine percent identified a specific subject, and 19 percent identified an alternative educational setting, including a juvenile detention facility. One student said that social interaction had been the best thing about school. A 20-year-old recalled her favorite part of school had been gym class because it was *"a relief."*

Participants also answered questions about their involvement in school-sponsored programs and activities. Two-thirds of students answered they had participated in one or more school-sponsored activities. Music and/or sports represented 50 percent of the activities the girls had joined while in school. One student mentioned a pregnancy club; another noted a Job Corps program.

The young women were asked to identify their own individual learning styles and identify the ways that teachers could best present material to them. Most students confirmed that *"being shown/hands on"* works best for them. Reading and listening were equally ranked in second place as effective learning channels. No one chose reading as a primary method of learning information.

Most students confirmed that "being shown/hands on" works best for them.

Students were asked to recall a favorite teacher and identify what he/she had done that was helpful. A third of the participants left this section blank. An 18-year-old student who left school in 10th grade wrote that she disliked all teachers. She cited the security guard in her school as being the most helpful. This was her second incarceration. Others described as helpful those teachers who took extra time to explain things and teachers who helped them to keep a positive attitude.

Teachers who were described as not helpful were those who put students on the spot in front of the class, or went too fast, or ignored student pleas of illness. A 17-year-old, with five incarcerations, wrote that she did not like most of her teachers because "they would just go through without stopping." The same student reflected that she had "loved art and math" but that "smoken pot" had made it hard to pay attention and had ultimately caused her to drop out of school.

The survey also asked respondents to look ahead and share information on what they desired to learn in the future. Four students left this item blank, but others expressed a variety of diverse goals. Twenty-four percent of respondents identified a specific skill or job title, including doctor and forensic scientist. A student aged 17 wrote that she would like to "learn to pay attention." Another, aged 18, wrote poignantly that she would like to understand her own reading problems. She had dropped out of school, she said, because she could not complete enough courses.

The young women took the opportunity offered in the survey to share comments and bits of advice with teachers and other adults who were trying to aid at-risk youth. Here are some of their comments:

- The youngest participant, aged 16, said simply: "... *you're not taking advice from an inmate ... stop acting so tough.*" She recalled 12 moves in her life and three school changes.
- A 19-year-old who had left school in ninth grade recommended: "... *show them you care, try to keep them away from the wrong crowd of friends and don't do any drugs around them ... just ignore them when they argue.*"
- A 19-year-old who left school in seventh grade advised: "... *don't push them too hard it will make it worse and they will resent you in the end.*" She added: "... *not everyone don't want to be a lawyer or really rich ... let us grow up to be us.*"
- A 17-year-old who left school in ninth grade suggested "... *sit them down and tell them what's right or wrong ... maybe if you have to reward them. ...*"
- A 17-year-old, incarcerated for the fourth time, cited numerous household moves and six changes to different schools. She wrote that she would like teachers to know this about her: "... *let them no if their willing 2 help me I will learn the Best way I can.*"

Conclusion

The survey results reported here represent one component of a comprehensive project that is being conducted through the Incarcerated Education Program. The researchers acknowledge that these survey results comprise only a snapshot of information shared by a small number of incarcerated females. The researchers acknowledge the potential disadvantages of drawing conclusions from self-reported data.

Still, our societal understanding of the causes and consequences of early school leaving behavior *must* include the stories and voices of young people who have left school early and who have become incarcerated. Incarcerated young people have much to tell us about their journeys to jail. These preliminary findings supplement a small but growing knowledgebase about young incarcerated women and their educational lives. We seek to share this information with parents, educators, and law enforcement professionals. Continued study will help in the development of better societal interventions that will encourage all young women to stay in high school and become better equipped to realize their full potential.

Acknowledgments

The authors would like to thank teachers in the Incarcerated Education Program for their insights and assistance with the project. Thanks also to teacher Joseph Powlina for assistance with data and to Deputy Joseph Caruso for photographic expertise. The authors are indebted to Sheriff Kevin Walsh, and Syracuse City School District Superintendent Daniel Lowengard, Chief Richard Carbery and Capt. Estéban Gonzalez for administrative support as this survey project was developed and as it goes forward.

References

Correctional Association of New York, 135 East 15th Street, N.Y. New York, *www.correctionalassociation.org. Women in Prison Fact Sheet 2007.*

Drapela, L. (2005). Does dropping out of high school cause deviant behavior? An analysis of the national education longitudinal study. *Deviant Behavior,* 26, 47–62.

Mageehon, A. (2003) Incarcerated women's educational experiences. *Journal of Correctional Education,* 54(4), 191–199.

Nelson, S., Olcott, L. (2006) Jail time is learning time. *Corrections Today,* February, p. 26–37.

Olcott, L. (2004) The best teaching job in the world. *American Jails,* (18) p. 44–51.

Sanger, D., Spilker, A., Williams, N., Velan, D. (2007). Opinions of female juvenile delinquents on communication, learning and violence. *Journal of Correctional Education,* 58(1) page 68–89.

Sinclair, M., Christenson, S., Thurlow, M. (2005). Promoting school completion of urban secondary youth with emotional or behavioral disabilities, *Exceptional Children,* 71(4) 465–467.

Wilson, R., Crocker R., Bobell, J. (1997). Learning style, brain modality and teaching preferences of incarcerated women at the Pocatello Women's Correctional Center, *Journal of Correctional Education,* 48(1) 4–6.

SIGNE NELSON is the coordinator of the Incarcerated Education Program in Syracuse, New York. LYNN OLCOTT, former GED teacher at the Onondaga County Justice Center, now teaches at the Cayuga Correctional Facility in Moravia, New York, and at SUNY–Cortland. For more information, contact Signe Nelson, Coordinator, Onondaga County Justice Center, 555 South State Street, Syracuse, NY 13202, or call 315–435–1726, extension 3.

Classroom Problems That Don't Go Away

Laverne Warner and Sharon Lynch

Wade runs "combat-style" beneath the windows of his school as he makes his getaway from his 1st-grade classroom. It is still early in the school year, but this is the third time Wade has tried to escape. Previously, his teacher has managed to catch him before he left the building. Today, however, his escape is easier, because Mrs. Archie is participating with the children in a game of "Squirrel and Trees" and Wade is behind her when he leaves the playground area. She sees him round the corner of the school, and speedily gives chase. When she reaches the front parking lot of their building, however, she cannot find him. Wade is gone!

Experienced and inexperienced teachers alike, in all grade levels, express concern about difficult classroom problems—those problems that don't ever seem to go away, no matter what management techniques are used. Wade's story and similar ones are echoed time and again in classrooms around the world as adults struggle to find a balance between correcting children's behavior and instructing them about self-management strategies.

Educators emphasize an understanding of appropriate guidance strategies, and teachers learn about acceptable center and school district policies. An abundance of books, videotapes, and other teacher resources are available to classroom practitioners to enhance their understanding of appropriate guidance strategies. Professional organizations such as the Association for Childhood Education International define standards of good practice. Textbooks for childhood educators define well-managed classrooms and appropriate management techniques (e.g., Marion, 2003; Morrison, 2001; Reynolds, 2003; Seefeldt & Barbour, 1998; Wolfgang, 2001).

Despite this preparation, educators daily face problems with guiding or disciplining children in their classrooms. Understanding the developmental needs of children and meeting their physical needs are two ingredients to happy classroom management. It is also important to look at the larger problems involved when children's misbehaviors are chronic to the point that youngsters are labeled as "difficult." Are these children receiving enough attention from the teacher? Are they developing social skills that will help them through interactions and negotiations with other children in the classroom?

Mrs. Archie's guidance philosophy is founded on principles that she believes are effective for young children. Taking time at the end of the day to reflect on Wade's disappearance, Mrs. Archie concluded that she had done what she could, as always, to develop a healthy classroom climate.

She strives to build a classroom community of learners and act with understanding in response to antisocial behavior in the classroom, and she knows that the vast majority of children will respond positively. Mrs. Archie's classroom layout promotes orderly activity throughout the day and is well-stocked with enough materials and supplies to keep children interested and actively engaged in their learning activities. Although the activities she provides are challenging, many simple experiences also are available to prevent children from being overwhelmed by classroom choices.

Furthermore, Mrs. Archie's attitude is positive about children, like Wade, who come from families that use punitive discipline techniques at home. Her discussions with Wade's mother prior to his escape had been instructive, and she thought that progress was being made with the family. Indeed, when Wade arrived at home the day he ran off, his mother returned him to school immediately.

So what is the teacher to do about children, like Wade, with chronic and intense behavioral difficulties? If serious behavior problems are not addressed before age 8, the child is likely to have long-lasting conduct problems throughout school, often leading to suspension, or dropping out (Katz & McClellan, 1997; Walker et al., 1996). Since the window of opportunity to intervene with behavior problems is narrow, childhood educators must understand the nature of the behavior problem and design an educative plan to teach the child alternative approaches.

The ABC's of the Problem

The first step in analyzing the behavior problem is to determine the "pay-off" for the child. Challenging behaviors usually fall into one of the following categories: 1) behavior that gets the child attention, either positive or negative; 2) behavior that removes the child from something unpleasant, like work or a task; 3) behavior that results in the child getting something she or he wants, like candy or a toy; and 4) behavior that provides some type of sensory stimulation, such as spinning around until the child feels dizzy and euphoric.

To understand the pay-off for the child, it is important to examine the ABC's of the behavior: the antecedents, behaviors, and consequences associated with the problem. The *antecedent* requires a record, which describes what was happening just prior to the incident. The actual *behavior* then can be described in observable, measurable terms: instead of saying that the misbehaving child had a tantrum, detail that he threw himself to the floor, screamed, and pounded his fists on the floor for four minutes. Finally, we examine the pay-off (*consequences*) for the behavior.

Did the behavior result in close physical contact as the child was carried into the adjoining room and the caregiver attempted to soothe him? Did the behavior result in his being given juice so that he could calm down? Did the behavior result in scolding by the teacher, providing the kind of intense individual attention that some youngsters crave because it is the only demonstration of love and caring they have experienced? When teachers and caregivers examine the ABC's of the behavior, they are better able to understand the child's motivation, establish preventive strategies, and teach alternative social skills the child can use to meet his or her needs.

Prevention Strategies

Mrs. Archie knows that she needs to learn specific strategies that will help her work with "difficult" behaviors, like those of Wade, because these problems certainly don't seem to go away on their own. The following intervention methods are designed to preempt anti-social behaviors and often are referred to as prevention strategies. It is always better to prevent the behavior as much as possible.

Accentuate the Positive

For the child who demonstrates inappropriate behavior to gain attention, the teacher should find every opportunity to give the child positive attention when he or she is behaving appropriately. Often, these opportunities to "catch the child being good" occur relatively early in the day. When children receive plenty of positive attention early in the day and the teacher continues to find opportunities for praise and attention as the day goes on, the child is not as likely to misbehave for attention as his need is already being met (Hanley, Piazza, & Fisher, 1997). This intervention is based on the principle of deprivation states. If the child is deprived of attention and is "hungry" for adult interaction, he will do anything to gain the attention of others, even negative attention.

Player's Choice

When educators see a negative pattern of behavior, they can anticipate that the child is likely to refuse adult requests. This is often referred to as "oppositional behavior." A teacher may remark, "It doesn't matter what I ask her to do, she is going to refuse to do it." One successful strategy for dealing with this type of oppositional behavior is to provide the child

with choices (Knowlton, 1995). This approach not only gives the child power and control, but also affords the child valuable opportunities for decision making. Example of choices include, "Do you want to carry out the trash basket or erase the chalkboard?," "Do you want to sit in the red chair or the blue chair?," or "Do you want to pick up the yellow blocks or the green blocks?"

The teacher must be cautious about the number of choices provided, however. Many children have difficulty making up their minds if too many choices are presented—often, two choices are plenty. Also, adults need to monitor their own attitude as they present choices. If choices are presented using a drill sergeant tone of voice, the oppositional child is going to resist the suggestions.

On a Roll

When adults anticipate that a child is going to refuse a request, teachers can embed this request within a series of other simple requests. This intervention is based on the research-based principles of high-probability request sequences (Ardoin, Martens, & Wolfe, 1999). The first step in this procedure is to observe the child to determine which requests she consistently performs. Before asking the child to perform the non-preferred request, ask her to do several other things that she does consistently. For example, 8-year-old Morgan consistently resists cleaning up the dollhouse area. While she is playing with the dollhouse, her teacher could ask her to "Give the dolls a kiss," "Show me the doll's furniture," and "Put the dolls in their bedrooms." After she has complied with these three requests, she is much more likely to comply with the request to "Put the dolls away now" or "Give them to me."

Grandma's Rule

This strategy often is referred to as the Premack Principle (Premack, 1959). When asking a child to perform an action, specifying what he or she will receive after completing it more often ensures its completion. Examples here include: "When you have finished your math problems, then we will go outside," "When you have eaten your peas, you can have some pudding," and "After you have rested awhile, we will go to the library."

A Spoonful of Sugar Helps the Medicine Go Down

This principle involves pairing preferred and non-preferred activities. One particular task that is difficult for preschoolers, and many adults, is waiting. Most of us do not wait well. When asking a child to complete a non-preferred activity such as waiting in line, pairing a preferred activity with the waiting will make it more tolerable.

Businesses and amusement parks use the principle of pairing when they provide music or exhibits for customers as they wait in line. Similarly, with young children, teachers can provide enjoyable activities as children wait. Suggested activities that can be used during waiting periods include singing, looking at books, reading a story, or holding something special such as a banner, sign, or toy.

Another difficult activity for many young children is remaining seated. If the child is given a small object to hold during the time she must remain seated, she may be willing to continue sitting for a longer period. The principle of pairing preferred and non-preferred activities also gives the child increasing responsibility for her own behavior, instead of relying on teacher discipline.

Just One More

This particular intervention is most effective when a child behaves inappropriately in order to escape a low-preference task. The purpose of the intervention is to improve work habits and increase time on task. The first step is to identify how long a particular child will work at a specific task before exhibiting inappropriate behavior. Once the teacher has determined how long a child will work on a task, the teacher can give the child a delay cue to head off misbehavior. Examples of delay cues are "Just one more and then you're finished," "Just two minutes and then you're finished," or "Do this and then you're finished."

In this intervention, a teacher sets aside preconceived ideas about how long children *should* work on a task and instead focuses on improving the child's ability to complete tasks in reference to his current abilities. As the children's challenging behaviors decrease, the adult gradually can increase the time on task, and the amount of work completed, before giving them the delay cue and releasing them from the task.

The More We Get Together

Another way to improve task completion is by making the job a collaborative effort. If a child finds it difficult to complete non-preferred activities, then the instructor can complete part of the task with the student. For example, when organizing the bookshelf, the adult completes a portion of the task, such as picking up the big books as the student picks up the little books. She prefaces that activity by stating, "I'll pick up the big books, and you pick up the little books." As the child becomes more willing to complete her part of the task, the caregiver gradually increases the work expectations for the child while decreasing the amount of assistance.

Communication Development

In addition to preventing inappropriate behavior, another tactic is replacing the problem behavior by teaching the child alternative behaviors. The key to this process is "functional equivalence." Teachers must determine the *function* or pay-off for the inappropriate behavior and then teach an alternative *equivalent* action that will service the same purpose as the negative behavior. This often is referred to as the "fair pair" rule (White & Haring, 1976). Rather than punishing the behavior, teaching children a better way to behave assists in meeting their needs.

Bids for Attention

The first step in addressing attention-seeking negative behaviors is to reduce their occurrence by providing plenty of attention for the child's appropriate behaviors. The next step is to teach the child appropriate ways to gain attention from others. Most children learn appropriate social skills incidentally from their family and teachers; some children, however, have learned negative ways to gain social attention. Some of the social skills that may need to be taught include calling others by name, tapping friends on the shoulder for attention, knowing how to join others in play, and raising one's hand to gain the teacher's attention. Numerous other social skills may require direct instruction. Any time a behavior is considered inappropriate, adults need to teach the child a better way to have his needs met.

When teaching social skills to chldren, break the skill into a maximum of three steps. Then model the steps and have the child demonstrate the skill. Provide positive and negative examples of the step and have the children label the demonstration as correct or incorrect. Use class discussion time to role-play and talk about when this particular social skill is appropriate. Throughout the day, set up situations that allow practice of the social skill and encourage the child to use the new skill. Finally, promote carry-over of the skill by communicating with the family about the social skills instruction in order for the child to practice the social skills outside of the classroom—on the playground, in the lunch room, and at home.

Ask for Something Else

If we know that the child has disruptive behaviors when presented with tasks that are disliked, then the teacher can present the child with an alternative task or materials, something she likes, *before* the problem behavior occurs. Then the child can be taught to ask for the alternative activity or object. When the child requests the alternative, provide it and preempt the negative behavior. In this way, children can learn to communicate their needs and prevent the challenging behavior from occurring.

Ask for Help

Many children behave disruptively because they are frustrated with a task. Teachers usually can determine when the child is becoming frustrated by observing and reading non-verbal communication signals. Possible signs of frustration might be sighing, fidgeting, reddening of the face, or negative facial expressions. Noticing these signs helps the teacher know that it is time to intervene. Rather than offering help when the child needs it, the teacher says, "It looks like you need some help. When you need help, you need to tell me. Now you say, 'I need help.'" After the child has responded by saying, "I need help," the teacher provides assistance. This strategy is much more effective if the group already has role-played "asking for help."

Ask for a Break

This strategy is similar to the two listed above; in this case, educators teach the child to ask for a break during a difficult and frustrating task. Prior to presenting the task, the teacher can explain that she knows that the activity can be difficult, but that the child can have a break after spending some time working hard at it. Then, the child can be taught to request a break while other students are engaged in various tasks.

Although teachers would like to think that instruction and activities are always fun for children and that learning should be child-directed, certain important activities must be mastered if children are to become successful in school. Especially as children progress into the primary grades, teachers expect them to work independently on pencil-and-paper tasks. Teaching youngsters communication skills that will help them handle frustration and low-preference activities will improve their outcomes as learners in school and in life.

Reviewing Options

Mrs. Archie, in reviewing her options for working with Wade, is gaining confidence in her ability to work more carefully with the family and with Wade to ensure his successful re-entry to her classroom. Her resolve is to continue developing a "community of learners" (Bredekamp & Copple, 1997) by helping Wade become a functioning member of her group. She intends to teach him how to enter a play setting, negotiate for what he wants in the classroom, and learn how to make compromises, while nurturing him as she would any child. These are goals that she believes will help turn around Wade's negative behavior.

Mrs. Archie also knows that her administrator is a caring woman, and, if necessary, Wade could be placed in another classroom so that he could have a "fresh start" with his entry into school. Her hope is that this will be a last-resort strategy, because she understands how much Wade needs a caring adult who understands him and his needs. Her phone call to Wade's mother at the end of the day will be friendly and supportive, with many recommendations for how the school can assist the family.

A Long-Term Plan

Most children with chronic difficult behaviors did not learn them overnight. Many of these children experience serious ongoing problems in their families. As teachers, we cannot change home dynamics or family problems. Sometimes a parent conference or parent education groups can be helpful, as the family learns to support a difficult child at home. With others, we do well to teach the child socially appropriate behavior in the classroom. As a child learns socially appropriate behavior in school, she learns that the behavior is useful in other settings. Often, the school is the only place where the child has the opportunity to learn prosocial behaviors. Children's negative behaviors may have, in a sense, "worked" for them in numerous situations for a substantial period of time. When we work to teach the child a better way to get his or her needs met, we must recognize that this process takes time and effort. When we as educators invest this time and effort with children during childhood, we are providing them with the tools that can make the difference in their school careers and in their lives.

References

Ardoin, S. P., Martens, B. K., & Wolfe, L. A. (1999). Using high-probability instruction sequences with fading to increase student compliance during transitions. *Journal of Applied Behavior Analysis, 32*(3), 339–351.

Bredekamp, S., & Copple, C. (Eds.). (1997). *Developmentally appropriate practice in early childhood programs* (Rev. ed.). Washington, DC: National Association for the Education of Young Children.

Hanley, G. P., Piazza, C. C., & Fisher, W. W. (1997). Noncontingent presentation of attention and alternative stimuli in the treatment of attention-maintained destructive behavior. *Journal of Applied Behavior Analysis, 30*(2), 229–237.

Katz, L., & McClellan, D. (1997). *Fostering children's social competence: The teacher's role.* Washington, DC: National Association for the Education of Young Children.

Knowlton, D. (1995). Managing children with oppositional defiant behavior. *Beyond Behavior, 6*(3), 5–10.

Marion, M. (2003). *Guidance of young children* (3rd ed.). Englewood Cliffs, NJ: Prentice Hall.

Morrison, G. (2001). *Early childhood education today* (8th ed.). Englewood Cliffs, NJ: Prentice Hall.

Premack, D. (1959). Toward empirical behavior laws: I. Positive reinforcement. *Psychological Review, 66,* 219–233.

Reynolds, E. (2003). *Guiding young children* (2nd ed.). Mountain View, CA: Mayfield.

Seefeldt, C., & Barbour, N. (1998). *Early childhood education: An introduction* (4th ed.). Columbus, OH: Merrill.

Walker, H. M., Horner, R. H., Sugai, G., Bullis, M., Sprague, J. R., Bricker, D., & Kaufman, M. J. (1996). Integrated approaches to preventing anti-social behavior among school-age children and youth. *Journal of Emotional and Behavioral Disorders, 4*(4), 194–209.

White, O. R., & Haring, N. G. (1976). *Exceptional teaching.* Upper Saddle River, NJ: Merrill/Prentice Hall.

Wolfgang, C. H. (2001). *Solving discipline and classroom management problems* (5th ed.). New York: John Wiley and Sons.

Laverne Warner is Professor, Early Childhood Education, and **Sharon Lynch** is Associate Professor of Special Education, Department of Language, Literacy, and Special Populations, Sam Houston State University, Huntsville, Texas.

UNIT 6

Communication Disorders

Unit Selections

Key Points to Consider

- Do students with limited English language proficiency in English speaking schools qualify for SPED under the category of Communication Disordered?

- How can assessment tools be selected and adapted for sensitivity to cross-cultural perspectives? What is the appropriate way to intervene when bilingual children have speech disorders?

- What can speech-language clinicians teach us about the assessment and remediation of communication and the improvement of reading skills?

Student Website

www.mhcls.com

Internet Reference

Issues in Emergent Literacy for Children with Language Impairments
   http://www.ciera.org/library/reports/inquiry-2/2-002/2-002.html

Speech and language impairments, although grouped together as a category of disability by the IDEIA (Individuals with Disabilities Education Improvement Act), are not synonymous. Language refers to multiple ways to communicate (for example by writing, signing, body movement, or voice), whereas speech refers to vocal articulation.

Many children have difficulty learning to read because of speech and/or language impairments. If they cannot receive language and/or express speech sounds correctly, the total lexicon makes less sense. Likewise, some children assessed as dyslexic (difficulty with the lexicon) are reading disabled primarily because of their disorders with speech and/or language. Telling these disorders apart can be challenging. Learning to communicate may also be difficult for children with hearing impairments, developmental disorders, some physical disorders (e.g., cerebral palsy), and some emotional disorders (e.g., elective mutism).

Speech is the vocal utterance of language. It is considered disordered in three underlying ways: voice, articulation, and fluency.

Voice involves coordinated efforts by the lungs, larynx, vocal cords, and nasal passages to produce recognizable sounds. Voice can be considered disordered if it is incorrectly phonated (breathy, strained, husky, hoarse) or if it is incorrectly resonated through the nose (hyper-nasality, hypo-nasality).

Articulation involves the use of the tongue, lips, teeth, and mouth to produce recognizable sounds. Articulation can be considered disordered if sounds are mispronounced, or if sounds are added, omitted, or substituted for other sounds, such as using the z sound for the s sound or w for l. Articulation disorders are more common in early childhood. Early intervention (see Unit 2) can be very effective in reducing distortions, additions, omissions, and substitutions.

Fluency involves appropriate pauses and hesitations to keep speech sounds recognizable. Fluency can be considered disordered if sounds are very rapid with extra sounds (cluttered) or if sounds are blocked or repeated, especially at the beginning of words. Stuttering is an example of a fluency disorder of speech. School-age boys not only stutter more than girls but require more speech-language therapy as part of special education. The chances of recovery from stuttering are greatest when intervention occurs before stuttering has been present for two or more years.

Language is the rule-based use of voice sounds, symbols, gestures, or signs to communicate. Language problems refer to the use of such devices in combinations and patterns that fail to communicate, fail to follow the arbitrary rules for that language, or lead to a delay in the use of communication devices relative to normal development in other areas (physical, cognitive, social).

The prevalence rates of speech and language disorders are high in primary school. The exact extent of the problem, however, has been questioned because assessment of communication takes a variety of forms. Shy children may be diagnosed with delayed language. Bilingual or multilingual children are often mislabeled as having a language disorder because they come from linguistically and culturally diverse backgrounds.

© Blend Images/Getty Images

Many bilingual children do not need the special services provided by speech-language clinicians but do benefit from instruction in English as a second language.

All children with language or speech disorders are entitled to assessment and remediation as early in life as the problem is realized. Because children's speech is not well developed between birth and age 3, most disorders are not assessed until preschool. Students with speech-language disorders are entitled to a free and appropriate education in the least restrictive environment possible and to transitional help into the world of work, if needed, after their education is completed.

Disordered language is usually more difficult to remedy than delayed language. Disordered language may be due to a receptive problem (difficulty understanding voice sounds), an expressive problem (difficulty producing the voice sounds that follow the arbitrary rules for that language), or both. Language disorders include aphasia (no language) and dysphasia (difficulty producing language). Many language disorders are the result of a difficulty in understanding the syntactical rules and structural principles of the language (form), or they are the result of a difficulty in perceiving the semantic meanings of the words of the language (content). Many language disorders are also due to a difficulty in using the language pragmatically, in a practical context (function).

Most speech and language impairments are remediated between pre-school and middle school. An exception to this is speech problems that persist due to physical impairments such as damage or dysfunction of lungs, larynx, vocal cords, or nasal passages. Another exception is language problems that persist due to concurrent disabilities such as deafness, autism, compromised mentation, traumatic brain injuries, or some emotional and behavioral disorders.

Speech-language clinicians usually provide special services to children with speech and language impairments in pull-out sessions in resource rooms. Computer technology is also frequently used to assist these children in both their regular education classes and in pull-out therapy sessions.

The first article addresses the confusion that exists over whether a child has a linguistic difference in speech/language or whether the child is, in fact, disabled in the area of communication. Students with limited English proficiency should not be labeled communication disordered unless they are significantly disabled in their mother tongue as well. However, many bilingual children do have phonological disorders in their mother tongue. Brian Goldstein and Leah Fabiano discuss their assessments and methods of remediation.

The second article discusses a two-stage program for assessment and remediation of early speech or language impairments. Working with young children in the areas of phonetic awareness, discrimination of faulty production of sounds, and listening to the sounds of language and correct articulation of sounds will not only correct communication disorders but improve reading skills.

Assessment and Intervention for Bilingual Children with Phonological Disorders

Monitoring phonological change across the two languages of bilingual children is important because it is possible that intervention provided in one language will generalize to the other language given the interdependence between the two languages.

BRIAN A. GOLDSTEIN AND LEAH FABIANO

An estimated 5.2 million bilingual children are enrolled in schools in the United States, a 61% increase since 1994 (National Center for English Language Acquisition and Language Instruction Education Programs, 2005). The increasing number of bilingual children has resulted in significant challenges to the provision of assessment and intervention services to bilingual children with phonological disorders (a term used here to apply to both segment- and pattern-based errors).

Providing assessment and intervention to children with such disorders is complicated given the lack of understanding of theories of bilingual phonological representation and the lack of knowledge of current best practices related to the assessment of and intervention for these children. The discussion below highlights theories of bilingual phonological representation and links those theories to models of assessment and intervention.

Theories of Bilingual Phonological Representation

Historically, researchers have posited two models of language representation for bilingual children. According to the Unitary System Model (e.g., Bhatia & Ritchie, 1999), bilingual children begin with a single phonological system that separates into two autonomous systems over time. In contrast, the Dual Systems Model maintains that bilingual children develop separate phonological systems for each language from birth that do not interact (e.g., Keshavarz & Ingram, 2002).

A third model, a variation of the Dual Systems Model known as the Interactional Dual Systems Model of phonological representation (Paradis, 2001), suggests that bilingual children possess two separate phonological systems with mutual influence. Various case and group studies have found support for the Interactional Dual Systems Model in that bilinguals use resources from both of their languages for efficiency in production while maintaining separation for language-specific elements (e.g., Brulard & Carr, 2003; Fabiano, 2006; Goldstein, Fabiano, & Iglesias, 2003; Johnson & Lancaster, 1998; Paradis, 2001).

Knowledge of phonological representation in bilinguals is helpful because it allows speech-language pathologists to distinguish a phonological *difference* from a *disorder*. Evidence-based assessment of phonological disorders in bilingual children should consider recent theories of bilingual phonological representation. By assessing the languages and determining how they interact, clinicians can make a valid diagnosis, determine the child's strengths and weaknesses, and plan for intervention.

Assessment of Bilingual Children

The following protocol for bilingual phonological assessment was developed based on the theoretical rationale that bilingual children maintain separation for some phonological elements while demonstrating interaction on others.

Step 1: Perform a Detailed Case History

In addition to what is normally obtained in a parent interview for a monolingual child, ask parents what a typical day is like for their child. In every situation mentioned, ask what language is typically spoken and what language the child uses during that task, or if both languages are heard/used. In addition, obtain the following information for bilingual children each time an assessment occurs: language history (when the child was exposed to and began to use each language); percent input in each language (hours per week the child *hears* each language); and percent output in each language (hours per week the child *uses* each language). It is important to remember that percent input and output are not static measures in that language environments shift over time (Pease-Alvarez, 2002).

Step 2: Obtain Speech Samples

Single-word and connected speech (conversation or narrative) samples should be obtained in both of the bilingual child's languages. It is important to collect speech samples in both languages because phonological acquisition will not be parallel across the bilingual child's two languages (Goldstein, Fabiano, & Washington, 2005). Developmental trajectories and structure of the two languages may be different for each language. As a result, the order of acquisition and phonological patterns will differ. Thus, phonological development in bilinguals is similar, but not identical, to monolinguals (e.g., Goldstein et al., 2005).

Step 3: Perform an Independent Analysis

Determine the phonetic inventory of the child in both languages using single-word and connected speech samples. Organize the inventory by place of articulation (e.g., bilabial, alveolar, etc.) and manner of articulation (e.g., stops, nasals, etc.). Obtaining a phonetic inventory in each language will aid in clinical decision-making and help to determine whether to take a phonetic or phonological approach to intervention.

Step 4: Perform a Relational Analysis

Relational analyses should be performed to examine overall consonant and vowel accuracy in each language, and accuracy of shared elements (i.e., common to both languages, such as /p/ between Spanish and English) and unshared elements (i.e., unique to each language, such as the Spanish trill). Analysis of shared and unshared elements should be examined because studies examining bilingual phonological representation have found, for example, significantly higher accuracy on shared elements compared with unshared elements, demonstrating interaction between the two languages (Fabiano, 2006; Fabiano & Goldstein 2004a, 2004b).

A phonological pattern analysis also should be included. The phonological pattern analysis should take into consideration that the type and frequency of phonological patterns vary across languages (Goldstein & Washington, 2001). For example, English allows three-member onset clusters and Spanish allows only two-member onset clusters. Because of this difference, cluster reduction is a phonological pattern that, at a given chronological age, would be developmental in English but "delayed" in Spanish.

Step 5: Perform an Error Analysis

In a substitution error analysis, one should examine targets (including phonemes that the child does not attempt to produce) and substitutes (phones the child is using in place of those target phonemes). In this analysis, one should account for cross-linguistic effects (using a phonological element specific to one language in the production of the other; for example, the Spanish trill /r/ found in an English production) and dialect features (Goldstein & Iglesias, 2001). Neither cross-linguistic effects nor dialect features should be scored as errors.

Intervention for Bilingual Children

Providing intervention to bilingual children with phonological disorders is challenging because there are relatively few research studies in this area. However, speech-language pathologists can use evidence that is known about phonological development in bilingual children, universal characteristics of phonological development, and the translation of theory into practice to guide decision-making about appropriate intervention services to bilingual children with phonological disorders. Consistent with the tenets of evidence-based practice, the process should begin with the clinical question (e.g., Justice & Fey, 2004).

Knowledge of phonological representation in bilinguals is helpful because it allows speech-language pathologists to distinguish a phonological *difference* from a *disorder*.

In treating bilingual children with phonological disorders, SLPs typically ask the question, "In which language do I treat?" That question, however, is not the appropriate one, because it mistakenly assumes that phonological development in bilingual children proceeds similarly in the child's two languages. Because the structure of each language is different (e.g., different phonemes, syllable types, word shapes, etc.) and development is not the same in each language (e.g., Goldstein, 2004), intervention will need to be tailored to the construct and development of each constituent language. A more precise question is, "When do I treat in each of the two languages?" (Goldstein, 2006).

To account for the nature of bilingual language development, Kohnert and Derr (2004) and Kohnert, Yim, Nett, Fong Kan, & Duran (2005) proposed two main approaches to providing intervention to bilingual children. It should be noted that these approaches are models based on underlying research on language (including phonological) development in bilingual children, although they have yet to be tested empirically. First, the Bilingual Approach proposes that SLPs should increase language skills common to both languages. In terms of phonology, this approach would mean that clinicians would begin intervention with constructs common to both languages (e.g., CV syllables, the phoneme /s/, initial consonant clusters). Thus, the initial treatment determination is the goal and not the language of intervention.

The Bilingual Approach would support beginning with goals in which one would treat constructs common to both languages or errors or error patterns exhibited with relatively equal frequency in both languages (Yavas & Goldstein, 1998). For example, this might mean that if unstressed syllable deletion were exhibited frequently in both languages, then that pattern might be an appropriate initial intervention target. Similarly, if /s/ was frequently in error in both languages, treatment might begin targeting that phoneme.

Second, the Cross-Linguistic Approach proposes that clinicians should focus on the linguistic skills unique to each language. This approach also will be necessary (likely in conjunction with the Bilingual Approach) because of the differences in the linguistic (in this case, phonological) structures of the two languages. For example, aspirated affricates exist in Hmong, but not in English, and can only be remediated in the one language. Additionally, SLPs might use a cross-linguistic framework based on types of errors and/or error rates (Yavas & Goldstein, 1998). For example, final consonant deletion is more common in the English of Spanish-English bilingual children than in their Spanish (Goldstein et al., 2005). Thus, intervention to decrease the use of that pattern will likely occur in English but not in Spanish. Finally, errors occurring in only one language would be targets for phonological intervention (e.g., backing in Language B but not in Language A).

Language of Intervention

Once the general approach is selected, then the initial language of intervention can be determined. The initial language of intervention will depend on a variety of factors such as language history (relative experience with each language), use in each language (how frequently the child utilizes each of the languages), proficiency in each language (how well the child understands and produces each language), environment (where and with whom the child uses each language), and family considerations (the family's goals) (Goldstein, 2006).

The child's phonological skills and errors/error patterns in each of the two languages will be a factor as well. That analysis might show that the child exhibits lower accuracy, more errors, and a higher frequency-of-occurrence on phonological patterns (e.g., cluster reduction) in Language A than in Language B. Thus, intervention would begin with Language A (all other factors being relatively equal).

In working with all children (bilingual and monolingual) with phonological disorders, SLPs need to determine how their goals will be implemented. The way in which goals are implemented may conform to a number of goal attack strategies: vertical, horizontal, and cyclical approaches (Fey, 1992). A "vertical approach" is one in which one goal is taught at a time until criterion is reached. A vertical-approach analogue for bilingual children might be implemented in one of two ways.

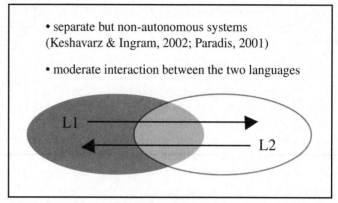

- separate but non-autonomous systems (Keshavarz & Ingram, 2002; Paradis, 2001)

- moderate interaction between the two languages

L1   L2

Interactional Dual Systems Model

Paradis J. *International Journal of Bilingualism*, Vol.5, no.1, March 2001, pp.19-38. Copyright © Kingston Press Ltd.

It might be used to focus on a goal that is specific to one language (e.g., trill in Spanish). Additionally, the SLP might consider how a target generalizes from one language to the other. So, remediation for /s/ occurs in English but is monitored but not targeted in Cantonese.

In a "horizontal approach," more than one goal is addressed in each session. A horizontal-approach analogue for bilingual children might be targeting one goal in Language A and one goal in Language B within the same session, although the targets would be divergent. For example, final consonants would be targeted in English, and aspirated affricates would be targeted in Hmong.

Finally, a "cyclical approach" is one in which a number of goals are addressed in a cyclical fashion, but only one goal is incorporated at a time within a session. A cyclical-approach analogue for bilingual children would be to rotate not only targets but also languages. For example, in Weeks 1–4, /s/ would be targeted in Language A and initial consonant clusters would be targeted in Language B. In Weeks 5–8, initial consonant clusters would be targeted in Language A with /s/ being the goal in Language B. (This example assumes, of course, that /s/ and clusters occur in both languages.)

Regardless of which goal attack strategy is used, patterns of phonological change should be monitored within and across the two languages (Grunwell, 1992). Monitoring these patterns serves to determine how the child's phonological system is changing during the course of intervention.

Monitoring phonological change across the two languages of bilingual children is important because it is possible that intervention provided in one language will generalize to the other language given the interdependence between the two languages (Paradis, 2001). There are a few studies that have examined this issue (Holm & Dodd, 1999; Holm, Dodd, & Ozanne, 1997; Holm, Dodd, Stow & Pert, 1998 in Holm & Dodd, 2001; Ray, 2002). Results from these studies indicate that intervention in English generally influences phonological skills in the other language. For example, Holm, Dodd, and Ozanne (1997) found that treatment of /s/ increased accuracy of that sound in both English and Cantonese. There were cases, however, in which phonological treatment in English did not affect skills in the other language. Holm, Dodd, Stow and Pert (1998 in Holm & Dodd, 2001) found that treatment of gliding did not generalize from English to Cantonese.

Unfortunately, for all these studies, intervention was provided in English only, and generalization to the other language was not always measured systematically. As a result, it is unclear if and/or how intervention in one language will generalize to the other language. It is likely, although untested, that intervention in one language will influence skills in the other language in a bi-directional manner (i.e., from Language A to Language B and vice versa). The interaction effect of providing intervention in more than one language is relatively unknown, but research on phonological development in bilingual children portends that such interaction is likely to occur.

A final consideration is the order in which goals are selected. For example, consider the targets for a monolingual English-speaking child with a severe phonological disorder. For that child, the SLP might begin intervention focusing on the inclusion of final consonants (i.e., decreasing final consonant deletion). That target would be appropriate given that, in English, final consonants are common, sounds occurring in word final position come from a large variety of sound classes, and sounds in word final position are critical for morphology.

Now consider the targets for a bilingual Spanish-English speaking child. In the child's English, focusing on final consonants still would be appropriate just as it was for the monolingual child. In Spanish, however, it would not be the most appropriate initial treatment target given that there are only five consonants in the language that occur at the end of a word (Hammond, 2001). In Spanish, a pattern such as unstressed syllable deletion would be a more fitting initial treatment target because the majority of words in Spanish are multisyllabic (Hammond, 2001). Thus, the order in which targets are remediated will be determined, in part, by the languages spoken by the child.

Assessing and treating bilingual children with phonological disorders is neither quick nor easy. However, understanding how the phonological system is represented in bilingual children leads to a comprehensive, least-biased assessment. Information from that broad and deep assessment then can be translated into appropriate intervention goals. Those goals likely will be different at different points in time for each of the child's two languages. Thus, it is not a matter of if, but when, both languages will be used during the intervention process. Doing so will allow bilingual children with phonological disorders to attain age-appropriate phonological skills in both languages.

BRIAN A. GOLDSTEIN is an associate professor in the Department of Communication Sciences, Temple University, Philadelphia. He is the author of *Cultural and Linguistic Diversity Resource Guide for Speech-Language Pathologists* and the editor of *Bilingual Language Development and Disorders in Spanish-English Speakers.* Contact him at briang@temple.edu. **LEAH FABIANO** is a postdoctoral fellow at the Center for Research in Language at the University of California, San Diego. Her research interests include bilingual phonological representation, development, and disorders in Spanish-English speaking populations. Contact her at lfabiano@mail.sdsu.edu.

A Speech-Language Approach to Early Reading Success

ADELE GERBER AND EVELYN R. KLEIN

We are both speech-language pathologists who, in earlier periods of our careers, have served as specialists in school settings. A substantial part of our caseloads consisted of young children with articulation delays and disorders to whom we provided therapy. One of the procedures we frequently employed was intensive training in speech-sound perception that enabled the children to develop a heightened awareness of the difference between their error production and the corresponding standard sound.

On several occasions, first-grade teachers told us that children receiving articulation therapy excelled in phonics. On the basis of this information, in 1970, I (Adele Gerber) designed a program called Beginning Reading Through Speech in a format appropriate for use in kindergarten and first-grade classrooms. Recently we have revised the procedures to a format suitable for use by tutors or teachers providing individual or small-group training for children needing help mastering emergent literacy and early reading skills.

Over the past few decades, teachers have been informed about results of extensive research that has produced compelling evidence of a strong relationship between phonological awareness and the acquisition of reading awareness—that is, the perception of skills (Chaney, 1998). In particular, professional development programs have placed a heavy emphasis on phonemic awareness—that is, the perception of the speech sounds that form words—and its relevance to the mastery of letter-sound correspondences required for phonic decoding of the written word.

> According to most theories of reading development today, phonological decoding is essential to reading.

Having served as a consultant in the Norristown, Pennsylvania Area School District, I received a request from the reading specialist to train teachers in the area of phonemic awareness, providing assistance in understanding the process and information about procedures for its development in children engaged in early reading acquisition. A corps of elementary school teachers participated in an inservice program that presented the rationale and procedures for a speech-language approach to early reading success.

This article describes this speech-language approach, which we designed to help young children learn to associate letters with consonant sounds and to assist children who are struggling with early reading skills. Here, we also provide rationale for this innovative approach and results showing its efficacy.

Rationale for the Speech-Language Approach

According to testimony from the International Reading Association before a congressional briefing regarding effectiveness of reading instruction, "If you want to make a difference, make it different." (National Institute of Child Health and Human Development, 2000). The speech-language approach does employ procedures that differ from traditional approaches to teach letter-sound associations, one of the essential building blocks of early reading success. This approach is unique because it stems from another discipline: speech-language-hearing science.

The necessity of phoneme awareness for reading success is supported by much evidence. Poor readers have deficits in this ability when compared to normal readers of the same age and younger (Badian, 2001; Goswami & Bryant, 1994; Wagner & Torgensen, 1987). According to most theories of reading development today, phonological decoding is essential to reading. The ability to learn the sound-letter associations for decoding printed words is directly related to awareness of the sounds of speech (Kamhi & Catts, 2002).

The Speech-Language Approach

This approach consists of two stages. Stage 1 contains six steps; Stage 2 consists of four steps.

Stage 1: Training Phonemic Awareness for Consonant-Sound Perception

A phoneme is the smallest discrete speech sound in a word that has the capability to distinguish one word from another. For example, the difference between *boy* and *toy* is determined by the initial phonemes /b/ and /t/. Because the sound is embedded in the meaningful context of a word, it is difficult for some children (and some adults) to perceive it as a discrete entity.

Failure in response to conventional phonics instruction is frequently due to attempts to match the abstract form of a letter to a sound that is not perceived.

Phonemic awareness development is critical to the speech-language pathologist's methods of treating articulation disorders. To heighten discrimination between a defective and a standard production of a speech sound, the phoneme is removed from the surrounding sounds in a word and presented in isolation (as a *phone*). Under this condition, the distinctive features of a speech sound are most apparent.

We designed the procedures in this approach to ensure success in a step-by-step progression from identification of each targeted consonant in isolation to recognition of the sound-letter correspondences in words.

According to a report from the National Reading Panel to the National Institute of Child Health and Human Development (2000), phonemic awareness training has caused reading and spelling improvement. The benefits have lasted beyond the end of training.

Step 1: Introduce the sound with a picture-sound symbol. Introduce each consonant sound with its associated picture-sound symbol. The sound picture and associated label capitalize on onomatopoeia (sounds that imitate what they denote). Cut out each of the 16 picture-sound symbols from Figure 1, and present them individually with a corresponding story that includes multiple productions of the sound in isolation. For example, a student is presented with a story (see Figure 2) about the sound of the letter. The *bubble sound,* /b/, is represented by a picture of a bubble displayed to the child (see Figure 3). We encourage teachers to develop their own stories similar in content and style to this example.

Step 2: Touch the picture of the sound symbol when hearing isolated sound. (This procedure applies to each new picture and sound.) Display a picture of the bubbles (picture-sound

Figure 1 The 16 picture-sound symbols.

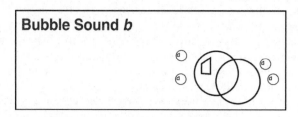

Bubble Sound _b_

(It is recommended to have a large glass ½ full of milk or another preferred drink, a straw, and a bubble blower with soapy water or bubble solution available, if possible). The sound of 'b' is produced as an isolated sound without the vowel sound as in 'buh'.

I'm going to tell you a story about Betty. Betty was a good little girl. She helped her mother make the beds. She never talked back. But there was one thing that she did that her mother did not like. Betty loved to blow bubbles in her glass of milk. Whenever she drank milk she would blow through her straw, like this. (demonstrate) She loved to hear the bubbly sound. The bubbles seemed to say, "b b b b b," etc.

Her mother said, "Betty, why do you like to blow bubbles in your glass?"

Betty said, "Because I love to hear the bubbles say, b b b b b."

Betty's mother said, "I'll buy you a bubble blower and you can blow all the bubbles you want." So Mother bought a little bottle of liquid bubbles and a bubble blower.

Betty blew lots of pretty bubbles. But one day she said to her mother, "Mommy, these bubbles are pretty, but they don't talk."

"What do you mean, the bubbles don't talk?" asked her Mother.

"They don't say, b b b b b," said Betty, "like my milky bubbles do."

"Well," said Mother, "I want you to drink your milk, not blow bubbles in it. But I want you to have fun, too. I have a good idea. I'll put the liquid bubbles in a glass and you can blow talking bubbles with your straw." So Mother put the liquid bubbles in a glass and Betty blew into it with a straw. She heard the bubbles say b b b b b any time she wanted to. But she drank her milk without blowing bubbles. So Mother was pleased, and Betty was happy with her talking bubble sound.

Can you make the bubble sound with me?

Figure 2 The bubble story for the /b/ sound.

symbol) on a workspace. Tell the child, "I will say some sounds. Some will be the bubble sound and some will be other sounds. When you hear the bubble sound, touch the bubbles." Produce a series of isolated consonant sounds; for example, "/b/, /l/, /b/, /b/, /f/, /k/, /b/," and so on.

Step 3: Touch the picture of the sound symbol when hearing the sound in syllables. After he achieves approximately 90% correct identification, tell the child: "I'm going to talk baby talk. That means I will talk like a baby. When you hear me say the bubble sound, touch the bubble." Produce a random series of

Figure 3 Picture-sound symbol and letter cards.

consonant-vowel (CV) nonsense syllables, some starting with the bubble sound. Say, "Ba-ba, fo-fo, bi-bi, sa-sa, ta-ta, ba-ba," and so on.

Step 4: Touch the picture of the sound symbol when hearing the sound in easy words. Following the child's approximately 90% correct identification, tell her, "I'm going to say some words. When you hear the bubble sound at the beginning of a word, touch the picture of the bubble. If it is the first word, touch this circle." Point to the circle on the left side, then continue, "And if it is the last word, touch this circle." Point to the circle on the right side. Produce a series of minimally contrastive CVC words that rhyme and include some that start with the /b/ sound. Use two drawn circles (one on the left side of page and one on the right side) to complete this step. Say, "Bat-hat; rake-bake, bin-fin; fill-bill," and so on.

Step 5: Touch the picture of the sound symbol when hearing sound in words. Following the child's approximately 90% correct identification, say, "I'm going to say words one at a time. Touch the picture of the bubble sound when you hear a word that begins with the bubble sound." Produce a randomized list of single words, starting with one-syllable words. If the child masters the task, increase the length of the words. Say, "Bark, house, boy, paint, sing, face, book, lady, tiger, big, party, Bobby, Carlos, Kim, Felix, Billy, Keisha, Luis, Tanya," and so on.

Step 6: Match the correct sound-symbol picture with one of four sounds. After completing Steps 1 through 5 with 4 of the 16 consonants sounds from Figure 1, display those four picture-sound symbols on the workspace. Tell the child, "I'm going to say words that start with different sounds. You point to the picture of the sound you hear at the beginning of each word." The first four picture-sound symbols recommended are: /b/, /f/, /m/, and /t/. Say, "boy, fun, basket, money, tie, fork, talk, big, milk," and so on.

Stage 2: Matching Letter to Sound— Introductory Systematic Phonics

Step 1: Introduce letters with corresponding picture sound symbols.
Display a picture-sound symbol card and a letter card beside it. Tell the child, "This is the letter that goes with the bubble sound. Its name is 'B.' This is the letter that goes with the angry cat sound. Its name is 'F.'" We recommend continuing with the four letters previously taught.

Step 2: Match the picture-sound symbols with letters.
Display a group of letter cards and a group of picture-sound symbol cards on the workspace in random order. (The number of cards displayed depends on the level of mastery demonstrated in Step 1.) Tell the child, "We are going to play a matching game. Here are some sound pictures and some letter cards. See how many letters and sound pictures you can match."

Step 3: Identify sound-symbol pictures with various words.
If the child achieves approximately 90% accuracy at Step 2, display a group of single-syllable word cards beginning with the targeted consonants; for example: bat, fan, man, tail. Tell the child, "I will say the word. You find the picture of the sound you hear at the beginning of the word. For example, if I say 'bat,' you point to the bubble sound picture."

Step 4: Match the beginning letters with the corresponding words.
If the child achieves approximately 90% accuracy at Step 3, display a group of corresponding consonant-letter cards. Tell the child, "I will say some words that begin with these sounds. You pick up the letter that matches the first sound you hear when I say the word." Produce a list of words in random order, matching the picture-sound symbols to the letters. Say one word at a time. We recommend that initially the words consist of single-syllable rhyming groups such as pat, fat, bat, mat, and so on. When the child achieves 90% accuracy at this level, introduce more varied word patterns.

Evidence of Effectiveness

The speech-language approach to early reading success was used in the Norristown, Pennsylvania, School District to reduce the incidence of students with reading delay. In an extended-day tutorial program staffed by classroom teachers, children in first and second grades who scored at the below basic level of reading on the Houghton Mifflin Emergent Literacy Test were scheduled in groups of five per instructor for one-half hour sessions three times per week. A midyear test of progress was administered after a period extending from October, 2001 to February, 2002. Table 1 reflects the pre-and posttest results secured at the beginning of March, 2002.

Table 1 Progress of Students on Tested Emergent Literacy Skills after 5 Months of Training

Emergent Literacy Subtest	Number Students/Grade	Percentage of Students	October 2001 Skill Level	March 2002 Skill Level
Rhyme	31/1st	100%	Below Basic	Proficient
Beginning Sounds	31/1st	100%	Below Basic	Proficient
Blending Onsets/Rimes	31/1st	100%	Below Basic	Proficient
Concepts of Print	31/1st	100%	Below Basic	Proficient
Letter Naming	31/1st	100%	Below Basic	Proficient
Segmenting Onsets/Rimes	31/1st	100%	Below Basic	Basic
Phoneme Blending	31/1st	100%	Below Basic	Basic
Phoneme Segmentation	31/1st	100%	Below Basic	Basic
Word Recognition	31/1st	100%	Below Basic	Basic
Fluency	31/1st	100%	Below Basic	Basic
Word Writing	31/1st	100%	Below Basic	Basic
Sentence Dictation	31/1st	100%	Below Basic	Basic
Rhyme	7/2nd	100%	Below Basic	Proficient
Concepts of Print	7/2nd	100%	Below Basic	Proficient
Letter Naming	7/2nd	100%	Below Basic	Proficient
Fluency	7/2nd	100%	Below Basic	Proficient
Beginning Sounds	7/2nd	100%	Below Basic	Proficient
Blending Onsets/Rimes	7/2nd	100%	Below Basic	Basic
Segmenting Onsets/Rimes	7/2nd	100%	Below Basic	Basic
Phoneme Blending	7/2nd	100%	Below Basic	Basic
Phoneme Segmentation	7/2nd	100%	Below Basic	Basic
Word Recognition	7/2nd	100%	Below Basic	Basic

Of the students tested, seven second-grade students had I.Q. scores in the 60–70 range. Although prior instruction throughout the first grade had not succeeded in the development of emergent literacy skills in these students at the basic or proficient levels, 5 months of instruction in this program achieved progress—to the basic or proficient level skills for all seven students, considered to be developmentally delayed.

The data in Table 1 indicate noteworthy gains that impressed the teachers who implemented the methods. In first grade, 5 of 12 tested areas (42%) showed improvement from below basic to proficient levels and 7 of 12 of the areas (58%) improved from below basic to basic levels for all 31 first graders. In the second grade, half the tested areas showed improvement from below basic to proficient, and the other half of the tested skills areas showed improvement from below basic to basic for all 7 second graders.

The effectiveness of this step-by-step approach to reading success evidenced by the reported gains was further reflected by the reactions of teachers. The reading specialist who was the administrator of the remedial reading program stated, "The teachers loved it." She further expressed her intent to introduce the program into kindergarten classrooms at the beginning of the next school year.

The effectiveness of this step-by-step approach to reading success evidenced by the reported gains was further reflected by the reactions of teachers.

Final Thoughts

The methods used in this program emphasized the importance of connecting the auditory signal of the letter sound to the visual letter. Onomatopoeias relating common items such as the roaring sound of a lion for the sound of /r/ or the sound of a hissing snake for /s/ are used to help make an imprint to associate the concrete sound with the abstract symbol. Tying in a high-interest story that captivates the young listener by using auditory bombardment with repetitive sounds embedded in a story line keeps the children engaged and ready to learn how to associate consonant sounds with letters.

Students need to have a strong understanding of spoken language before they can understand written language. Our goal is to reduce the incidence of students with reading delay. As reading specialists in an urban-school setting where our less-skilled readers tend to have difficulty identifying, separating, and blending sound segments, we incorporated the speech/language approach in our extended day tutorial reading program. The gains have been noteworthy.

—Reported from teachers in the Norristown School District, 2002

Studies have demonstrated that in early intervention, including phonological awareness, phonetic decoding, letter naming, sound knowledge, whole-word identification, and writing skills, along with reading connected text can be very effective (Vellutino, Scanlon, & Sipay, 1996). From an extensive review of research and practice in the area of emergent literacy, Whitehurst & Lonigan (1998) determined that well-developed language skills, letter knowledge, and some form of phonological sensitivity are necessary for reading and writing and that the origins of these components of emergent literacy are found during the preschool years (Treiman, Tincoff, Rodruquez, Mouzaki, & Frances, 1998).

The early intervention methods used in the speech-language approach incorporate these skills and combine memory-enhancing strategies with phoneme awareness to help prevent problems during emergent literacy and the early reading period. This program approach has been found effective with beginning readers in first and second grades who were functioning at below basic level of early reading prior to instruction and at basic and proficient levels after training.

References

Badian, N. A. (2001). Phonological and orthographic processing: Their roles in reading prediction. *Annals of Dyslexia, 51*, 179–199.

Chaney, C. (1998). Preschool language and metalinguistic skills are links to reading success. *Applied Psycholinguistics, 19*, 433–446.

Goswami, U., & Bryant, P. (1994). *Phonological skills and learning to read.* Hove, UK: Lawrence Erlbaum.

Kamhi, A. G., & Catts, H. W. (2002). The language basis of reading: Implications for classification and treatment of children with reading disabilities. In K. G. Butler & E. R. Silliman (Eds.), *Speaking, reading, and writing in children with language learning disabilities* (pp. 45–72). Mahwah, NJ: Lawrence Erlbaum.

National Reading Panel. (2000). Teaching children to read: An evidence-based assessment of the scientific research literature on reading and its implications for reading instruction (NIH Publication No. 00-4769.) Report of the National Reading Panel. National Institute of Child Health and Human Development. Washington, DC.

Treiman, R., Tincoff, R., Rodriguez, K., Mouzaki, A., & Frances, D. J. (1998). The foundations of literacy: Learning the sounds of letters. *Child Development, 69*(6), 1524–1540.

Vellutino, F. R., Scanlon, D. M., & Sipay, E. R. (1996). Toward distinguishing between cognitive and experiential deficits as primary sources of difficulty in learning to read: The importance of intervention in diagnosing specific reading disability. In B. Blachman (Ed.), *Foundations of reading acquisition and dyslexia: Implications for early intervention* (pp. 347–379). Mahwah, NJ: Lawrence Erlbaum.

Wagner, R. K., & Torgensen, J. K. (1987). The nature of phonological processing and its causal role in the acquisition of reading skills. *Psychological Bulletin, 101*, 192–212.

Whitehurst, G. J., & Lonigan, C. J. (1998). Child development and emergent literacy, *Child Development, 69*, 848–872.

ADELE GERBER, Professor Emeritus, Temple University, Department of Communication Sciences, Philadelphia, Pennsylvania. **EVELYN R. KLEIN** (CEC Chapter #388), Assistant Professor, Department of Speech, Language, Hearing Science, La Salle University, Philadelphia, Pennsylvania. Address correspondence to Adele Gerber, 600 East Cathedral Road, H316, Philadelphia, PA 19128 (e-mail: adeleg410@aol.com).

UNIT 7

Hearing and Visual Impairments

Unit Selections

Key Points to Consider

- Should children with profound hearing loss use American Sign Language (ASL), or English, as their primary language?

- Do all students with blindness learn to read Braille?

- How can tactile strategies support learning for students with visual impairments and other severe disabilities?

Student Website

www.mhcls.com

Internet References

Info to Go: Laurent Clerc National Deaf Education Center
   http://clerccenter.gallaudet.edu/InfoToGo/index.html
The New York Institute for Special Education
   http://www.nyise.org/index.html

The number of children with deafness or blindness has been greatly reduced in recent years. These are now considered low incidence disabilities due to earlier, more adequate prenatal care, preventive medicine, health maintenance, and medical technology. In the future, with knowledge of the human genome and with the possibility of genetic manipulation, all genetic causes of blindness and deafness may be eliminated. Now and in the future, however, environmental factors will probably still leave many children with hearing and vision impairments.

Hearing impairments are rare, and the extreme form, legal deafness, is rarer still. A child is assessed as hard-of-hearing for purposes of receiving special educational services if he or she needs some form of sound amplification to comprehend oral language. A child is assessed as deaf if he or she cannot benefit from amplification. Educational deafness means the student cannot be taught using sound (hearing). Vision and tactile modes are used instead.

When children are born with impaired auditory sensations, they are put into a classification of children with congenital (at or dating from birth) hearing impairments. When children acquire problems with their hearing after birth, they are put into a classification of children with adventitious hearing impairments. If the loss of hearing occurs before the child has learned speech and language, it is called a prelinguistic hearing impairment. If the loss occurs after the child has learned language, it is called a postlinguistic hearing impairment.

Children whose hearing losses involve the outer- or middle-ear structures are said to have conductive hearing losses. Conductive losses involve defects or impairments of the external auditory canal, the tympanic membrane, or the ossicles. Children whose hearing losses involve the inner ear are said to have sensorineural hearing impairments.

Since 1999 The Newborn and Infant Hearing Screening and Intervention Act in the United States has provided incentives for states to test the hearing of newborns before hospital discharge. Most states now offer this test for a small fee. When an infant is diagnosed with deafness or hearing loss, an appropriate early education can begin immediately under the auspices of IDEIA (see Unit 2).

Children with visual disabilities that cannot be corrected are the smallest group of children who qualify for special educational services through the Individuals with Disabilities Education Improvement Act (IDEIA). Legally, a child is considered to have low vision if acuity in the best eye, after correction, is between 20/70 and 20/180 and if the visual field extends from 20 to 180 degrees. Legally, a child is considered blind if visual acuity in the best eye, after correction, is 20/200 or less or if the field of vision is restricted to an area of less than 20 degrees (tunnel vision). These terms do not accurately reflect a child's ability to see or read print.

The educational definition of visual impairment focuses on what experiences a child needs in order to be able to learn. One must consider the amount of visual acuity in the worst eye, the perception of light and movement, the field of vision (a person "blinded" by tunnel vision may have good visual acuity in only a very small field of vision), and the efficiency with which

© Scott T. Baxter/Getty Images

a person uses any residual vision. A child is educationally blind if he or she cannot use vision to learn. Hearing and tactile modes are used instead.

Public Law 99-457, fully enacted by 1991, mandated early education for children with disabilities between ages three and five in the least restrictive environment. This has been reauthorized as PL102-119, which requires individualized family service plans outlining what services will be provided for parents and children, by whom, and where. These family service plans (IFSPs) are updated every six months. This early childhood extension of IDEIA has been especially important for babies born with low vision or blindness.

In infancy and early childhood, many children with low vision or blindness are given instruction in using the long cane as soon as they become mobile. Although controversial for many years, the long cane is increasingly being accepted. A long cane improves orientation and mobility and alerts persons with visual acuity that the user has a visual disability. This warning is very important for the protection of persons with blindness/low vision.

Children with visual impairments that prevent them from reading print may be taught to read braille. Braille is a form of writing using raised dots that are "read" with the fingers. In addition to braille, children who are blind are taught with Optacon scanners, talking books, talking handheld calculators, closed-circuit televisions, typewriters, and special computer software.

Students with vision or hearing impairments whose disabilities can be ameliorated with assistive devices can usually have their individualized needs met appropriately in inclusive classrooms. Students with visual or hearing disorders whose problems cannot be resolved with technological aids, however, need the procedural protections afforded by law. They should receive special services from age of diagnosis through age 21, in the least restrictive environment, free of charge, with semiannually updated individualized family service plans (IFSPs) until age three and annually updated individualized education plans (IEPs) and eventually individualized transition plans (ITPs)

through age 21. The numbers of children and youth who qualify for these intensive specialized educational programs are small.

Many professionals working with individuals who are deaf feel that communities of others who are deaf and who use sign language is less restrictive than a community of people who hear and who use oral speech. The debate about what has come to be known as the deaf culture has not been resolved.

The first article in this unit deals with the debate over the oral-English language approach to education of students with profound hearing loss, and the use of the alternate language, American Sign Language (ASL). Advances in medicine and technology have allowed many young children to have cochlear implants. These devices allow them to decipher some sounds and succeed with an oral education in English. Other children do better when they use ASL as their primary language and use English only as a second language, if at all. The current feeling among many educators is to try whatever works best for each individual child. Not everyone agrees with this stance. The report by Burton Bollag explains why.

The Debate over Deaf Education

Technological changes are shaking up the teaching of the hearing impaired.

BURTON BOLLAG

D aniel S. Koo was born deaf. When he was 4 he started attending a public school where he spent part of each week getting intensive training in speaking and listening with the help of hearing aids.

He remembers those early years as increasingly frustrating because, try as he might, he could not understand what his teachers were saying. By fourth grade he was falling behind academically, and his parents transferred him to another public school, which practiced a little-used method, called cued speech. As teachers spoke, they would make rapid hand movements near their mouths to visually represent the sounds they were producing.

"The light bulb just went on," recalls Mr. Koo, and a world of learning opened to him. He attended the University of Maryland at College Park—attending classes with the help of an interpreter—and went on to graduate studies at Gallaudet University, in Washington, where all his classes were taught in American Sign Language. Today he is a postdoctoral fellow in neurolinguistics at Georgetown University Medical Center.

Mr. Koo's academic success is all the more remarkable when compared with the academic performance of most deaf students. According to the latest nationwide survey, the average deaf 18-year-old reads below the fourth-grade level. Despite decades of efforts, the scores have remained largely unchanged.

"Historically we have taught deaf students material way below their conceptual level since we taught them through English," says Gabriel A. Martin, chair of the communication-disorders and deaf-education department at Lamar University.

The solution, he says, is teaching deaf children through American Sign Language—their one "native" tongue. But the issue is highly controversial. Opponents say that concentrating on signing can undermine young children's acquisition of English, and largely relegates them to being able to communicate only with other deaf people.

For more than two centuries, educators of the deaf—and the college departments that train them—have debated the best way to teach deaf children. At one end of the spectrum are those who favor the "oral" method, training teachers to concentrate on developing speech and hearing skills. At the other end are those who advocate a "bilingual" approach, teaching primarily in American Sign Language and promoting English as a second language.

Scientific studies have been inconclusive in demonstrating an inherent superiority of one method over the other. But earlier detection of deafness in infants—some 45 states now require screening at birth—and recent advances in medical technology are resulting in greater hearing in a larger portion of deaf children. The development is shifting the debate in favor of the oral approach.

That is beginning to have profound effects on the work of the country's 74 academic departments of deaf education. "I know in talking to my colleagues there is a growing recognition that the kids have changed," says Harold A. Johnson, director of Kent State University's deaf-education teacher-preparation program.

Hearing More

One of the most pervasive new influences on deaf children has been the introduction of cochlear implants. The devices, first approved in 1984, bring sounds from an external hearing aid directly to the auditory nerve. The size of a needle, the devices are surgically inserted under the skin at the base of the skull, just behind the ear, where they take over the function of a damaged inner ear—the most common cause of deafness.

However, the sounds the implants produce are different, and less complete, than what is heard by people with normal hearing. People who get cochlear implants must be trained to decipher the new sounds. In addition, for the first months they must have their implants regularly "mapped"—or fine-tuned—to improve clarity and adjust volume levels.

According to the Food and Drug Administration, approximately 13,000 adults and 10,000 children had received implants by 2002, the latest year for which data are available. But the technology continues to improve, and the number of people receiving implants is increasing rapidly.

The trend is a source of anxiety to some deaf people, who feel that it may lead to an erosion of the gains they have won in recent decades in antidiscrimination legislation, and undercut their hard-won dignity. Benjamin J. Bahan, a professor of deaf studies at Gallaudet University who has been deaf since he was 4, worries that as more deaf children are given an oral education, the teaching of American Sign Language may be abandoned.

"Let those kids be bilingual," he said in an e-mail message. "After all with their implants off they are DEAF."

Yet the implants are already affecting the work of Gallaudet. With 1,900 students, it is the world's only university devoted to the deaf. Part of its mission is the development of teaching methods and materials for the more than 71,000 severely deaf children in the United States. The university runs a model elementary school and middle school on its large campus in Washington.

Up until now, Gallaudet's goal has been to make all 370 schoolchildren it enrolls fully fluent in both English, or at least written English, and American Sign Language. But educators say they are seeing a growing number of children with implants whose improved hearing would allow them to benefit from a more oral-based education.

"Teachers come here trained in a more visual approach," says Debra B. Nussbaum, coordinator of the model schools' Cochlear Implant Education Center. But, she adds, "we've been talking about how to change our strategies."

Supporters of the oral approach say far too few teachers are being trained in that orientation. "In the last 10 to 15 years there has been a dramatic increase in demand" for oral education, says Susan T. Lenihan, director of the deaf-education program at Fontbonne University, in St. Louis. Deaf-education departments "should recognize this shift in the population," she says, and train more teachers equipped to work with deaf people with cochlear implants.

Perhaps the strongest trend in academic departments in recent years has been a growing openness to try whatever works with individual children.

Yet like many institutions, Gallaudet is moving cautiously and, so far, appears committed to maintaining a strong sign-language component in its model schools. "I do a lot of workshops across the country," says Ms. Nussbaum. "I'm hearing about kids with cochlear implants who didn't do as well as the doctors thought they would." Some children have found so little benefit from the devices that they have stopped using them, educators say.

Gallaudet wants to make sure none of the youngsters in its model schools end up like countless children in exclusively oral programs over the years: without any language—barely knowing English, but never having learned sign language. Not only are such children deprived of a developed means of communication, but with no language in the early years—the critical time for learning languages—their cognitive development may be permanently stunted, scholars say.

Communication was on the minds of many Gallaudet students when they demonstrated last week against a new president chosen by the institution's board of trustees. Protesting students accuse the new president, Jane K. Fernandes, a deaf person who only learned sign language as an adult, of having a haughty and aloof style.

While educators struggle to get the balance right between oral and visual forms of communication, perhaps the strongest trend in academic departments in recent years has been a growing openness to try whatever works with individual children. "Our students are prepared to use a wide range of teaching approaches," says T. Alan Hurwitz, vice president of the Rochester Institute of Technology and dean of its National Technical Institute for the Deaf, which enrolls approximately 60 students in a graduate education program. More important than the method used, says Mr. Hurwitz, who was born deaf and spoke through a signing interpreter, is "detecting deafness very early, getting parents involved early, and having good teachers."

Checkered History

While the popularity of different approaches has gone up and down, the root of the debate over the proper way to teach the deaf goes back more than 200 years.

In 1771 the abbé Charles-Michel de l'Epée, a young priest, founded the first public school for the deaf, in Paris. He based the language of instruction on a system of hand signs he had observed deaf French people using to communicate with one another.

During the 19th century, deaf children in America were taught mainly in sign language. But there was a competing approach, championed by, among others, Alexander Graham Bell, the inventor of the telephone, who was married to a deaf woman. The backers of this oral approach argued that sign language was a form of savagery that kept its users isolated from the rest of humanity. The oral approach won out when the International Congress of Educators of the Deaf, meeting in Milan in 1880, decreed that deaf people should be taught spoken language, not sign language.

For much of the 20th century, deaf children in America received a predominantly oral education. Sign language continued being passed down surreptitiously in the dormitories of the residential schools where most deaf children were then sent. Those caught signing were sometimes forced to sit on their hands.

The 1960s brought another shake-up, inspired by the civil-rights movement and buttressed by the work of William C. Stokoe Jr., a Chaucer scholar at Gallaudet. Mr. Stokoe published several influential works demonstrating that American Sign Language was not just a collection of gestures, but a true language with its own rules and grammatical structures. Indeed scholars, and deaf people fluent in both languages, say American Sign Language is as rich a medium as English for conveying even complex, intellectual ideas.

The development was liberating for deaf-education departments. Several new communications systems involving hand signs were developed, including cued speech, which proved so helpful to Mr. Koo.

The majority of departments moved toward an approach often referred to as "total communication," whose professed aim is to work with a variety of methods to find what works best for each child. In reality, many departments settled into a reliance on "signed English," which is not a real language like ASL, but a practice of translating spoken English, word for word. Critics say signed English is a sloppy compromise, allowing a person to speak and sign at the same time, but conveying considerably less information to a deaf listener than does ASL.

To the disappointment of many scholars, this flourishing of new methods brought virtually no improvement in the test scores of deaf schoolchildren. Some scholars have reacted, ironically, by pulling to one extreme or the other: either a bilingual approach that relies chiefly on American Sign Language, or an exclusively oral approach that excludes signing altogether.

While the bilingual approach is intellectually appealing to many academics (most agree that American Sign Language is the easiest "tongue" for deaf children to master), scholars readily acknowledge its one major drawback. About 97 percent of deaf children are born to hearing parents, and, educators say, those parents are typically unwilling or unable to master sign language. That means that children whose education is based on American Sign Language will communicate better with teachers and other deaf people than with their own parents.

"It challenges the whole notion of what it means to be a parent," says Carol J. Erting, chair of Gallaudet's education department. "Emotionally, it's just really, really hard."

More recently, the continued improvements in medical technology—digital hearing aids that work better than the traditional analog ones, and continually improving cochlear implants—have made the oral approach increasingly attractive.

While cochlear implants are bringing new hope, they are also heating up old controversies. K. Todd Houston, executive director of the Alexander Graham Bell Association for the Deaf and Hard of Hearing, the leading group promoting oral education for deaf children, asserts that "there is a window of opportunity to stimulate auditory pathways," which may be missed if a child is exposed at an early age to a signing environment. Many scholars do not agree. With bilingualism and even multilingualism common in many parts of the world, they ask, why shouldn't a deaf child be fluent in English and sign language?

Mr. Koo, the neurolinguist, says that if he and his wife have any deaf children, he will raise them bilingually, in American Sign Language and cued English, the method that involves speaking and making hand signs around the mouth to represent the sounds.

"ASL exposes children to the world's knowledge," he says, "and it incorporates self-esteem and aspects of deaf culture." Mastering English "gives them access to the richness of the English world, like Shakespeare and idioms.

"I cherish them both," he says.

Using Tactile Strategies with Students Who Are Blind and Have Severe Disabilities

JUNE E. DOWNING AND DEBORAH CHEN

Vision is a primary sense for learning. Teachers use pictures, photographs, and a variety of color-coded materials in their instruction. They also use demonstrations and considerable modeling, which requires the students' visual attention. Many students with severe and multiple disabilities have considerable difficulty understanding verbal information and so rely heavily on visual information (Alberto & Frederick, 2000; Hodgdon, 1995; Hughes, Pitkin, & Lorden, 1998).

But what about students who cannot perceive visual cues—or access verbal information? When students have severe and multiple disabilities, teachers must resort to alternative teaching strategies to provide effective and accessible instruction.

If these students are also blind or have limited vision, however, they need instructional materials that provide relevant tactile information. This article describes specific tactile strategies to support instruction of students who have severe and multiple disabilities and who do not learn visually.

When students have severe and multiple disabilities, teachers must resort to alternative teaching strategies to provide effective and accessible instruction.

Getting in Touch

A teacher's instructional style certainly influences what a student learns. Teachers engage their students by providing visual and auditory information. They convey their mood through facial expressions, body language, and tone of voice. They give directions by gestures, pointing, and spoken words. If students cannot receive or understand these modes of communication, the teacher must use alternative strategies. The primary alternatives are tactile. The teacher must convey his or her instructional expectations, mood, and information through physical and direct contact with the student. Teaching through the sense of touch may be unfamiliar and uncomfortable for most teachers, including those with training in special education. Teachers should become aware of how they interact with the student through touch. To be most effective with tactile teaching, teachers must consider many issues:

- What impressions are conveyed to a student when he or she is touched?
- Do the teacher's hands convey different information depending on their temperature, tenseness of tone, speed of movement, and degree of pressure?
- Are teachers aware of the range of emotions that they can communicate through touch?
- Where do they touch the student (e.g., palms, back of hands, arms, legs, chest)?
- Do they touch the student's bare skin or clothing over the skin?
- How do students respond to different types of tactile input?

To be maximally effective, teachers must become aware of, interpret, monitor, and modify their tactile interactions from the student's perspective.

Tactile Modeling

Sighted students learn from demonstrations and through imitation. Students who are blind or have minimal vision need opportunities to feel the demonstrator's actions by touching the parts of the body or objects involved in the actions (Smith, 1998). For example, in a cooking class, a classmate demonstrates how to make meringue by whipping egg whites. The student who is blind can feel the peer's hand holding the bowl, the other hand grasping the electric mixer. This way, the student who is blind can "see" what his or her classmate is demonstrating. Like other tactile adaptations, the use of tactile modeling requires careful planning on the part of the teacher and extra time for the student to benefit from this instructional strategy.

Tactile Mutual Attention

Sighted students visually examine and make observations about something they are looking at together. The student with minimal or no vision should have opportunities for shared exploration with classmates through tactile mutual attention (Miles, 1999). For example, during a unit of study on masks, the student and a classmate may tactilely examine an African mask, placing their hands together as they explore the relatively smooth parts of the mask and find the leather strips, beads, and decorative feathers that border the mask. This way the student has a joint focus and shares observations with a classmate. Sighted classmates will have many creative ideas of ways to use tactile modeling and tactile mutual attention with peers who are blind and have additional disabilities (see Figure 1).

Tactile Learning and Teaching

When students with severe disabilities are unable to use their vision effectively for obtaining information, they require tactile information that is accessible to their hands or other parts of their body. Tactile information, however, has different characteristics from visual.

Unlike vision, touch provides a fragment of the whole; the student must put together a series of tactile impressions to understand what other students are looking at. For example, fourth-grade students are studying different aspects of life in the desert. One student, who is deaf and blind and does not know American Sign Language, is feeling a large desert tortoise. One hand is near the tail, and the other hand is feeling one edge of the shell near the tortoise's head. It will take this student considerable time and effort to tactilely examine and discover the physical characteristics of a tortoise, while his classmates can see that it is a tortoise in one glance.

> **Unlike vision, touch provides a fragment of the whole; the student must put together a series of tactile impressions to understand what other students are looking at.**

Certain concepts are easier to convey tactilely than others. Abstract concepts are much more difficult to adapt tactilely than more concrete facts. For instance, it is much easier to teach about helium using balloons than it is to teach historical events. The teacher must ensure that the tactile representation is truly representative of the concept and is relevant and meaningful to the student. For example, to teach that the solid state of water is ice, the use of raised (tactile) lines in waves to represent water and raised (tactile) straight lines to represent ice is not

1. Select the message that you want to communicate to the student (e.g., greeting, reassurance, encouragement, praise, redirection, demonstration).
2. Decide how best to communicate that message through the type of touch (i.e., duration, pressure, movement) and where to touch the student (e.g., back of hand, shoulder, or knee).
3. Identify how you will let the student know that you are close (e.g., by saying his name) before touching him or her (e.g., on the elbow).
4. Discuss whether and how to examine an item with the student (e.g., by having two students examine an African mask).
5. Decide whether and how to use tactile modeling (e.g., by asking a classmate to show the student how to blow up a balloon).
6. Observe the student's reactions to your tactile interactions and modify the interaction accordingly.
7. Identify how you will end the interaction (e.g., let the student know that you are leaving by giving him a double pat on the shoulder).

Figure 1   Considerations for interacting through touch.

meaningful or understandable to most students with severe and multiple disabilities. In contrast, the use of water (wet, liquid) and ice (cold, solid) would clearly represent the critical aspects of the topic of study.

The educational team must decide what aspects of a lesson can be represented tactilely to make instruction most easily understood. At times, the best tactile representation may be tangential to the specific subject. For example, for a lesson on Lewis and Clark and their exploration of the West, artifacts of the Old West (e.g., pieces of clothing, fur, leather pieces, a whip, and tools) can be used to provide a tactile experience for the student with no usable vision. Such items would also benefit the entire class. Acting out the event using objects as props also adds clarity and interest to a seemingly abstract topic.

Obviously, students with different skills and abilities will develop different concepts of the topic of study. For example, whereas fifth-grade students without disabilities in geometry class learn how to find the area of a square, a student who has severe and multiple impairments, including blindness, may just be learning to sort square shapes from round ones. General and special educators need to understand such differences and still challenge students to learn what they can.

Presenting Tactile Information

You can provide visual (e.g., pictures or sign language) and auditory (e.g., speech) information to several students at once. These so called *distance senses* are quick and efficient. In contrast, tactile information requires individual physical contact and takes more time to understand. You must allow extra time for presentation of tactile information so the student has an opportunity to touch, handle, examine, and eventually synthesize and understand information (Downing & Demchak, 2002). Here are some reminders:

- Decide how to introduce an item to the student.
- The item should be accessible so the student can detect its presence and then manipulate it to determine its identity or relationship to familiar experiences.
- Touching the item to some part of the student's body (e.g., arm or side or back of hand) is less intrusive than manipulating the student's hand to take the item and therefore, such an approach is recommended (Dote-Kwan & Chen, 1999; Miles, 1999; Smith, 1998). Some students are timid about tactile exploration because they are wary and careful about handling unfamiliar or disliked materials.

Allow extra time for presentation of tactile information so the student has an opportunity to touch, handle, examine, and eventually synthesize and understand information.

A teacher or peer may introduce a new object to the student, by holding the object, and placing the back of his or her hand under the student's hand. The student is more likely to accept the touch of a familiar hand than that of an unfamiliar object. Slowly the teacher or peer can rotate his or her hand until the student is touching the object. This way the student has physical support while deciding whether to touch and examine the object (Dote-Kwan & Chen, 1999). After the student detects the presence of the item, he or she is more likely to take the item and explore it (if physically possible).

Ideally, students will use their hands to explore; however, some students have such severe physical disabilities that they may use touch receptors in their tongue, on their cheeks, or inside of their arms. In all cases, you need to encourage the student's active participation (even if only partial) in accessing information.

Providing Effective Tactile Representation

To determine whether tactile information is truly representative of a specific concept, the representation must be tactilely salient and meaningful. Because it is natural for sighted teachers to have a visual perspective, it is difficult to make tactile adaptations that make sense tactilely. For example, tactile outlines of items (e.g., string glued to a drawing of a house) may be used to represent different concepts but may not be recognized tactilely or understood by the student. Although miniatures are

1. Identify the objective of the lesson or the instructional concept.
2. Select the materials to convey this concept.
3. Close your eyes and examine the material with your hands.
4. Take a tactile perspective, not visual, when deciding how and what to present.
5. If the entire concept (e.g., house) is too complicated to represent through a tactile adaptation, then select one aspect of the concept (e.g., key) for the tactile representation.
6. Consider the student's previous tactile experiences. What items has he or she examined?
7. How does the student examine materials through the sense of touch?
8. Decide how the item will be introduced to the student.
9. Identify what supports the student needs to tactilely examine the item.
10. Decide what language input (descriptive words) will be used to convey the student's experience of the material.

Figure 2 Considerations for developing tactile adaptions.

convenient because of their size and are easy to handle, they are based on visual characteristics of the objects they represent. For example, a small plastic dog has no tactile characteristics in common with a real dog. Similarly, a miniature of a house, while visually recognizable, does not resemble a house when examined tactilely. A key that the student has used to open the front door of his house will form a more accurate concept of "house."

Experiment with what can be perceived tactilely by blindfolding yourself and examining the adaptation using only your sense of touch. In addition, avoid misconceptions as much as possible. For example, in a kindergarten classroom, a student brought a glass paperweight with a rose in it for show and tell. He talked about the rose as he passed it around the class. When a classmate who has no vision and limited language was allowed to hold the paperweight, he was confused when told "it's a rose." More appropriate language should be used to describe what this student is experiencing (e.g., "round," "smooth," "heavy," and "glass"). If this student is to understand the meaning of "rose," then you need to provide a real rose, so the student can perceive its shape, texture, size, and scent (see Figure 2 for other considerations).

Hyperresponsivity to Touch

Some students demonstrate strong reactions to tactile information, even though this may be the best way for them to receive information. These reactions are often referred to as *tactile defensiveness* and treated as a negative characteristic of the student. Some people have a low sensory threshold and are hyperreactive or hyperresponsive to certain sensory stimulation (Williamson & Anzalone, 2001). Tactile responsivity is simply the degree to which an individual responds to tactile stimulation. Some individuals can tolerate considerable and varied amounts of tactile input without much reaction (e.g., tactile hyporesponsivity), while others are very sensitive to certain types of tactile input (tactile hyperresponsivity). These responses vary from person to person. Some people can wear certain fabrics next to their skin while others cannot.

Teachers must be aware of and respect these individual differences. Teachers should not take students' hands and physically make them touch materials if they are not willing to do so (Smith, 1998). If students are forced to have aversive tactile experiences, they are less likely to explore tactilely. The term tactile defensiveness has a negative connotation that may interfere with effective intervention. If the student has a sensory modulation problem that results in hyperresponsiveness, then the educational team should include an occupational therapist. Creative ways to bypass this problem and assist the student to handle tactile information are needed.

A Team Effort

Making appropriate tactile accommodations (instructional strategies or materials) cannot be left to one member of the team (i.e., the teacher certified in the area of visual impairment). A team effort is required, with different team members contributing their skills, knowledge, experiences, and ideas (Downing, 2002; Silberman, Sacks, & Wolfe, 1998). A special educator specifically trained in the area of visual impairments and blindness can be helpful with teaching ideas and tactile resources. Depending on this teacher's professional training and experiences, however, he or she may be unfamiliar with the types of accommodations a particular student may need. The student who is blind, has spoken language, and reads braille has very different learning needs from those of a student who does not speak, does not read braille, and has limited receptive language.

Relying on one specialist to meet the tactile needs of a student who is blind with additional severe disabilities should be avoided. The ideas of all members of the team are needed, including family members and classmates who do not have disabilities (Downing, 2002). This way tactile adaptations and strategies are more likely to be used at home and school and with peers.

Team members should consider how the student perceives information through touch, the student's best physical position, the student's ability to move different parts of his body, and past experiences with tactile information. Family members can provide insight on the student's tactile experiences and preferences. Occupational therapists can provide valuable information on the student's use of his hands, responsivity to tactile items, and strategies to decrease hyperresponsivity. Physical therapists can help with positioning considerations and adaptive equipment that support tactile exploration. In

collaboration with the general educator, the teacher certified in visual impairments can provide ideas for making tactile adaptations to instructional materials. Classmates can be asked for their ideas on how to use tactile modeling or to gather objects and tactile materials that can make a lesson more meaningful.

The ideas of all members of the team are needed, including family members and classmates who do not have disabilities.

Final Thoughts

Meeting the learning needs of students who have severe disabilities and who do not have clear access to visual information is a significant instructional challenge. Teaching through touch is unfamiliar and perhaps awkward for most sighted people, but learning though touch is essential for students who are blind or have minimal vision. Effective use of tactile strategies must consider the individual student's needs and abilities, learning environment, and task. These strategies can best support students' learning when there is a concerted effort on the part of the educational team, additional time for the presentation of tactile information, and systematic evaluation of adaptations.

References

Alberto, P. A., & Frederick, L. D. (2000). Teaching picture reading as an enabling skill. *TEACHING Exceptional Children, 33*(1), 60–64.

Dote-Kwan, J., & Chen, D. (1999). Developing meaningful interventions. In D. Chen (Ed.), *Essential elements in early communication visual impairments and multiple disabilities* (pp. 287–336). New York: American Foundation for the Blind Press.

Downing, J. E. (2002). Working cooperatively: The role of team members. In J. E. Downing (Ed.), *Including students with severe and multiple disabilities in typical classrooms: Practical strategies for teachers* (2nd ed., pp. 189–210). Baltimore: Paul H. Brookes.

Downing, J. E., & Demchak, M. A. (2002). First steps: Determining individual abilities and how best to support students. In J. E. Downing (Ed.), *Including students with severe and multiple disabilities in typical classrooms: Practical strategies for teachers* (2nd ed., pp. 37–70). Baltimore: Paul H. Brookes.

Hodgdon, L. A. (1995). *Visual strategies for improving communication. Vol. 1: Practical supports for school and home.* Troy, MI: QuirkRoberts.

Hughes, C., Pitkin, S. E., & Lorden, S. W. (1998). Assessing preferences and choices of persons with severe and profound mental retardation. *Education and Training in Mental Retardation and Developmental Disabilities, 33*, 299–316.

Miles, B. (1999). *Talking the language of the hands to the hands.* Monmouth, OR: DBLINK, The National Information Clearinghouse on Children Who Are Deaf-Blind. (ERIC Document Reproduction Service No. ED 419 331)

Silberman, R. K., Sacks, S. Z., & Wolfe, J. (1998). Instructional strategies for educating students who have visual impairments with severe disabilities. In S. Z. Sacks & R. K. Silberman (Eds.), *Educating students who have visual impairments with other disabilities* (pp. 101–137). Baltimore: Paul H. Brookes.

Smith, M. (1998). Feelin' groovy: Functional tactual skills. Retrieved January 24, 2000, from http://www.tsbvi.edu/Outreach/seehear/summer98/groovy.htm

Williamson, G. G., & Anzalone, M. (2001). *Sensory integration and self regulation in infants and toddlers: Helping very young children interact with their environment.* Washington, DC: Zero to Three. (ERIC Document Reproduction Service No. ED 466 317)

JUNE E. DOWNING (CEC Chapter #29), Professor; and **DEBORAH CHEN** (CEC Chapter #918) Professor, Department of Special Education, California State University, Northridge. Address correspondence to June E. Downing, Department of Special Education, California State University, Northridge, 18111 Nordhoff St., Northridge, CA 91330-8265 (e-mail: june.downing@csun.edu).

The development of this article was supported by the U.S. Department of Education, Office of Special Education and Rehabilitative Services Grant # H3224T990025. The content, however, does not necessarily reflect the views of the U.S. Department of Education, and no official endorsement should be inferred.

From *Teaching Exceptional Children*, by June E. Downing and Deborah Chen, Vol. 36, no. 2, November/December 2003, pp. 56–60. Copyright © 2003 by Council for Exceptional Children. Reprinted by permission.

UNIT 8

Physical and Health Impairments

Unit Selections

Key Points to Consider

- What is needed for writing explicit, functional accommodations for students with physical and health impairments?

- How do students with ADHD differ from their non-ADHD special-education peers? Do they receive necessary and appropriate services?

- Why is prescribing drugs for growing children both an art and a science? Too much? Too little? How do physicians make determinations about dosages which allow meaningful education to occur?

- What is the overlap between teens with ADHD and substance use?

Student Website
www.mhcls.com

Internet References

Association to Benefit Children (ABC)
   http://www.a-b-c.org
An Idea Whose Time Has Come
   http://www.boggscenter.org/mich3899.htm
Resources for VE Teachers
   http://www.cpt.fsu.edu/tree//ve/tofc.html
The Family Center on Technology and Disability
   http://www.fctd.info

Two civil rights laws, Section 504 of the Rehabilitation Act (1973) and the Americans with Disabilities Act (1990), prohibit discrimination against students with disabilities. They also mandate reasonable accommodations for them in education. Together with the Individuals with Disabilities Education Improvement Act of 2004 (IDEIA) and the No Child Left Behind Act of 2001 (NCLB), the United States has clearly articulated its desire that students with physical and health impairments be given equal access to free and appropriate public education, in the least restrictive environment. These laws also mandate nondiscriminatory, multidisciplinary assessments, individualized educational programs, and parental participation.

Children and youth with physical and health impairments can be divided into classifications of mild, moderate, and profound. Within most impairments, the same diagnosis may not produce the same degree of disability. For example, children with cerebral palsy may be mildly, moderately, or profoundly impaired.

Physical impairments are usually defined as those that hinder physical mobility or the ability to use one or more parts of the skeletomuscular system of the body. These problems may be neurological (brain or spinal cord) or skeletomuscular (muscles or skeletal bones). Regardless of etiology, the child with a physical impairment usually has a problem with mobility. He or she may need crutches or other aids in order to walk or may be in a wheelchair.

Health impairments are usually defined as those that affect stamina and one or more systems of the body: the cardiovascular, respiratory, gastrointestinal, endocrine, skin, lymphatic, urinary, reproductive, sensory, or nervous systems. Children with health impairments usually have to take medicine or follow a medical regimen in order to attend school. The degree of impairment (mild, moderate, profound) is usually based on limitations to activity, duration of problem, and extent of other problems.

Attention-deficit hyperactive disorder (ADHD) is formally recognized as a health impairment. Often children with ADHD are also assessed as learning disabled, gifted, or as emotionally-behaviorally disordered. It is possible for a child with ADHD to have characteristics of all of these categories.

Physical and health impairments are not always mutually exclusive. Many times a child with a physical impairment also has a concurrent or contributing health impairment, and vice versa. In addition, children with physical and health impairments may also have concurrent conditions of educational exceptionality.

Some children with physical and health impairments have only transitory impairments; some have chronic but non-worsening impairments; and some have progressive impairments that make their education more complicated as the years pass and may even result in death before the end of the developmental/educational period.

Each of the dimensions defined in the preceding paragraphs makes educational planning for children with physical and health impairments very complicated.

The reauthorization of IDEIA in 2004 mandated that schools must pay for all medical services required to allow physically or health-impaired students to attend regular education classes. The only exceptions are the actual fees for physician-provided

© Photodisc Collection/Getty Images

health services. Thus, if children need ambulances to transport them to and from school, the schools must pay the tab. Federal appropriations for special educational services only pay about 10 percent of the bills. Thus high-cost special needs students can quickly drain the funds of state and local education departments.

Teachers may resent the need to spend teacher time giving medications or providing quasi-medical services (suctioning, changing dressings, or diapers) for students with health impairments in the many U.S. schools that no longer have school nurses.

Resentment is common in parents of nondisabled students who feel that the education of high-cost students with disabilities robs their children of teacher time, curriculum, and supplies to which they should be entitled. More than 95 percent of students with special needs attend regular schools today. About three percent attend separate schools and about two percent are served at home, in hospitals, or in residential facilities.

When physical or health impairments are diagnosed in infancy or early childhood, an interdisciplinary team usually helps plan an individualized family service plan (IFSP) that includes working with parents, medical and/or surgical personnel, and preschool special-education providers (see Unit 2).

When the physical or health impairment is diagnosed in the school years, the school teachers collaborate with outside agencies, but more of the individualized educational planning (IEP) is in their hands. Children who have physical or health impairments usually need psychological as well as academic support. Teachers need to help them in their peer interactions. Teachers should also work closely with parents to ensure a smooth transition toward a lifestyle that fosters independence and self-reliance. By middle school, individualized transition plans (ITPs) should be developed. They should be implemented throughout high school and until age 21 when the students move to adult living, and they must be updated every year. Schools are held accountable for their success in helping students with physical and health impairments to make smooth transitions to maturity, independent living, and self-sufficiency.

The first selection for this unit is an overview of some of the accommodations that school systems must make to ensure that students with disabilities receive an appropriate education. MaryAnn Byrnes points out that the teaching profession is about creating a level playing field and giving all students an equal chance to participate in education. Writing explicit accommodations can make this possible.

In the next article in this unit, the author, Timothy Wilens, discusses the overlap between teens with ADHD and substance use disorder (SUD).

In the last article, "Trick Question," Michael Fumento questions the diagnosis of ADHD. Many have declared this label as a hoax, and the use of medication to treat it a conspiracy to make boys more docile. The article presents evidence that it is a neurological disorder that can usually be successfully treated with medication.

Writing Explicit, Unambiguous Accommodations

A Team Effort

Academic accommodations are intended to increase access to education for students with disabilities. Although the concept seems simple, implementation is challenging because of the ambiguous wording of some accommodations. This article reviews confusing aspects of frequently encountered accommodations. Research-based guidelines for writing explicit, functional accommodations are suggested and illustrated with student examples.

MARYANN BYRNES

Consider two fourth-grade students. Ed has an emotional/behavioral disorder and needs to be able to leave the class to see his counselor. Lydia, who has a specific learning disability in the area of written language, needs to be seated near supportive peers who can help with note taking. Even though different seating arrangements are required to provide access, the individualized education programs (IEPs) for both Lydia and Ed list only *preferential seating* as an accommodation. How would teachers know where Ed and Lydia should sit?

Accommodations stimulate energetic discussions in IEP meetings. Occasionally, special education teachers wonder why accommodations are not implemented by general education teachers. Some struggles may occur when there is confusion about the intent of a particular IEP accommodation. Practical, research-based guidelines for writing accommodations, emphasizing how to avoid the pitfalls of ambiguity, provide a solution to this problem.

Accommodations Overview

Although educators frequently use the term very broadly, accommodations reflect a legal directive to provide educational access to students with disabilities. Both Section 504 of the Rehabilitation Act of 1973 and the Americans with Disabilities Act of 1990 require organizations to provide reasonable accommodations so individuals with disabilities have equal access to programs, activities, and services. The Individuals with Disabilities Education Act (IDEA), reauthorized in 2004 as the Individuals with Disabilities Education Improvement Act, empowers IEP teams to identify accommodations that facilitate access to

instruction. Beginning with its 1997 reauthorization, IDEA and the No Child Left Behind Act of 2001 require IEP teams to consider accommodations for large-scale assessments.

Academic accommodations have been defined as "practices and procedures in the areas of presentation, response, setting, and timing/scheduling that provide equitable access during instruction and assessment for students with disabilities" (Thompson, Morse, Sharpe, & Hall, 2005, p. 17). Accommodations can be necessary for students on either a 504 plan or an IEP. Accommodations are not intended to make school easier but to make learning and assessment accessible to students with disabilities.

Like a curb cut in the sidewalk, an appropriate academic accommodation removes a barrier to performance, reducing the impact of a disability (Thompson, Morse, et al., 2005; Ysseldyke et al., 2001) so that a student can more accurately demonstrate what he or she knows and can do (Thurlow & Bolt, 2001). Think about a math test taken by a student with a specific learning disability in reading. A poor score on this test might reflect content knowledge but might also reflect the student's difficulty reading the written directions or the problems presented. Students without a reading disability would not encounter this challenge. An accommodation directing that test material be read aloud to this student compensates for the effect of the disability and enables him or her to more accurately demonstrate math knowledge (Fletcher et al., 2006).

A well-chosen accommodation is often described as creating a "level playing field" (Fuchs & Fuchs, 2001; Thompson, Lazarus, Thurlow, & Clapper, 2005; Thompson, Morse, et al., 2005), defined as "a state of equality; an equal opportunity" ("Level Playing Field," n.d.). When barriers posed by a disability are removed, students with disabilities have an equal chance to participate in education.

Accommodation Confusion

Creating this level playing field does not seem to be an easy task. Confusion about accommodations has been documented by a number of studies. Parker (2006) found that general education teachers had difficulty discriminating learning strategies from accommodations. Secondary general education faculty studied by Maccini and Gagnon (2006) were also unsure and implemented fewer accommodations in teaching and testing than did their special education colleagues.

Perhaps some of this difficulty stems from differing views of the exact meaning of some accommodations. Byrnes (in press) found that general education and special education teachers held very different interpretations about the meanings of three frequently encountered accommodations: (a) extended time, (b) scribing, and (c) preferential seating.

If one term (e.g., *preferential seating*) refers to a range of classroom changes, it is understandable that teachers could be confused about how to accurately implement a particular accommodation. To ensure that students with disabilities have effective access to learning, teams must be explicit in selecting and describing the accommodations deemed necessary.

Guidelines for Writing Explicit Accommodations

Neither IDEA nor Section 504 is specific about how to select accommodations. Individualized education program teams have little formal advice about this essential decision for assessment (Edgemon, Jablonski, & Lloyd, 2006), let alone instruction. This important element of an educational plan appears to be very perplexing.

To reduce the confusion of ambiguous accommodations, a set of guidelines for selecting and writing explicit accommodations provides a concrete plan to increase educational access. Built on a model proposed by Ofiesh, Hughes, and Scott (2004) for selecting assessment accommodations for postsecondary students with learning disabilities, these guidelines include the following five steps: (a) state the disability, (b) describe the educational impact of the disability, (c) consider upcoming educational tasks, (d) identify barriers related to the disability, (e) write unambiguous accommodations. Table 1 demonstrates these steps for Ed (the student with an emotional/behavioral disorder) and Lydia (the student with a specific learning disability in written language), highlighted at the beginning of this article.

Step 1: State the Disability

Each IEP includes the name of the student's disability. Use this as a beginning point to discuss accommodations, anchoring the conversation in issues of disability and access.

Step 2: Describe the Educational Impact of the Disability

Describe the characteristics of the disability that affect the student's education. The audience is general education teachers, parents, and students. Tell the reader exactly how the student's disability impacts his or her school experience. What functional difference does the disability make? What about the disability makes learning challenging?

Consider each student as an individual rather than by category. This is especially important because some disabilities, such as health impairments, emotional/ behavioral disabilities, and learning disabilities, include an array of disorders. Use descriptions rather than disability labels or academic jargon (e.g., *processing disorder*) that might not be clear to parents or general education teachers.

Teams would be wise to also consider a student's areas of strength as well as how cultural, linguistic, or ethnicity characteristics influence education. Such student characteristics may be important as the team describes the disability and selects accommodations.

Step 3: Consider Upcoming Educational Tasks

Although some disability characteristics might remain relatively constant (e.g., level of hearing or visual acuity), curriculum expectations change across grades. Although students are not expected to read fluently in kindergarten, they are expected to use reading as a tool in later grades. Young children participate in short, structured tasks; older students will be required to manage their time to accomplish longer tasks in a range of subject areas.

In collaboration with general education colleagues, educational activities the student will encounter during the duration of the IEP should be reviewed. Understanding the curriculum expectations for the next school year prepares the team to decide which barriers must be addressed (Bolt & Thurlow, 2004).

Step 4: Identify Barriers Related to the Disability

It is tempting to discuss accommodations as generalities, seeking whatever might help the student do better in class. However, if the goal is to level the playing field, the team's task is to locate the bumps in that field.

Before accommodations are selected, it is essential to explore situations in which the student's disability blocks equal access to upcoming educational activities (Ysseldyke et al., 2001). Information from the previous three steps will help identify the barriers that must be addressed. These discussions are good opportunities to build on the respective strengths of educators and therapists.

Step 5: Write Unambiguous Accommodations

Once a barrier is identified, it is time to write an explicit, unambiguous accommodation that levels the playing field. Describe exactly the actions the team believes must be taken to remove

Table 1 Writing Explicit Accommodations for Ed and Lydia

Step	Ed	Lydia
1. State the disability	Emotional/behavioral disorder	Specific learning disability in written language
2. Describe the educational impact of the disability	Possesses strong content knowledge Has difficulty concentrating when distracted by thoughts and concerns related to traumatic life events Anxiety sometimes triggered by reading material content Thoughts can return to home life if Ed is not engaged with a topic Can refocus after meeting with his counselor for discussion and/or time out Without support, Ed's anxiety can cause him to act out in class	Reading and comprehending grade-level material are areas of strength Responds readily and accurately to oral questions and written multiple-choice tests Struggles to put thoughts on paper in conventional sentences Written ideas often presented in phrases or incomplete sentences Works very slowly when required to take class notes or write short answer items or essays
3. Consider upcoming educational tasks	In fourth grade, Ed and Lydia will be expected to read longer text selections independently and interpret them; write essays and short reports; use text material in mathematics assignments; and begin to take notes in class. In this school, fourth-grade students are not required to plan time to write semester-long projects or conduct extensive Internet and library searches on specified topics.	
4. Identify barriers related to the disability	Increased amount of independent work may make Ed vulnerable to being distracted by his internal concerns Specially designed instruction will help Ed learn to manage this anxiety During this period, Ed will need his counselor to help him relax and focus Ed and his teacher have agreed on a silent signal he can use to indicate his need to see the counselor It would be helpful if he could leave the room without attracting attention to himself	Increased amount of written work and note taking will be a challenge given Lydia's written language disability Specially designed instruction will focus on improving written language skills During this period, Lydia will need to have some way to get written class notes and also to record her responses to class tasks and tests
5. Write unambiguous accommodations	Seating near the classroom door so Ed can unobtrusively leave to meet with his counselor	Seating near helpful peers who will share class notes Seating in a group of helpful peers who will scribe group assignments Easy access to a computer equipped with voice-to-print software

barriers related to the impact of the disability. Precisely where should this student sit if this change makes learning more accessible?

Remember that the goal is not to change expectations but to help the student participate without the effects of the disability. Accommodations are not intended to make learning easier but to make learning accessible.

Team members, including students and parents, should discuss exactly what each understands is meant by every proposed accommodation. Reword, or define, terms that are unique to a specific grade or school. This process ensures the meaning of each accommodation is shared. As can be seen from the examples for Ed and Lydia, explicit accommodations do not need to be lengthy, just specific.

Table 2   Explicit Alternatives to Preferential Seating

Disability Type	Impact of the Disability	Explicit Seating Accommodation
Attention	Distracted by classroom activity but responds to quieter environment	With easy access to carrel
	Easily drawn away from tasks, into the conversation/activities of others	Desk set apart from student clusters
	Easily distracted by sounds and movement	Away from the window
	Distracted by the sounds and activity of students at the computer	Away from the computer
	Unable to sit in one seat for more than a short period of time	In either of two assigned desks
	Responds well to regular reinforcement for on-task behavior	Close to adult administering reinforcement
	Has difficulty attending in large group instruction	Near the center of instruction
Emotional/behavioral	Easily influenced by the behavior of others	Near positive role models
	Makes uncontrollable sounds and movement	In location where this behavior does not distract others
	Sometimes teased by others because of unusual behavior	Away from provocative peers
	Bolts from room	Away from the door
	Utilizes counseling services to manage bursts of anxiety	Near the door, for quiet departure
	Fears unexpected interactions with others	With back to wall
Academic	Has significant difficulty decoding; makes good use of computer software that reads print	Near the computer, with earphones so voice output does not disturb others
	Can express thoughts orally but has difficulty doing so in writing due to decoding challenges	With access to scribe, in a location where their interaction does not affect other students
	Can express thoughts orally but has difficulty doing so in writing due to slow writing speed	Near peers who will provide class notes and record group discussions
	Is developing skill using voice-to-print software (rather than a scribe) for written tasks	Near the computer
Health	Develops allergic reaction to dust and pollen	Away from the window
	Develops allergic reaction to dust	Away from heating vent
	Needs quick access to lavatory on a frequent basic	Near the door
	Needs larger amount of room to move with walker	So that moving to and from the seat is not blocked by physical obstacles
Sensory	Has difficulty clearly seeing objects more than 5 feet away	Near the center of instruction, within the range of visual acuity
	Supplements available hearing through lip-reading	Near the center of instruction
	Uses a hearing aid to enhance acuity	Away from doors, windows, and noisy vent

Explicit Alternatives to Preferential Seating

The prevalence of some ambiguous accommodations can seem overwhelming. Teams may need help replacing the ambiguous with the explicit; it takes practice to generate specific descriptions. An extensive array of explicit alternatives for one common, ambiguous accommodation is contained in Table 2. Similar charts can be created for other accommodations that have multiple interpretations.

Several disability characteristics—attention, behavior, academic, health, and sensory—are listed in Table 2. Each of these might require different seating. The impact of the disability characteristic is described briefly and paired with an explicit seating accommodation that enhances access.

Although not every student requires preferential seating, this accommodation was selected because it generated the largest number of conflicting interpretations from educators in one study (Byrnes, in press). Notice that there are six different descriptions of how attention difficulties can impact the school experience. Each calls for a particular interpretation of preferential seating.

The importance of eliminating ambiguity is apparent throughout Table 2. Some preferred seats are very different from others. One student will need to be close to the door, while another must be seated away from the door. Using the ambiguous phrase *preferential seating* might actually increase a student's difficulties instead of increasing access.

Each explicit alternative increases the likelihood that teachers will know precisely where the student should sit. Linking an explicit accommodation to disability characteristics will help everyone understand how the accommodation removes a barrier to learning.

Maximize the Value of Explicit Accommodations

The value of explicit accommodations is not limited to clarity in the IEP meeting. Their effectiveness is seen in daily implementation of a student's plan. Team members can adopt four practices to increase the likelihood that accommodations will be implemented as intended. These require attention to (a) the number of accommodations selected, (b) specificity about use of accommodations, (c) the process for reviewing accommodations, and (d) special considerations during transitions.

Keep Lists of Accommodations Concise

Individualized education programs often contain accommodations that some think might be good to have rather than what is appropriate to the student's disability. Remember that accommodations are legal entities. Educators are mandated to implement them. Explicit, functional accommodations targeting the impact of the disability are easier for people to understand, remember, and implement.

Specify When an Accommodation Is Needed

Some IEPs include statements that a particular accommodation should be provided "as needed." Teachers, parents, and students might disagree about what is needed. Be sure to write exactly what must be done to ensure the student has access. Relying on others to decide when an accommodation is needed invites confusion.

Review Accommodations Regularly

Each time the IEP is updated, consider whether a student's accommodations remain appropriate. Students change and so does curriculum. Specially designed instruction might have helped a student attain skills, making a current accommodation unnecessary in the next year. For example, once a student has learned the skill of taking notes, there may be no need for a note taker as an accommodation. In contrast, upcoming curriculum demands might require different accommodations. Lydia did not need a note taker in early grades but does require this accommodation later in school, when students are expected to use this skill.

While deliberating appropriate accommodations, seek those that promote independence so the student becomes more self-reliant. For example, using voice-to-print software might replace scribing by an adult.

Clarify during Transitions

Although explicit accommodations communicate clearly what needs to happen to ensure access, it is important to review expectations with new teachers, especially if the student transfers schools, even within districts. Similarly, if a new student's IEP contains an accommodation that seems ambiguous, take the time to clarify its intent with the teachers who wrote the IEP. This small investment of time will ensure that everyone understands what needs to be done to provide access.

Summary

Instructional accommodations are intended by law to ensure that students with disabilities have equal access to education. They encompass the areas of presentation, response, setting, and timing/scheduling. There is little formal guidance about selecting and communicating the accommodations that will level the playing field and create this access.

Compounding the problem, terms used for accommodations can be interpreted in multiple ways. *Preferential seating* was used as one example of an ambiguous accommodation. Teachers have interpreted this one term to signal a wide range of locations, including the front of the room, the back of the room, and away from windows and heating vents. Educators on the same team could be implementing different versions of preferential seating. Choosing the wrong interpretation could unintentionally create more barriers than it removes.

Educators can reduce ambiguity and confusion by writing explicit, functionally based accommodations. A five-step set of guidelines is described and illustrated for two students with different disabilities.

Steps 1 and 2 of the guidelines begin with the disability. Special education teachers can start by describing characteristics that affect classroom learning and assessment. Parents, students, and other educators can contribute their observations.

The next two steps of the guidelines focus on the curriculum in place for the duration of the IEP. In Step 3, general education teachers lead with their knowledge of upcoming expectations in curriculum and instruction. In Step 4, team members collaborate to identify barriers that might arise when the characteristics of the student's disability encounter the expected curriculum and instruction.

In Step 5 of the guidelines, team members write an unambiguous accommodation. This describes exactly what should be done to level the playing field and increase student access.

Reducing ambiguity by applying these guidelines helps all team members, including parents and students, expect the same action from each chosen accommodation. This shared understanding increases the likelihood that the team's intentions will be implemented. When this occurs, students with disabilities have the best opportunity to demonstrate what they know and can do.

References

Americans with Disabilities Act, 42, U.S.C.A. § 12101 *et seq.* (1990).

Bolt, S. E., & Thurlow, M. L. (2004). Five of the most frequently allowed testing accommodations in state policy: Synthesis of research. *Remedial and Special Education, 25,* 141–152.

Byrnes, M. (in press). Educators' interpretations of ambiguous accommodations. *Remedial and Special Education.*

Edgemon, E. A., Jablonski, B. R., & Lloyd, J. W. (2006). Large-scale assessments: A teacher's guide to making decisions about accommodations. *TEACHING Exceptional Children, 38*(3), 6–11.

Fletcher, J. M., Francis, D. J., Boudousquie, A., Copeland, K., Young, V., Kalinowski, S., et al. (2006). Effects of accommodations on high-stakes testing for students with reading disabilities. *Exceptional Children, 72,* 136–150.

Fuchs, L. S., & Fuchs, D. (2001). Helping teachers formulate sound test accommodation decisions for students with learning disabilities. *Learning Disabilities Research & Practice, 16,* 174–181.

Individuals with Disabilities Education Improvement Act of 2004, 20 U.S.C.A. § 1400 *et seq.* (2005).

Level playing field. (n.d.). Dictionary.com *unabridged (v 1.0.1).* Retrieved September 14, 2006, from http://dictionary.reference .com/search?q=level playing field&r=66

Maccini, P., & Gagnon, J. C. (2006). Mathematics instructional practices and assessment accommodations by secondary special and general educators. *Exceptional Children, 72,* 217–234.

No Child Left Behind Act of 2001, 20 USC § 6301 *et seq.* (2002).

Ofiesh, N. S., Hughes, C., & Scott, S. S. (2004). Extended test time and postsecondary students with learning disabilities: A model for decision making. *Learning Disabilities Research & Practice, 19,* 57–70.

Parker, B. (2006). Instructional adaptations for students with learning disabilities: An action research project. *Intervention in School and Clinic, 42,* 56–58.

Section 504, Rehabilitation Act, 29 U.S.C.A. § 794 (1973).

Thompson, S. J., Lazarus, S. S., Thurlow, M. L., & Clapper, A. T. (2005). *The role of accommodations in educational accountability systems* (Topical Review 8). College Park, MD: Institute for the Study of Exceptional Children and Youth.

Thompson, S. J., Morse, A. B., Sharpe, M., & Hall, S. (2005). *Accommodations manual: How to select, administer, and evaluate use of accommodations for instruction and assessment of students with disabilities* (2nd ed.). Retrieved June 22, 2006, from http://osepideasthatwork.org/toolkit/ accommodations.asp

Thurlow, M. L., & Bolt, S. E. (2001). *Empirical support for accommodations most often allowed in state policy* (Synthesis Report 41). Minneapolis: University of Minnesota, National Center on Educational Outcomes.

Ysseldyke, J., Thurlow, M., Bielinski, J., House, A., Moody, M., & Haigh, J. (2001). The relationship between instructional and assessment accommodations in an inclusive state accountability system. *Journal of Learning Disabilities, 34,* 212–220.

MARYANN BYRNES, EdD, is an associate professor in the Graduate College of Education at the University of Massachusetts Boston and immediate past president of the Massachusetts Council for Exceptional Children. Her current research interests include special education policy, assessment, and accommodations. Address: MaryAnn Byrnes, University of Massachusetts Boston, Graduate College of Education, 100 Morrissey Blvd., Boston, MA 02125; e-mail: maryann.byrnes@ umb.edu.

ADHD and the SUD in Adolescents

Timothy E. Wilens

Overlap between ADHD and SUD

The overlap between Attention Deficit Hyperactivity Disorder (ADHD) and alcohol or drug abuse (referred to here as substance use disorders [SUD]) in adolescents has been an area of increasing clinical, research, and public health interest. ADHD onsets in early childhood and affects from 6 to 9 percent of children and adolescents worldwide (Anderson, et al., 1987) and up to 5 percent of adults (Kessler, in press). Substance use disorders (SUD) usually onset in adolescence or early adulthood and affect between 10 to 30 percent of U.S. adults, and a less defined, but sizable number of juveniles (Kessler, 2004). The study of comorbidity between SUD and ADHD is relevant to both research and clinical practice in developmental pediatrics, psychology, and psychiatry with implications for diagnosis, prognosis, treatment, and healthcare delivery.

In adolescent studies incorporating structured psychiatric diagnostic interviews assessing ADHD and other disorders in substance abusing groups have indicated that from one third to one-half of adolescents with SUD have ADHD (DeMilio, 1989; Milin, et al., 1991). Data largely ascertained from adult groups with SUD also show an earlier onset and more severe course of SUD associated with ADHD (Carroll & Rounsaville, 1993; Levin & Evans, 2001).

ADHD as a Risk Factor for SUD

The association of ADHD and SUD is particularly compelling from a developmental perspective as ADHD manifests itself earlier than SUD; therefore, SUD as a risk factor for ADHD is unlikely. Thus, it is important to evaluate to what extent ADHD is a precursor of SUD. Prospective studies of ADHD children have provided evidence that the groups with conduct or bipolar disorders co-occurring with ADHD have the poorest outcome with respect to developing SUD and major morbidity (Biederman, et al., 1997; Mannuzza, et al., 1993). As part of an ongoing prospective study of ADHD, differences in the risk for SUD in ADHD adolescents (mean age 15 years) compared to non-ADHD controls were found. The controls were accounted for by comorbid conduct or bipolar disorders (Biederman, et al., 1997); however, we also show that the age of risk for SUD onset in non-comorbid ADHD is approximately 17 years in girls and 19 years old for boys (Biederman, et al., 2006a; Milberger, et al., 1997b).

SUD Pathways Associated with ADHD

An increasing body of literature shows an intriguing association between ADHD and cigarette smoking. It has been previously reported that ADHD was a significant predictor for early initiation of cigarette smoking (before age 15) and that conduct and mood disorders with ADHD put youth at particularly high risk for early onset smoking (Milberger, et al., 1997a) (*see Figure below*). Data also suggest that one-half of ADHD smokers go on to later SUD (Biederman, et al., 2006b); not surprising given that not only does smoking lead to peer group pressures and availability of illicit substances; but that nicotine exposure may make the brain more susceptible to later behavioral disorders and SUD (Trauth, et al., 2000). Furthermore, nicotinic modulating agents are increasingly being evaluated for the treatment of ADHD (Wilens, et al., 2006). Of interest, very recent NIDA-funded prospective data suggests that stimulant treatment of

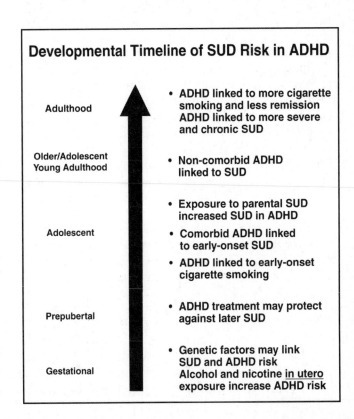

Developmental Timeline of SUD Risk in ADHD

Adulthood
- ADHD linked to more cigarette smoking and less remission ADHD linked to more severe and chronic SUD

Older/Adolescent Young Adulthood
- Non-comorbid ADHD linked to SUD

Adolescent
- Exposure to parental SUD increased SUD in ADHD
- Comorbid ADHD linked to early-onset SUD
- ADHD linked to early-onset cigarette smoking

Prepubertal
- ADHD treatment may protect against later SUD

Gestational
- Genetic factors may link SUD and ADHD risk Alcohol and nicotine in utero exposure increase ADHD risk

ADHD reduces not only the time to onset but also the incidence of cigarette smoking (Monuteaux, et al., 2004).

The precise mechanism(s) mediating the expression of SUD in ADHD remains to be seen. The self-medication hypothesis is compelling in ADHD considering that the disorder is chronic and often associated with demoralization and failure, factors frequently associated with SUD in adolescents. Moreover, we recently found that among substance abusing adolescents with and without ADHD, ADHD adolescents reported using substances more frequently to attenuate their mood and to help them sleep. No evidence of differences in types of substances has emerged between ADHD and nonADHD substance abusing teens (Biederman, et al., 1997). In addition, the potential importance of self-medication needs to be tempered against more systematic data showing the strongest relationship between ADHD and SUD being mediating by the presence of comorbidity in addition to familial contributions such as exposure to parental SUD during vulnerable developmental phases.

Diagnosis and Treatment Guidelines

Evaluation and treatment of comorbid ADHD and SUD should be part of a plan in which consideration is given to all aspects of the teen's life. Any intervention in this group should follow a careful evaluation of the adolescent including psychiatric, addiction, social, cognitive, educational, and family evaluations. A thorough history of substance use should be obtained including past and current usage and treatments. Although no specific guidelines exist for evaluating the patient with active SUD, experience has shown that at least one month of abstinence is useful in accurately and reliably assessing for ADHD symptoms. Semi-structured psychiatric interviews or validated rating scales of ADHD are invaluable aids for the systematic diagnostic assessments of this group.

The treatment needs of individuals with SUD and ADHD need to be considered simultaneously; however, the SUD needs to be addressed initially (Riggs, 1998). If the SUD is active, immediate attention needs to be paid to *stabilization of the addiction(s)*. Depending on the severity and duration of the SUD, adolescents may require inpatient treatment. Self help groups offer a helpful treatment modality for many with SUD. In tandem with addiction treatment, SUD adolescents with ADHD require intervention(s) for the ADHD (and if applicable, comorbid psychiatric disorders).

Medication serves an important role in reducing the symptoms of ADHD and other concurrent psychiatric disorders. Effective agents for adolescents with ADHD include the stimulants, noradrenergic agents, and catecholaminergic antidepressants (Wilens, et al., 2002). Recent findings from a metanalysis of 10 studies of open and controlled trials suggest that medications used in adolescents and adults with ADHD plus SUD have only a meager effect on the ADHD, but have little effect on substance use or cravings (Riggs, et al., 2004; Schubiner, et al., 2002; Wilens, et al., 2005). Of interest, no evidence exists that treating ADHD pharmacologically through an active SUD

exacerbates the SUD—consistent with work of Grabowski et al. (2004) who have used stimulants to block cocaine and amphetamine abuse. Not surprisingly, work by Volkow et al. (1998) have demonstrated important differences between binding at the dopamine transporter between methylphenidate and cocaine resulting in very different abuse liabilities.

Summary

There is a strong literature supporting a relationship between ADHD and SUD. Both family-genetic and self-medication influences may be operational in the development and continuation of SUD in ADHD. Adolescents with ADHD and SUD require multimodal intervention incorporating addiction and mental health treatment. Pharmacotherapy in ADHD and SUD individuals needs to take into consideration timing, misuse and diversion liability, potential drug interactions, and compliance concerns.

While the existing literature has provided important information on the relationship of ADHD and SUD, it also points to a number of areas in need of further study. The mechanism by which untreated ADHD leads to SUD, as well as the risk reduction of ADHD treatment on cigarette smoking and SUD needs to be better understood. Given the prevalence and major morbidity and impairment caused by SUD and ADHD, prevention and treatment strategies for these adolescents need be further developed and evaluated.

References

Anderson, J.C., Williams, S., McGee, R., & Silva, P.A. (1987). DSM III disorders in preadolescent children. Prevalence in a large sample from the general population. *Arch Gen Psychiatry* 44: 69–76.

Biederman J., Monuteaux M., Mick, E. et al. (2006a). Young Adult Outcome of Attention Deficit Hyperactivity Disorder: A Controlled 10 year Prospective Follow-Up Study. *Psychol Med* 36: 167–179.

Biederman, J., Monuteaux, M., Mick, E., et al. (2006b). Is Cigarette Smoking a Gateway Drug to Subsequent Alcohol and Illicit Drug Use Disorders? A Controlled Study of Youths with and without ADHD. *Biol Psychiatry* 59: 258–64.

Biederman, J., Wilens, T. & Mick, E. et al. (1997). Is ADHD a risk for psychoactive substance use disorder? Findings from a four year follow-up study. *J Am Acad Child Adolesc Psychiatry* 36: 21–29.

Carroll, K.M. & Rounsaville, B.J. (1993). History and significance of childhood attention deficit disorder in treatment-seeking cocaine abusers. *Comrpehensive Psychiatry* 34: 75–82.

DeMilio, L. (1989). Psychiatric syndromes in adolescent substance abusers. *Am J Psychiatry* 146: 1212–1214.

Grabowski, J., Shearer, J., Merrill, J. & Negus, S.S. (2004). Agonist-like, replacement pharmacotherapy for stimulant abuse and dependence. *Addict Behav* 29: 1439–1464.

Kessler, R.C. (in press). A recent replication of the National Comorbidity Study estimating the prevalence of adult ADHD among persons 18–44 in the US. *Psychol Med.*

Kessler, R.C. (2004). The epidemiology of dual diagnosis. *Biol Psychiatry* 56: 730–7.

Levin, F.R. & Evans, S.M. (2001). Diagnostic and treatment issues in comorbid substance abuse and adult attention-deficit hyperacity disorder. *Psychiatric Annals* 31: 303–312.

Mannuzza, S., Klein, R.G., Bessler, A., Malloy, P. & LaPadula, M. (1993). Adult outcome of hyperactive boys: Educational achievement, occupational rank, and psychiatric status. *Arch Gen Psychiatry* 50: 565–576.

Milberger, S., Biederman, J., Faraone, S., Chen, L. & Jones, J. (1997a). ADHD is associated with early initiation of cigarette smoking in children and adolescents. *J Am Acad Child Adolesc Psychiatry* 36: 37–44.

Milberger, S., Biederman, J., Faraone, S., Wilens, T. & Chu, M. (1997b). Associations between ADHD and psychoactive substance use disorders: Findings from a longitudinal study of high-risk siblings of ADHD children. *Am J Addict* 6: 318–329.

Milin, R., Halikas, J.A., Meller, J.E. & Morse, C. (1991). Psychopathology among substance abusing juvenile offenders. *J Am Acad Child Adolesc Psychiatry* 30: 569–574.

Riggs, P.D. (1998). Clinical approach to treatment of ADHD in adolescents with substance use disorders and conduct disorder. *J Am Acad Child Adolesc Psychiatry* 37: 331–332.

Riggs, P.D., Hall, S.K., Mikulich-Gilbertson, S.K., Lohman, M. & Kayser, A. (2004). A Randomized Controlled Trial of Pemoline for Attention-Deficit/Hyperactivity Disorder in Substance-Abusing Adolescents. *J Am Acad Child Adolesc Psychiatry* 43: 420–429.

Schubiner, H., Saules, K.K. & Arfken, C.L. et al. (2002). Double-blind placebo-controlled trial of methylphenidate in the treatment of adult ADHD patients with comorbid cocaine dependence. *Exp Clin Psychopharmacol* 10: 286–94.

Trauth, J.A., Seidler, F.J. & Slotkin, T.A. (2000). Persistent and delayed behavioral changes after nicotine treatment in adolescent rats. *Brain Res* 880: 167–72.

Volkow, N., Wang, G. & Fowler, J. et al. (1998). Dopamine transporter occupancies in the human brain induced by therapeutic doses of oral methylphenidate. *Am J Psychiatry* 155: 1325–1331.

Wilens T., Monuteaux M., Snyder L., Moore B.A. (2005). The clinical dilemma of using medications in substance abusing adolescents and adults with ADHD: What does the literature tell us? *J Child Adolesc Psychopharmacol* 15: 787–98.

Wilens T., Verlinden M.H., Adler L.A., Wozniak P.A. & West S.A. (2006). ABT-089, A Neuronal Nicotinic Receptor Partial Agonist, for the Treatment of Attention-Deficit/Hyperactivity Disorder in Adults: Results of a Pilot Study. *Biol Psychiatry* 59: 1065–70.

Wilens, T.E., Biederman, J. & Spencer, T.J. (2002). Attention Deficit/ Hyperactivity Disorder across the Lifespan. *Ann Rev Med* 53: 113–131.

DR. TIMOTHY E. WILENS is Associate Professor of Psychiatry at Harvard Medical School in Boston, Massachusetts. In addition, he is Director of the Substance Abuse Services in the Pediatric Psychopharmacology Clinic at Massachusetts General Hospital.

Dr. Wilens earned his BS in literature, science, and arts at the University of Michigan Honors College, and his MD at the University of Michigan Medical School in Ann Arbor. His peer reviewed articles concerning the relationship of Attention Deficit Hyperactivity Disorder (ADHD), bipolar disorder, and substance abuse and related topics number more than 170. Dr. Wilens has also published more than 65 book chapters, and 225 abstracts and presentations for national and international scientific meetings. He may be contacted at Twilens@ partners.org.

Acknowledgments—This research was supported by NIH BOI DA14419 and K24 DA016264 to TW.

Trick Question

A liberal 'hoax' turns out to be true.

MICHAEL FUMENTO

It's both right-wing and vast, but it's not a conspiracy. Actually, it's more of an anti-conspiracy. The subject is Attention Deficit Disorder (ADD) and Attention Deficit Hyperactivity Disorder (ADHD), closely related ailments (henceforth referred to in this article simply as ADHD). Rush Limbaugh declares it "may all be a hoax." Francis Fukuyama devotes much of one chapter in his latest book, *Our Posthuman Future,* to attacking Ritalin, the top-selling drug used to treat ADHD. Columnist Thomas Sowell writes, "The motto used to be: 'Boys will be boys.' Today, the motto seems to be: 'Boys will be medicated.'" And Phyllis Schlafly explains, "The old excuse of 'my dog ate my homework' has been replaced by 'I got an ADHD diagnosis.'" A March 2002 article in *The Weekly Standard* summed up the conservative line on ADHD with this rhetorical question: "Are we really prepared to redefine childhood as an ailment, and medicate it until it goes away?"

Many conservative writers, myself included, have criticized the growing tendency to pathologize every undesirable behavior—especially where children are concerned. But, when it comes to ADHD, this skepticism is misplaced. As even a cursory examination of the existing literature or, for that matter, simply talking to the parents and teachers of children with ADHD reveals, the condition is real, and it is treatable. And, if you don't believe me, you can ask conservatives who've come face to face with it themselves.

Myth: ADHD Isn't a Real Disorder

The most common argument against ADHD on the right is also the simplest: It doesn't exist. Conservative columnist Jonah Goldberg thus reduces ADHD to "ants in the pants." Sowell equates it with "being bored and restless." Fukuyama protests, "No one has been able to identify a cause of ADD/ADHD. It is a pathology recognized only by its symptoms." And a conservative columnist approvingly quotes Thomas Armstrong, Ritalin opponent and author, when he declares, "ADD is a disorder that cannot be authoritatively identified in the same way as polio, heart disease or other legitimate illnesses."

The Armstrong and Fukuyama observations are as correct as they are worthless. "Half of all medical disorders are diagnosed without benefit of a lab procedure," notes Dr. Russell Barkley, professor of psychology at the College of Health Professionals at the Medical University of South Carolina. "Where are the lab tests for headaches and multiple sclerosis and Alzheimer's?" he asks. "Such a standard would virtually eliminate all mental disorders."

Often the best diagnostic test for an ailment is how it responds to treatment. And, by that standard, it doesn't get much more real than ADHD. The beneficial effects of administering stimulants to treat the disorder were first reported in 1937. And today medication for the disorder is reported to be 75 to 90 percent successful. "In our trials it was close to ninety percent," says Dr. Judith Rapoport, director of the National Institute of Mental Health's Child Psychiatry Branch, who has published about 100 papers on ADHD. "This means there was a significant difference in the children's ability to function in the classroom or at home."

Additionally, epidemiological evidence indicates that ADHD has a powerful genetic component. University of Colorado researchers have found that a child whose identical twin has the disorder is between eleven and 18 times more likely to also have it than is a non-twin sibling. For these reasons, the American Psychiatric Association (APA), American Medical Association, American Academy of Pediatrics, American Academy of Child Adolescent Psychiatry, the surgeon general's office, and other major medical bodies all acknowledge ADHD as both real and treatable.

Myth: ADHD Is Part of a Feminist Conspiracy to Make Little Boys More Like Little Girls

Many conservatives observe that boys receive ADHD diagnoses in much higher numbers than girls and find in this evidence of a feminist conspiracy. (This, despite the fact that genetic diseases are often heavily weighted more toward one gender or the other.) Sowell refers to "a growing tendency to treat boyhood as a pathological condition that requires a new three R's—repression, re-education and Ritalin." Fukuyama claims Prozac is being used to give women "more of the alpha-male feeling," while Ritalin is making boys act more like girls. "Together, the two sexes are gently nudged toward that androgynous median personality. . . that is the current politically correct outcome in American society." George Will, while acknowledging that Ritalin can be helpful, nonetheless writes of the "androgyny agenda" of "drugging children because they are behaving like children, especially boy children." Anti-Ritalin conservatives frequently invoke Christina Hoff Sommers's best-selling 2000 book, *The War Against Boys.* You'd never know that the drug isn't mentioned in her book—or why.

"Originally I was going to have a chapter on it," Sommers tells me. "It seemed to fit the thesis." What stopped her was both her survey of the medical literature and her own empirical findings. Of one child she personally came to know she says, "He was utterly miserable, as was everybody around him. The drugs saved his life."

Myth: ADHD Is Part of the Public School System's Efforts to Warehouse Kids Rather than to Discipline and Teach Them

"No doubt life is easier for teachers when everyone sits around quietly," writes Sowell. Use of ADHD drugs is "in the school's interest to deal with behavioral and discipline problems [because] it's so easy to use Ritalin to make kids compliant: to get them to sit down, shut up, and do what they're told," declares Schlafly. The word "zombies" to describe children under the effects of Ritalin is tossed around more than in a B-grade voodoo movie.

Kerri Houston, national field director for the American Conservative Union and the mother of two ADHD children on medication, agrees with much of the criticism of public schools. "But don't blame ADHD on crummy curricula and lazy teachers," she says. "If you've worked with these children, you know they have a serious neurological problem." In any case, Ritalin, when taken as prescribed, hardly stupefies children. To the extent the medicine works, it simply turns ADHD children into normal children. "ADHD is like having thirty televisions on at one time, and the medicine turns off twenty-nine so you can concentrate on the one," Houston describes. "This zombie stuff drives me nuts! My kids are both as lively and as fun as can be."

Myth: Parents Who Give Their Kids Anti-ADHD Drugs Are Merely Doping up Problem Children

Limbaugh calls ADHD "the perfect way to explain the inattention, incompetence, and inability of adults to control their kids." Addressing parents directly, he lectures, "It helped you mask your own failings by doping up your children to calm them down."

Such charges blast the parents of ADHD kids into high orbit. That includes my Hudson Institute colleague (and fellow conservative) Mona Charen, the mother of an eleven-year-old with the disorder. "I have two non-ADHD children, so it's not a matter of parenting technique," says Charen. "People without such children have no idea what it's like. I can tell the difference between boyish high spirits and pathological hyperactivity. . . . These kids bounce off the walls. Their lives are chaos; their rooms are chaos. And nothing replaces the drugs."

Barkley and Rapoport say research backs her up. Randomized, controlled studies in both the United States and Sweden have tried combining medication with behavioral interventions and then dropped either one or the other. For those trying to go on without medicine, "the behavioral interventions maintained nothing," Barkley says. Rapoport concurs: "Unfortunately, behavior modification doesn't seem to help with ADHD." (Both doctors are quick to add that ADHD is often accompanied by other disorders that are treatable through behavior modification in tandem with medicine.)

Myth: Ritalin Is "Kiddie Cocaine"

One of the paradoxes of conservative attacks on Ritalin is that the drug is alternately accused of turning children into brain-dead zombies and of making them Mach-speed cocaine junkies. Indeed, Ritalin is widely disparaged as "kiddie cocaine." Writers who have sought to lump the two drugs together include Schlafly, talk-show host and columnist Armstrong Williams, and others whom I hesitate to name because of my longstanding personal relationships with them.

Mary Eberstadt wrote the "authoritative" Ritalin-cocaine piece for the April 1999 issue of *Policy Review,* then owned by the Heritage Foundation. The article, "Why Ritalin Rules," employs the word "cocaine" no fewer than twelve times. Eberstadt quotes from a 1995 Drug Enforcement Agency (DEA) background paper declaring methylphenidate, the active ingredient in Ritalin, "a central nervous system (CNS) stimulant [that] shares many of the pharmacological effects of amphetamine, methamphetamine, and cocaine." Further, it "produces behavioral, psychological, subjective, and reinforcing effects similar to those of d-amphetamine including increases in rating of euphoria, drug liking and activity, and decreases in sedation." Add to this the fact that the Controlled Substances Act lists it as a Schedule II drug, imposing on it the same tight prescription controls as morphine, and Ritalin starts to sound spooky indeed.

What Eberstadt fails to tell readers is that the DEA description concerns methylphenidate *abuse.* It's tautological to say abuse is harmful. According to the DEA, the drugs in question are comparable when "administered the same way at comparable doses." But ADHD stimulants, when taken as prescribed, are neither administered in the same way as cocaine nor at comparable doses. "What really counts," says Barkley, "is the speed with which the drugs enter and clear the brain. With cocaine, because it's snorted, this happens tremendously quickly, giving users the characteristic addictive high." (Ever seen anyone pop a cocaine tablet?) Further, he says, "There's no evidence anywhere in literature of [Ritalin's] addictiveness when taken as prescribed." As to the Schedule II listing, again this is because of the potential for it to fall into the hands of abusers, not because of its effects on persons for whom it is prescribed. Ritalin and the other anti-ADHD drugs, says Barkley, "are the safest drugs in all of psychiatry." (And they may be getting even safer: A new medicine just released called Strattera represents the first true non-stimulant ADHD treatment.)

Indeed, a study just released in the journal *Pediatrics* found that children who take Ritalin or other stimulants to control ADHD cut their risk of future substance abuse by 50 percent compared with untreated ADHD children. The lead author speculated that "by treating ADHD you're reducing the demoralization that accompanies this disorder, and you're improving the academic functioning and well-being of adolescents and young adults during the critical times when substance abuse starts."

Myth: Ritalin Is Overprescribed across the Country

Some call it "the Ritalin craze." In *The Weekly Standard,* Melana Zyla Vickers informs us that "Ritalin use has exploded," while Eberstadt writes that "Ritalin use more than doubled in the first half of the decade alone, [and] the number of schoolchildren taking the drug may now, by some estimates, be approaching the *4 million mark.*"

A report in the January 2003 issue of *Archives of Pediatrics and Adolescent Medicine* did find a large increase in the use of ADHD medicines from 1987 to 1996, an increase that doesn't appear to be slowing. Yet nobody thinks it's a problem that routine screening for high blood pressure has produced a big increase in the use of hypertension medicine. "Today, children suffering from ADHD are simply less likely to slip through the cracks," says Dr. Sally Satel, a psychiatrist, AEI fellow, and author of *PC, M.D.: How Political Correctness Is Corrupting Medicine.*

Satel agrees that some community studies, by the standards laid down in the APA's *Diagnostic and Statistical Manual of Mental Disorders (DSM),* indicate that ADHD may often be over-diagnosed. On the other hand, she says, additional evidence shows that in some communities ADHD is *under*-diagnosed and *under*-treated. "I'm quite concerned with children who need the medication and aren't getting it," she says.

There *are* tremendous disparities in the percentage of children taking ADHD drugs when comparing small geographical areas. Psychologist Gretchen LeFever, for example, has compared the number of prescriptions in mostly white Virginia Beach, Virginia, with other, more heavily African American areas in the southeastern part of the state. Conservatives have latched onto her higher numbers—20 percent of white fifth-grade boys in Virginia Beach are being treated for ADHD—as evidence that something is horribly wrong. But others, such as Barkley, worry about the lower numbers. According to LeFever's study, black

children are only half as likely to get medication as white children. "Black people don't get the care of white people; children of well-off parents get far better care than those of poorer parents," says Barkley.

Myth: States Should Pass Laws That Restrict Schools from Recommending Ritalin

Conservative writers have expressed delight that several states, led by Connecticut, have passed or are considering laws ostensibly protecting students from schools that allegedly pass out Ritalin like candy. Representative Lenny Winkler, lead sponsor of the Connecticut measure, told *Reuters Health,* "If the diagnosis is made, and it's an appropriate diagnosis that Ritalin be used, that's fine. But I have also heard of many families approached by the school system [who are told] that their child cannot attend school if they're not put on Ritalin."

Two attorneys I interviewed who specialize in child-disability issues, including one from the liberal Bazelon Center for Mental Health Law in Washington, D.C., acknowledge that school personnel have in some cases stepped over the line. But legislation can go too far in the other direction by declaring, as Connecticut's law does, that "any school personnel [shall be prohibited] from recommending the use of psychotropic drugs for any child." The law appears to offer an exemption by declaring, "The provisions of this section shall not prohibit *school medical staff* from recommending that a child be evaluated by an appropriate medical practitioner, or prohibit school personnel from consulting with such practitioner, with the consent of the parent or guardian of such child." [Emphasis added.] But of course many, if not most, schools have perhaps one nurse on regular "staff." That nurse will have limited contact with children in the classroom situations where ADHD is likely to be most evident. And, given the wording of the statute, a teacher who believed a student was suffering from ADHD would arguably be prohibited from referring that student to the nurse. Such ambiguity is sure to have a chilling effect on any form of intervention or recommendation by school personnel. Moreover, 20-year special-education veteran Sandra Rief said in an interview with the National Education Association that "recommending medical intervention for a student's behavior could lead to personal liability issues." Teachers, in other words, could be forced to choose between what they think is best for the health of their students and the possible risk of losing not only their jobs but their personal assets as well.

"Certainly it's not within the purview of a school to say kids can't attend if they don't take drugs," says Houston. "On the other hand, certainly teachers should be able to advise parents as to problems and potential solutions.... [T]hey may see things parents don't. My own son is an angel at home but was a demon at school."

If the real worry is "take the medicine or take a hike" ultimatums, legislation can be narrowly tailored to prevent them; broad-based gag orders, such as Connecticut's, are a solution that's worse than the problem.

The Conservative Case for ADHD Drugs

There are kernels of truth to every conservative suspicion about ADHD. Who among us has not had lapses of attention? And isn't hyperactivity a normal condition of childhood when compared with deskbound adults? Certainly there are lazy teachers, warehousing schools, androgyny-pushing feminists, and far too many parents unwilling or unable to expend the time and effort to raise their children properly, even by their own standards. Where conservatives go wrong is in making ADHD a scapegoat for frustration over what we perceive as a breakdown in the order of society and family. In a column in *The Boston Herald,* Boston University Chancellor John Silber rails that Ritalin is "a classic example of a cheap fix: low-cost, simple and purely superficial."

Exactly. Like most headaches, ADHD is a neurological problem that can usually be successfully treated with a chemical. Those who recommend or prescribe ADHD medicines do not, as *The Weekly Standard* put it, see them as "discipline in pill-form." They see them as pills.

In fact, it can be argued that the use of those pills, far from being liable for or symptomatic of the Decline of the West, reflects and reinforces conservative values. For one thing, they increase personal responsibility by removing an excuse that children (and their parents) can fall back on to explain misbehavior and poor performance. "Too many psychologists and psychiatrists focus on allowing patients to justify to themselves their troubling behavior," says Satel. "But something like Ritalin actually encourages greater autonomy because you're treating a compulsion to behave in a certain way. Also, by treating ADHD, you remove an opportunity to explain away bad behavior."

Moreover, unlike liberals, who tend to downplay differences between the sexes, conservatives are inclined to believe that there are substantial physiological differences—differences such as boys' greater tendency to suffer ADHD. "Conservatives celebrate the physiological differences between boys and girls and eschew the radical-feminist notion that gender differences are created by societal pressures," says Houston regarding the fuss over the boy-girl disparity among ADHD diagnoses. "ADHD is no exception."

But, however compatible conservatism may be with taking ADHD seriously, the truth is that most conservatives remain skeptics. "I'm sure I would have been one of those smug conservatives saying it's a made-up disease," admits Charen, "if I hadn't found out the hard way." Here's hoping other conservatives find an easier route to accepting the truth.

MICHAEL FUMENTO is a senior fellow at the Hudson Institute in Washington, D.C., where he is completing his latest book, tentatively titled *Bioevolution: How Biotechnology Is Changing our World,* due this spring from Encounter Books.

UNIT 9

Severe Disabilities/ Multiple Disabilities

Unit Selections

Key Points to Consider

- Does expensive assistive technology really enhance the educational performance of students with severe disabilities/multiple handicaps? How long should it be used?

- Can students with traumatic brain injuries benefit from reentry into general education classes? How can this be accomplished successfully?

Student Website

www.mhcls.com

Internet References

Activity Ideas for Students with Severe, Profound, or Multiple Disabilities
   http://www.palaestra.com/featurestory.html
Severe and/or Multiple Disabilities
   http://www.nichcy.org/pubs/factshe/fs10txt.htm

For most of the twentieth century, children with multiple disabilities (MD) were kept hidden in their parents' homes or put into institutions. Any father or mother presenting such a child at a public school for admission was ridiculed and turned away. The Individuals with Disabilities Education Improvement Act (IDEIA) in the United States has turned this around. Such children may now be enrolled in general education classes if that is appropriate. They are entitled to a free education in the least restrictive environment that serves their needs. IDEIA has allowed millions of students, who once would have been written off as "uneducable" to be given some form of schooling.

A child placed in the category of severe or multiple disabilities (MD) has two or more co-occurring areas of exceptionality. Each child with MD is very special and very needy. Consider the physicist, Steven Hawking, who has a brilliant mind but cannot communicate or move without augmentative technology. While many MD students have some intellectual disabilities, many have normal or above normal intellect. Their impairments may be developmental disabilities, communication impairments, autism, traumatic brain injuries, emotional and behavioral disorders, visual impairments, hearing impairments, physical impairments, health impairments, or any combinations of these.

The practice of deinstitutionalization (removing individuals from hospitals and large residential institutions and keeping them in their own homes) and the legal initiatives requiring free and appropriate public education in the least restrictive environment have closed some of the cracks through which these children once fell.

Schools are attempting to provide students with severe or MD with the best education possible. Often, when schools fail, it is some condition(s) outside the school's control that share the onus of responsibility. Schools, when they fail to be effective, usually provide inadequate services due to lack of professional development. Without adequate teacher preparation, and sufficient teaching support, education of all children in inclusive classrooms becomes infeasible. Professional development must be both improved and expanded to give regularized education a leg to stand on.

The lay public is often unprepared for children with traumatic brain injuries and other forms of severe or MD to be accepted for inclusion in public schools. Advocates for the rights of disabled individuals have used the term "handicapism" to describe this prejudice and discrimination directed at disabled students. The greater the disability, the greater the evinced prejudice. A disability (not able) is not the same as a handicap (hindrance, not at an advantage). The words should not be used interchangeably. A person who is not able to do something (walk, see, hear) has a disability but does not have to be handicapped. Schools and communities may impose handicaps (hindrances) by preventing the student with the disability from functioning in an alternative way. Thus, if a student who cannot walk can instead locomote in a wheelchair, he or she is not handicapped. If a building or classroom has no ramps, however, and is inaccessible to a wheelchair user, then the school has imposed a handicap by preventing access to that particular property of the environment. If a student cannot use vocal cords to communicate, and

© Digital Vision/Punchstock/Punchstock

is provided with an augmentative and alternate communication (AAC) system, he or she is not handicapped. If a building or classroom has no power supply or other provisions for use of the AAC system, then the environment again has imposed a handicap. There are millions of ways in which properties of our environments and characteristics of our behavior prevent children with severe or multiple disabilities from functioning up to their potentialities.

Some public schools have resisted the regular education initiative (REI) that calls for general education classes rather than special education classes to be primarily responsible for the education of students with more severe and multiple disabilities. The inclusive school movement, which supports the REI, would have special education teachers become consultants, resource specialists, collaborative teachers, or itinerant teachers rather than full-time special education teachers. Most educators agree that an appropriate education for each child with a disability may require a continuum of services. Some children, especially those with multiple disabilities, may require an environment more restrictive than a general education classroom for at least part of the day in order to get the type of assistance they need to function up to their potentialities. Teacher education typically does not offer comprehensive preparation for working with children with severe or MD who require extensive special educational services. In addition, children with severe or MD often require related services (for example, chemotherapy, physical therapy, psychotherapy, transportation) to enable them to learn in a classroom environment. Hopefully, teacher preparation, in-service education, and professional development sessions will address some of these concerns of service delivery in the near future.

Many children and youth with MD suffer from a lack of understanding, a lack of empathy, and handicapist attitudes that are directed at them. They present very special problems for teachers to solve. Often the message they hear is, "Just go away." The challenge of writing an appropriate individualized education program (IEP) is enormous. Updating the IEP each year and preparing an individualized transition plan (ITP), which will allow the student with severe or MD to function as independently as possible after age 21, is mandated by law. These students must be served. Teachers must be given the time and support needed to do so. Excuses such as no time, no money, and no personnel to provide appropriate services are unacceptable. Teachers can expect progress and good results, even with the most severely multiply disabled.

The first article in this unit "Monitor That Progress" by Howard Parette and his associates discusses the use of assistive technology (AT) for students with severe or multiple disabilities. Such technology is used not only to teach, but also to measure progress in education as mandated by No Child Left Behind. It is expensive. The authors suggest that the use of AT be carefully evaluated with data collection and interpretation. If it is not effective, IEP planning should re-evaluate and change it.

The second article in this unit suggests that students with traumatic brain injuries should be allowed to reenter public schools despite a range of cognitive, physical, and social-emotional disorders that may affect their education. The author, Julie Bowen, gives a variety of specific research-based learning strategies that aide this process. Educators who work with all students with MDs can benefit from these behavioral and instructional interventions.

Monitor That Progress!

Interpreting Data Trends for Assistive Technology Decision Making

HOWARD P. PARETTE ET AL.

Although IDEA requires consideration of assistive technology (AT) when developing individualized education programs (IEPs) for all students with disabilities, little guidance has been offered to date regarding the role of data in the AT decision-making process. How can IEP teams use classroom data to help them evaluate the effectiveness of AT solutions—both when considering implementation and assessing the usefulness of continuing AT use?

The mandate of the No Child Left Behind Act of 2001 (NCLB) has placed increasing pressure on public schools to ensure that students with disabilities make progress in the general education curriculum. For the approximately 7 million school-age children with disabilities in the United States, "taking full advantage of their rights to a high quality education requires support to learn in ways that work with their needs" (Silver-Pacuilla, 2005, p. 3). The role of AT in supporting such progress has emerged as an important factor for teachers and policy makers to ensure that all students demonstrate progress. The federal definition of AT is often cited; the Individuals With Disabilities Education Improvement Act of 2004 (IDEA) describes it as "any item, piece of equipment, or product system, whether acquired commercially, modified, or customized, that is used to increase, maintain, or improve functional capabilities of individuals with disabilities" (20 U.S.C. § 1401(251)). A working definition for teachers in the context of progress monitoring might be "a tool or strategy that allows a person to do a task they could not do without the tool *at the expected performance level*" (Parette, 2006).

IDEA requires that AT devices (20 U.S.C. § 1401(1)) and AT services (20 U.S.C. 1401(2)) be "considered" when developing student IEPs. Although some guidance has been provided regarding the consideration process (cf. Center for Technology in Education & Technology and Media Division, 2005; Chambers, 1997; Edyburn, 2005; Watts, O'Brien, & Wojcik, 2004; Zabala, 1995), teachers have relatively little direction regarding how to use individual student data in this process. Others have described subjective data tools for AT consideration (see box, "Additional Resources") that reflect sensitivity to the importance of students being self-determined and self-aware AT users. Such uses of AT, however, are beyond the scope of this

article, where the emphasis is on assessment data clearly linked to classroom curricula.

Curriculum-based measurement (CBM; Deno, 1985, 2003) provides a framework for understanding the role of regular classroom assessment in tracking student competency in basic skill areas such as reading, spelling, written language (Deno, 2003) and mathematics (Calhoon & Fuchs, 2003). With CBM, "student performance is assessed frequently on standardized tasks representing year-long curriculum and scores on these reliable and valid tests . . . are displayed graphically" (Stecker & Fuchs, 2000, p. 128). Teachers apply decision-making rules to the graphed data to determine whether instructional program adjustments are needed (Stecker & Fuchs). CBM resources are available both in print (Shinn, 1998; Shinn & Hubbard, 1992) and online (AIMSweb, 2007). Because AT is compensatory rather than instructional, it is not always clearly linked to CBM measures, though CBM does provide a framework for understanding the role of the teacher in collecting classroom data to make decisions about student progress. We also note that the expected performance levels established by CBM (e.g., words per minute when handwriting) may not be applicable to AT use (e.g., words per minute when using a keyboard or voice recognition system), and thus a "normed" grade-level performance is not available.

The Importance of Data in AT Consideration

Arguably, the question must be asked, "How can an effective AT decision be made without data to support its impact on basic skill acquisition by the student?" There are two important phases in the AT consideration process when data is crucial. The first phase is the period *before* a decision is made to try, acquire, or purchase a particular AT solution (i.e., during the IEP development process). It is well recognized that AT abandonment often results when inappropriate or ineffective AT devices are selected for students with disabilities (Galvin & Donneil, 2002; Phillips & Zhao, 1993). The need to make effective decisions, then, is especially important given most schools' limited fiscal resources for purchasing

AT; they have a vested interest in being good stewards of these resources. The IEP team collaboratively performs decision making at this level, essentially completing a problem-solving process (Friend & Cook, 2003) that begins by identifying the problem. This involves more than naming the problem (e.g., the student cannot communicate or has difficulty writing); problem identification requires that the extent of the discrepancy between current and desired performance is identified and confirmed through multiple sources of information (i.e., data; Friend & Cook). Taken together, these issues provide a sound justification for the need for data that supports the team decision to try, acquire, or purchase AT.

The second important phase is *after* implementing the AT solution. Once a team decides to move forward with trying a strategy or acquiring or purchasing a particular tool, it is important to collect ongoing data while the student uses the AT solution. There are two separate questions to answer during the implementation phase:

- Does the AT enhance performance?
- Is the AT needed over time to support continued educational progress?

Data provide trends that either support the immediate effectiveness of AT in enhancing performance and support ongoing use, or signal that the AT should be discontinued and/or reconsidered, either short- or long-term. In all instances, data can assist teachers in making effective decisions regarding whether a particular AT solution makes sense for a student, appears to be effective and enhances the child's performance in an academic area, and continues to support educational progress.

A Classroom Approach for Evidence-Based Practice

Most teachers are familiar with classroom assessment approaches (cf. Howell & Nolet, 2000; Oosterhof, 1999; Popham, 2002), although they may be less familiar with implementing such approaches when students use AT to perform academic tasks. The data collection approach should accommodate several considerations when documenting whether a particular AT strategy or device is effectively helping the student develop competencies in basic skill areas. The student's performance should be documented both using the AT solution and without using the AT solution, thus providing performance lines for comparison to the student's expected performance on an academic task. This approach constitutes what AT outcomes researchers call a *concurrent time series* design (Smith, 2000). "Concurrent," assumes that comparisons are made both with and without the AT. The "time" element implies that a reasonable period of time is allotted for data collection to ascertain whether the AT is effective. The "series" component assumes that multiple assessments occur during the allotted time period to develop a student performance line (what the student actually does) that is compared to an expected performance line (level of acceptable student performance).

The question of whether AT initially enhances performance is similar to the question of whether a behavioral intervention changes student behavior. When a behavior change is needed, a teacher will implement an intensive set of procedures thought to enhance behavioral performance after establishing a stable baseline of performance. This is followed by one of several design variations whose purpose is to establish whether the intervention is responsible for any behavior change (Barlow & Hersen, 1984; Tawney & Gast, 1984). One method is the withdrawal design (ABAB) in which the intervention is withdrawn for a period of time (often equal to the period of the intervention), then reinstated. For AT users with hightech solutions this often occurs naturally (albeit unintentionally) when an augmentative and alternative communication (AAC) device or computer malfunctions for several days. Seeking to minimize the time spent without any intervention in place (multiple withdrawal sessions), the alternating treatments design uses rapidly alternating conditions of intervention and no intervention, or alternates two different interventions. During an initial AT intervention, this might mean alternating the text-to-speech screen reader or portable keyboarding device (such as an Alphasmart™ Neo) between available and not available. In this design, the time of day (morning vs. afternoon) or content subject (language arts vs. social studies) must be counterbalanced across days so that the AT is available and not available an equal number of times each morning or for each content subject. Although these assessment designs would establish the initial effectiveness of an AT in enhancing performance, a number of substantive criticisms weigh against their use.

When the behavior or skill is of clear social or academic significance, the ABAB design—withholding treatment (in this case the AT) for 3 to 5 days to establish a data trend—is not supportable; an alternating treatments design will produce the same evaluation. However, although the alternating treatments design produces a demonstration of effectiveness, it requires that the student be without the AT for as many days or sessions as it is available. Again, for a socially or academically significant skill, is this a cost-effective solution? Neither of these designs addresses the question of whether the AT should be maintained over time, beyond the initial demonstration of effectiveness. If AT is a *compensatory* intervention, then the student needs it over time. If, on the other hand, the student acquires the skill for which the AT was compensating, either through continued direct instruction or as a result of using the AT, then the AT is either no longer needed or it was actually an *instructional* intervention, not compensatory.

Modeled on the multiple baseline probe design (Tawney & Gast, 1984), the concurrent time series design addresses all of the previous concerns. Using scheduled, concurrent probes of student performance without the AT, it can assess the initial effectiveness of the AT in enhancing the performance while minimizing the effect of AT withdrawal, and it also can assess the long-term effect on student performance in the academic area. As we will discuss, these two separate questions can be addressed through scheduling of the no-AT probes. There are other considerations in using this approach:

- *Similar conditions need to be maintained between AT and no-AT probes.* For example, a writing sample collected during daily journal writing with no AT cannot be compared to a book report collected with AT (different genre); a math sample collected in the general

Table 1 Issues for IEP Team Consideration

When using . . .	The Team Should Ask . . .
Preassessments and ongoing assessments	• Are the assessments measuring the same thing? If not, how do they differ (e.g., fluency vs. comprehension; computation vs. reasoning; narrative vs. expository writing)?
	• What are the practicalities for implementation of data-gathering? Has a standard procedure been developed and documented? How long does it take?
	• Who will gather the data? If teachers, aides, and others, is interrater reliability an issue?
	• If the student skill being assessed using AT is a CBM measure, how is it determined? What resources are available to the teacher? How does the team know that the CBM measures what is intended to be measured?
	• What is the expected level of performance of the student on the targeted tasks being assessed? Are expected levels available when use of AT changes the response mode?
Data-based decision making	• If a concurrent time series design is used, what design features need to be considered to ensure that conditions such as time of day, instructional format, setting, medications, or other factors are not affecting student performance?
	• How can we assure cost-effective use of teacher and student time?
	• Are scoring rules available? Are graphs being maintained? Are decisions being made using the graphed data?

education class without AT cannot be compared to a math sample collected in 1:1 instruction in the resource room with AT (different instructional conditions).

• *The assessments should be cost effective.* Scheduling of probes also requires considering their cost-effectiveness. If a 5- or 10-minute writing sample produces a 50 to 100 word sample, then a 30-minute sample is not needed.

• *Data samples must be scored and graphed immediately* after they have been collected to be useful in decision making.

Collecting Data

During IEP development, where the question is the effectiveness of the AT in enhancing performance, conduct frequent (daily or weekly) assessments to gather the necessary information for decision making. This data is used to determine whether a particular AT solution effects a difference in student performance on a targeted curricular task. Data may be collected by a teacher or an aide, depending on the nature of the data (e.g., spelling performance can easily be assessed by an aide, whereas observational data such as increased communication interactions with others in a group activity might better be assessed by a teacher during a classroom activity).

During AT implementation, where the question is whether to continue the AT, the teacher or aide (again, depending on the complexity of the task and the form of the classroom data) should collect assessment data on at least a monthly basis. At this point, it's appropriate to consider the school district's

scheduling of CBM (e.g., concurrently conduct the AT/no AT probes in conjunction with the district's quarterly assessments). Regularly scheduled data collection ensures that the AT solution continues to positively impact student performance on targeted curricular tasks across time. The key to scheduling is to be cost-effective, assessing often enough to be sensitive to behavior changes and infrequently enough to conserve time and resources. Table 1 presents some considerations for an IEP team when making decisions about assessing and implementing AT solutions.

Regularly scheduled data collection ensures that the AT solution continues to positively impact student performance on targeted curricular tasks across time.

Interpreting Classroom AT Data Trends

The following sections present case scenarios regarding specific types of AT being considered for students with disabilities, both during the first phase (IEP development) and second phase (implementation). Each graph (see Figures 1 through 8) assumes a concurrent time series design for data collection, and incorporates multiple data points. The straight line in each graph

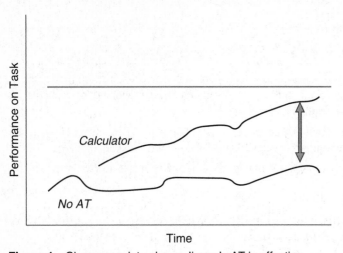

Figure 1 Classroom data shows Jimmy's AT is effective.

Note: Copyright 2006 by the Special Education Assistive Technology (SEAT) Center at Illinois State University. Used with permission.

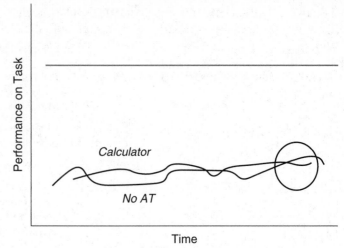

Figure 2 Classroom data shows Jimmy's AT is ineffective.

Note: Copyright 2006 by the Special Education Assistive Technology (SEAT) Center at Illinois State University. Used with permission.

represents an expected level of student performance deemed appropriate for any particular task (e.g., 8 out of 10 correct math problems; 15 out of 20 correct spelling words).

Data for Initial IEP Consideration
Is the AT Effective?
Jimmy's IEP team wants to consider purchasing a talking calculator to assist him in completing 2-digit subtraction problems. Jimmy's learning disability inhibits his ability to understand the process of completing these types of problems, and the talking calculator is viewed as a means of potentially compensating for the disability. The classroom teacher takes one assessment of his performance in the morning, having Jimmy complete a worksheet of 10 two-digit subtraction problems without using the calculator. In the afternoon, another assessment is taken while allowing Jimmy to use the talking calculator. She continues to take assessments over a 3-week period, using the same format (a worksheet with 10 two-digit subtraction problems). What might the data show?

The AT is Effective. Over the 3-week period, the data trend of Jimmy's performance using the calculator reflects a positive trend, with a substantial gap between his performance with and without the calculator (see Figure 1). Based on this data, the team could reasonably assume that the talking calculator had a positive influence on his performance level for this specific academic task.

The AT Is Ineffective. Alternatively, over the 3-week period, the trend lines suggest that Jimmy's performance is comparable with and without the talking calculator (Figure 2). Because the AT seems to make no appreciable difference in Jimmy's performance, the team may reasonably assume that the talking calculator is ineffective and should not be considered for purchase and continued implementation. Interestingly, at a later point in the data collection process the two trend lines cross (inside circle) and it appears that Jimmy's ability to perform the academic task may actually be improving. The team might explore why this is occurring—is direct instruction beginning to have an impact, or can some other influence account for the data trend?

One AT Solution Is Better than Others
Juanita has difficulty with 3-digit division problems having a 2-digit divisor. Her IEP team has discussed three different options that might increase her academic performance on a 10-problem worksheet. First, the team wanted to examine use of a task-analysis procedure incorporating visual strategies (i.e., pictures associated with components of completing this type of division problem). Second, the team thought that using a large-face calculator might prove effective. Third, the team recommended a trial period of a software application that would require Juanita to use appropriate place value and location of numerals in the division process. The teacher implemented each of these potential solutions, including no AT use, with worksheet completion daily over a 4-week period. Four very distinct trend lines emerged when the data were charted (see Figure 3).

It appears that each of the three AT solutions resulted in higher performance on the division task than no AT. The large-face calculator resulted in performance that was closest to the expectations for students. Interestingly, the software application resulted in performance that exceeded expectations and thus may be overcompensating for the student; it does more than is needed. Overcompensation can be problematic in that children may rely on the technology to such an extent that learning new skills or maintaining those previously learned is not deemed to be important. Thus, in this particular scenario, the most effective solution for Juanita was the calculator, and the team could reasonably move forward with its purchase and implementation in her daily classroom activities.

Acquisition Phase—Is It Working?
Yolanda continues to have difficulty with 3-digit multiplication problems. Her IEP team decided to see if implementing the MathPad™ software program would increase her performance in completing daily worksheet problems. Over a 2-week period the data reflected relatively little difference in performance whether Yolanda used the software or not, although after 2 weeks a positive trend line began to appear in favor of the software (see Figure 4).

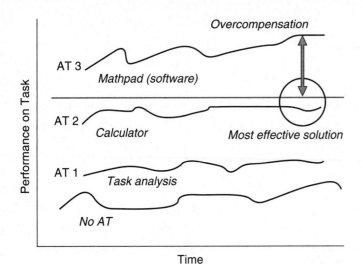

Figure 3 Classroom data for Juanita shows one AT solution Is better than others.

Note: Copyright 2006 by the Special Education Assistive Technology (SEAT) Center at Illinois State University. Used with permission.

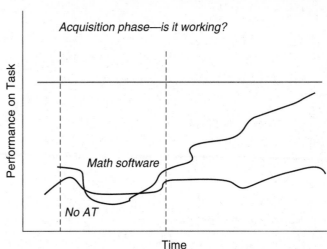

Figure 4 Classroom data reflects Yolanda's AT learning curve.

Note: Copyright 2006 by the Special Education Assistive Technology (SEAT) Center at Illinois State University. Used with permission.

The classroom data reflects a real-life phenomenon that all teachers and students confront when working with technology: It takes time to learn how to use a device, and our performance may actually decrease initially during that learning curve! In Yolanda's case there was a slight dip in performance early on when MathPad™ was first implemented, followed by a steady rise until her performance crossed the no-AT trend line. Teachers should be aware that when testing certain AT solutions, they may not be able to make decisions in just a few days or weeks. There is no rule of thumb regarding how long a team should continue implementing an AT solution to ascertain whether it will be effective. The more complex the device and its features, the greater the probability that an acquisition phase will be embedded in a data trend that shows no or little improvement until the child is familiar with its features and comfortable using the device.

Continuing Use of the AT

Once data have provided support necessary to justify purchase, acquisition, and/or implementation of an AT solution [whether it is a strategy or device), it is necessary to ensure that the AT continues to be effective over time. The student's IEP should include statements regarding use of the device, and teachers have an obligation to monitor the student's use of the AT in academic settings to facilitate decision making regarding progress and performance. The following sections present examples of data trends for particular students over the course of an academic year, followed by interpretation discussions.

The AT Continues to Be Effective

Dargan had problems with spelling accuracy in one-page composition English assignments. The IEP team approved use of spell-check software early in the year, when initial data indicated that it made a difference in expected performance. Over time, the teacher continued to obtain data regarding Dargan's

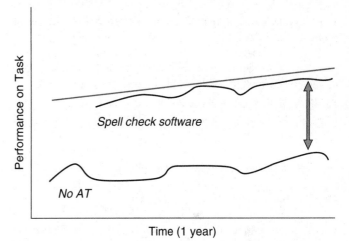

Figure 5 Classroom data supports continuing use of Dargan's AT.

Note: Copyright 2006 by the Special Education Assistive Technology (SEAT) Center at Illinois State University. Used with permission.

spelling accuracy in onepage composition assignments, both with and without use of the spell-check software.

The data trends indicated a substantial gap between performance both with and without use of the spell check software (see Figure 5). When using the software, Dargan's performance consistently approached what would be expected; thus, the team unequivocally accepted AT as effective, and Dargan's IEP reflected ongoing use of the spellcheck software in writing assignments.

Direct Instruction Makes A Difference!

Let's assume that over the course of the academic year, Dargan's teacher administers writing probes on a regular basis, both after direct instruction (no AT) is routinely provided and while he uses the spell-check software for targeted writing assignments. The resulting data reflect two interesting trends: Both direct instruction

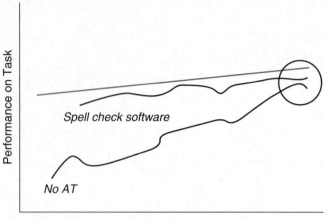

Figure 6 Classroom data for Dargan reflects impact of AT and direct instruction.

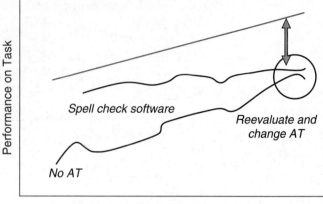

Figure 7 Classroom data indicates Dargan's AT should be reevaluated.

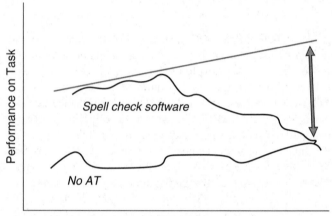

Figure 8 Classroom data shows Dargan's AT is ineffective

(no AT) and use of the spell-check software enable Dargan to approach an expected level of performance (see Figure 6).

Without maintaining such data, a teacher may not be aware that a student's proficiency in a particular academic skill area is actually increasing over time without reliance on the AT. In Figure 6, the performance line for the no-AT strategy (direct instruction) almost crosses the performance line for Dargan's use of the spell-check software. When such a trend is reflected, the IEP team may wish to reconsider continuing use of the AT in favor of more traditional classroom teaching strategies.

Reevaluate and Change!

What if, over the course of the academic year, the teacher's classroom data indicate a different kind of trend (see Figure 7)? Initially, the spell-check software indicated a substantial difference in Dargan's performance, but over time the trend line stabilized and became somewhat flat. The no-AT strategy (direct instruction) impact continued to increase until they both began to level off in close proximity to one another. In this instance, the team might reconsider use of the spell-check software, as near the end of the data collection period its effect appeared to be comparable to the no-AT strategy. The team might wish to reevaluate Dargan's AT options regarding supporting spelling skills. They might also infer that direct instruction is having a positive effect and may be preferred to using AT.

The AT Is Ineffective

Ideally, after a team invests time and effort into the AT consideration process and makes a decision regarding strategies and devices to be implemented in classroom settings, the student would continue to show progress when using the device. However, in an alternative Dargan scenario the data trends over time indicate a decline in spelling skill proficiency using the spell-check software (see Figure 8). Although his performance trend line continues to exceed the performance line for no AT (direct instruction) until later in the data collection process, at one point the performance is comparable.

AT strategies or devices are intended to help students do things they could not do without the device, at an expected performance level. Thus, a team could reasonably assume that as long as data indicates that the student's performance level using AT exceeds the performance level without the AT, use of the strategy or device should be maintained. In instances such as those presented in Figure 8, however, the decrease in proficiency reflected by a declining trend line for the spell-check software is an area of concern for the IEP team, and requires close monitoring to establish the cause of the decline. It may be, for example, that new demands to use more difficult vocabulary have had a negative impact on spelling performance, even with assistance.

Final Thoughts

The role of curriculum-based data in educational decision making, particularly with regard to the AT consideration process, has become increasingly important. NCLB and other demands for school accountability require teachers to be more thoughtful about all decisions regarding students with disabilities; progress and success in the general education curriculum has become an integral societal expectation (Behavioral Research and Teaching & American Institutes for Research, 2006). Teachers can increase their effectiveness as participants in IEP meetings by collecting and sharing meaningful data that drives decision making. Understanding data trends generated by use of a concurrent time series approach can contribute immensely to more effective AT consideration.

Understanding data trends generated by use of a concurrent time series approach can contribute immensely to more effective AT consideration.

References

AIMSweb. (2007). *AIMSweb progress monitoring and response to intervention, system.* Retrieved February 8, 2007, from http://aimsweb.com/

Barlow, D. H., & Hersen, M. (1984). *Single case experimental designs* (2nd ed.). Oxford, England: Pergamon Press.

Behavioral Research and Teaching, University of Oregon, & American Institutes for Research, Washington, DC. (2006). *Including students with disabilities in large-scale assessment: Executive summary.* Retrieved April 27, 2006, from http://osepideasthatwork.org/toolkit/tk_lrgAssmnt_ES.asp

Calhoon, M. B., & Fuchs, L. S. (2003). The effects of peer-assisted learning strategies and curriculum-based measurement on mathematics performance of secondary students with disabilities. *Remedial and Special Education, 24,* 235–245.

Center for Technology in Education & Technology and Media Division of the Council for Exceptional Children. (2005). *Considering the need for assistive technology within the individualized educational program.* Arlington, VA: Council for Exceptional Children.

Chambers, A. C. (1997). *Has technology been considered? A guide for IEP teams.* Reston, VA: Council for Exceptional Children.

Deno. S. L. (1985). Curriculum-based measurement: The emerging alternative. *Exceptional Children, 52,* 219–232.

Deno, S. L. (2003). Developments in curriculum-based measurement. *The Journal of Special Education, 37,* 184–192.

Edyburn, D. L. (2005). Assistive technology and students with mild disabilities: From consideration to outcome measurement. In D. Edyburn, K. Higgins, & R. Boone (Eds.), *Handbook of special education technology research and practice* (pp. 239–270). Whitefish Bay, WI: Knowledge by Design.

Friend, M., & Cook, L. (2003). *Interactions: Collaboration skills for school professionals* (4th ed.) Boston: Allyn & Bacon.

Galvin, J. C., & Donnell, C. M. (2002). Educating the consumer and caretaker on assistive technology. In M. J. Scherer (Ed.), *Assistive technology: Matching device and consumer for successful rehabilitation* (pp. 153–167), Washington, DC: American Psychological Association.

Howell, K. W., & Nolet, V. (2000). *Curriculum-based evaluation: Teaching and decision making* (3rd ed.). Belmont, CA: Wadsworth Thompson Learning.

Individuals With Disabilities Education Improvement Act of 2004, 20 U.S.C. § 1400 et seq. (2004).

No Child Left Behind Act of 2001, 20 U.S.C. 6301 et seq. (2001).

Oosterhof, A. (1999). *Developing and using classroom assessments* (2nd ed.). Upper Saddle River, NJ: Merrill. Prentice Hall.

Parette, P. (2006, March). *Assessment for assistive technology.* Workshop presented at the National Association of School Psychologists 2006 Annual Convention, Anaheim, CA.

Phillips, B., & Zhao, H. (1993). Predictors of assistive technology abandonment. *Assistive Technology, 5,* 36–45.

Popham W. J. (2002). *Classroom assessment: What teachers need to know* (3rd ed.). Boston: Allyn and Bacon.

Shinn, M. R. (Ed). (1998). *Advanced applications of curriculum-based measurement.* New York: Guilford.

Shinn, M. R., & Hubbard, D. D. (1992). Curriculum-based measurement and problem-solving assessment: Basic procedures and outcomes. *Focus on Exceptional Children, 24*(5), 1–20.

Silver-Pacuilla, H. (2005). *Moving towards solutions. Assistive & learning technology for all students.* Washington, DC: National Center for Technology Innovation.

Smith, R. O. (2000). Measuring assistive technology outcomes in education. *Diagnostique, 25,* 273–290.

Stecker, P. M., & Fuchs, L. S. (2000). Effecting superior achievement using curriculum-based measurement: The importance of individual progress monitoring. *Learning Disabilities Research and Practice, 15,* 128–134.

Tawney, J. W., & Gast, D. L. (1984). *Single-subject research in special education.* Columbus, OH: Merrill.

Watts, E. H., O'Brien, M., & Wojcik, B. W. (2004). Four models of assistive technology consideration: How do they compare to recommended educational assessment practices? *Journal of Special Education Technology, 19*(1), 43–56.

Zabala, J. (1995). *The SETT framework: Critical areas to consider when making informed assistive technology decisions.* Retrieved April 27, 2006, from http://sweb.uky.edu/~jszaba0/SETTintro.html

Additional Resources

Wisconsin Assistive Technology Initiative (http://www.wati.org)

The Family Center on Technology and Disability (http://www.fctd.info)

Assistive Technology Training Online Project, School of Public Health and Health Professions, University of Buffalo (http://atto.buffalo.edu)

HOWARD P. PARETTE (CEC IL Federation), Kara Peters, Professor of Assistive Technology; **GEORGE R. PETERSON-KARLAN** (CEC IL Federation), Professor of Special Education; and **BRIAN W. WOJCIK** (CEC IL Federation), Coordinator, Special Education Assistive Technology Center, Illinois State University, Normal. **NORA BARDI** (CEC IL Federation), Assistive Technology Specialist, Unit 5 Community Schools, Normal, Illinois.

Address correspondence to Howard P. Parette, SEAT Center, Illinois State University, Normal, IL 61790-5910 (e-mail: hpparet@ilstu.edu).

UNIT 10

Gifted or Talented

Unit Selections

Key Points to Consider

- What can reduce the social isolation of students who are gifted and learning disabled?

- Would you add anything to the 5-step program to help teachers enhance their technology integration skills?

Student Website

www.mhcls.com

Internet References

Hoagies' Gifted: Educators
http://www.hoagiesgifted.org/educators.htm

The Council for Exceptional Children
http://www.cec.sped.org/index.html

The International Society for Technology Education
http://www.iste.org

The Individuals with Disabilities Education Improvement Act (IDEIA) mandates special services for children with disabilities, but not for children with exceptional gifts or talents. The monies spent to provide special services for three children with high-cost disabilities could pay for accelerated lessons for a classroom full of college-bound students with intellectual giftedness. Should schools in the twenty-first century be more egalitarian? IDEIA mandates appropriate education but not sameness of quantity or degree of knowledge for every child. Are we inclined to push compensatory education of students with shortcomings in learning, while leaving students with a gift for learning to cope for themselves to counterbalance the equation? Do we want educational parity?

Since many textbooks on exceptional children include children with special gifts and talents, and since these children are exceptional, they will be included in this volume. Instructors who deal only with the categories of disabilities covered by IDEIA may simply omit coverage of this unit.

The Omnibus Education Bill of 1987 provided modest support for gifted and talented identification and the education of students with giftedness in the United States. It required, however, that each state foot the bill for the development of special programs for children with exceptional gifts and talents. A few states have implemented accelerated or supplemental education for the gifted. Most states have not.

Giftedness can be viewed as both a blessing and a curse. Problems of jealousy, misunderstanding, indignation, exasperation, and even fear are often engendered in people who live with, work with, or get close to a child with superior intelligence. Are children with giftedness at a disadvantage in our society? Do their powerful abilities and potentialities in some area (or areas) leave them ridiculed or bored in a regular classroom? Children with special gifts and talents may be deprived of some of the opportunities with which less-exceptional children are routinely provided.

Students who are gifted tend to ask a lot of questions and pursue answers with still more questions. They can be incredibly persistent about gathering information about topics that engage them. They may, however, show no interest at all in learning about topics that do not. They may be very competitive in areas where they are especially skilled, competing even with teachers and other adults. They may seem arrogant about their skills, when, in their minds, they are only being honest.

Many children and youth with special gifts and talents have extraordinary sensitivity to how other people are reacting to them. As they are promoted through elementary school into middle school and high school, many such children learn to hide their accomplishments for the secondary gain of being more socially acceptable or more popular. Because they have not been challenged or have been discouraged from achieving at their highest potentialities, underachievement becomes a problem. They have poor study habits as a result of not needing to study. They may be unmotivated, intensely bored, and discouraged by the educational programs available to them.

Researchers who have studied creative genius have found that most accomplished high achievers share one childhood similarity. Their parents recognized their special abilities early

© Randy Faris/Corbis

and found tutors or mentors who would help them develop their skills. This is true not only of mathematicians and scientists but also of world-class sports players, musicians, artists, performers, writers, and other producers of note.

Educational programs that refuse to find tutors or mentors, to encourage original work, or to provide special education in the skill areas of students with gifts are depriving potential producers of the depth and breadth of their talents.

The earlier that children with special gifts and talents are recognized, the better. The sooner they are provided with enriched education, the more valuable their future contributions will become. Children from all ethnic backgrounds, from all socio-economic levels, and from both sexes can have exceptional gifts and talents. Researchers have reported that parents of gifted persons seldom have any special creative skills or talents of their own, by which to predict exceptionality.

The assessment of children with special gifts and talents, especially in the early childhood years, is fraught with difficulties.

Should parents nominate their own children when they see extraordinary skills developing? How objective can parents be about their child's ability as it compares to the abilities of other same-aged children? Should measures of achievement be used (recitals, performances, art, reading levels, writings)? Many parents are embarrassed by their child's extraordinary aptitudes. They would rather have a popular child or a child more like his or her peers, than an exceptional child.

In the first article Emily Williams King describes students who are twice-exceptional: both exceptionally gifted and learning-disabled, a not uncommon phenomenon. Their school work may be patronizingly simple yet they may fail at certain tasks. Their self-concept and social skills suffer. Ms. King suggests a variety of ways to help. When gifted students with diverse learning styles really connect with new information, their education can have lasting effects for the greater good of all humanity. The ability of twice-exceptional students to succeed cannot be underestimated or ignored.

The last article in this unit, "Creating a Personal Technology Improvement Plan for Teachers of the Gifted" gives a 5-step program to help teachers enhance their technology integration skills. Kevin Besnoy discusses conducting needs assessments, writing long and short term goals, accessing resources, implementing strategies, and evaluating progress.

Addressing the Social and Emotional Needs of Twice-Exceptional Students

Emily Williams King

Children who are both gifted and have a learning disability (gifted/LD) face numerous challenges in the classroom and in life. These students often feel as though they are a part of two worlds, one as a student with a disability and the other as a student with outstanding abilities. Being classified as having a disability and being gifted, sometimes called twice-exceptional, can be quite confusing. These students often wonder, for example, "Why am I so good at math but need special help with reading? Where do I fit in?"

In addition to the challenge of having a disability, gifted/LD students may experience increased frustration resulting from heightened expectations and higher standards for achievement that go along with being gifted (Coleman, 2001). Because these students are labeled as "gifted," they may be expected to be strong in all areas, when in fact their strength may lie in only one or two areas (Strop, 2003).

As a result of these expectations, school can be very frustrating for a twice-exceptional student. Most curricula require students to depend on basic academic skills, such as reading, arithmetic, and writing, which can be areas of difficulty for many children who are gifted/LD. Because of their ongoing conflict between intellectual strengths and academic struggles, many students who are gifted/LD develop low self-concepts after starting school (Swesson, 1994). These students have also been shown to have difficulty with social skills and often report feelings of not fitting in with their peers (Vespi & Yewchuk, 1992). Therefore, recognizing and supporting the social and emotional needs of twice-exceptional students are just as important as addressing their academic needs. We must appropriately identify and serve students who are gifted/LD in order to maximize their potential both inside and outside the classroom.

Types of Gifted/LD Students

Students who are both gifted and have learning disabilities exhibit superior intellectual ability as well as a significant discrepancy between their level of performance in a particular area, such as reading, mathematics, spelling, or written language, as compared with their performance in areas of strength (McCoach, Kehle, Bray, & Siegle, 2001; see box, "Possible Characteristics of Twice-Exceptional Students"). The literature defines three types of students who are gifted/LD:

Many students who are gifted/LD develop low self-concepts after starting school.

1. The first group consists of students who are identified as gifted and have subtle learning disabilities (Baum, 1994). These students may have a large vocabulary and excellent verbal abilities, whereas their handwriting and spelling abilities contradict this image (Baum, 1994). Students in this category also achieve on grade level, thus causing their learning disability to be overlooked. Identification of their disabilities could offer these students an understanding of their academic difficulties (Baum, 1994).

2. The second group of students who are gifted/LD consists of those who are unidentified. In other words, their abilities and disabilities "mask" each other. These students' superior intelligence seems to compensate for their undiagnosed learning disability (Baum, 1994). They usually receive instruction in the general classroom and often perform at grade level, so no "red flags" are raised. However, these students are often functioning below their potential. The talents of students in this group often emerge in specific content areas, becoming noticed later in life. This group of students may also suffer from mild depression (Baum, 1994).

3. The third group contains those students identified as both gifted and LD. They are identified more often than those in the previous two groups because they stand out in the classroom. These bright students often fail in school and are noticed because of their disability, not because of their talents. Because little attention is given to their strengths, these students become more aware of their difficulties in learning, feeling academic failure more often than success. Over time, this negative outlook on school can lead to disruptive classroom behavior and feelings of low self-concept (Baum, 1994).

Identification of Gifted/LD Students

Identifying children who are both gifted and LD poses a challenge to teachers and school psychologists. Both teachers and parents can have difficulty associating failing grades and incomplete assignments with giftedness (Swesson, 1994). A central issue in the complexity of identifying students who are gifted/ LD is that their giftedness may mask their learning disability and that their learning disability may mask their giftedness (McCoach, et al. 2001). Although these students have varying patterns of strengths and weaknesses, they may appear to have average abilities and achievement in the classroom. This masking of abilities is also apparent in the identification of giftedness with fullscale IQ scores. These students' learning disability may in fact lower their IQ score so dramatically that they do not qualify for gifted services (Waldron & Saphire, as cited in McCoach et al., 2001). Because students who are gifted/LD appear to have hidden gifts and at the same time have the ability to compensate for their learning disabilities, educators and psychologists must look for unique characteristics to identify this population of students.

Because many students who are gifted/LD have creative interests that may not be nurtured in the classroom, their behavior may be drastically different in their home environment. Parents should be involved in the identification process to offer insight into their child's activities outside of school (Rivera, Murdock, & Sexton, 1995). In many cases, students who are gifted/LD continually experience failure in school while successfully learning and creating at home, where they can put extended effort into their hobbies and interests (Baum,

1984). Developing a collaborative relationship between parents and teachers will also facilitate productive intervention strategies.

Emotional Concerns of Gifted/LD Students

Twice-exceptional students are often caught between two worlds. Many of these students are internally motivated and have strong beliefs in their abilities, much like gifted students, yet they repeatedly fail at certain tasks, similar to children with LD. One group of students who are gifted/LD reported having "some idea that they could not make their brain, body, or both do what they wanted each to do" (Schiff, Kaufman, & Kaufman, 1981, p. 403)

[Some gifted/LD] students' superior intelligence seems to compensate for their undiagnosed learning disability.

Because of a strong belief in their abilities, gifted students also tend to have high expectations of their achievement level that are not always realistic (Vespi & Yewchuk, 1992). Therefore, a student who is gifted/LD may experience failure much more often than he or she expects, which can result in a fear of failure with future tasks. This fear can lead to frustration with, and feelings of anxiety toward, academic tasks as these students become aware of the discrepancy between their potential ability and their performance (Vespi & Yewchuk).

Students who are gifted/LD also report experiencing frustrating dichotomies of feeling both confused and bored, not understanding why they are good at some tasks and not others. The mixed messages that twice-exceptional students seem to get concerning their abilities often leave them with the feeling that they must prove they are smart (Rizza & Baum, personal communication, April 7, 2005). As a result, some students who are gifted/LD report avoiding or rushing through academic tasks in which they fear failure, often because completing the task seems more important than the quality of their work. Vespi and Yewchuk (1992) reported that not attending to a task also appears to be a way that such students cope with the anticipated frustration of a difficult task. Students who are gifted/LD often use their memory skills to hide their deficits. Hiding their deficits can develop into coping skills (Coleman, 1992).

The disappointments that twice-exceptional students experience in the classroom can often be observed in their behavior. These students may be disruptive, aggressive, and easily frustrated in the classroom environment (Fetzer, 2000). Students who are gifted/LD commonly daydream, doodle instead of listen, and may act impulsively when given directions (Fetzer). However, these students have been shown to persevere with difficult tasks when they are given encouragement and support (Vespi & Yewchuk, 1992).

Possible Characteristics of Twice-Exceptional Students

- Discrepancy between verbal and written work.
- Creativity.
- Excel on tasks requiring abstract concepts.
- Difficulty on tasks requiring memorization of isolated facts.
- Anxiety.
- Depression.
- Acting-out behavior.
- Poor organization.
- Poor motivation.
- Active problem solvers.
- Analytic thinkers.
- Strong task commitment when topic is personally meaningful.
- Withdrawal/shyness.
- Discrepancy between out-of-school talents and classroom performance.

Source: Baum, 1984 and Swesson, 1994.

Self-Concept of Gifted/LD Students

Students who are gifted/LD and who have difficulty coping with the discrepancy between their abilities and disabilities, may develop a low self-concept. Global self-concept is defined as the "general evaluation of one's self worth as a person" (Harter, Whitesell, & Junkin, 1998, p. 655). Students may also develop more specific self-concepts, such as an academic self-concept, which "refers to individuals' knowledge and perceptions about themselves in achievement situations" (Bong & Skaalvik, 2003, p. 6). Because of their experiences of failure in school, many children with learning disabilities have lower self-concepts than normally achieving students (Cooley & Ayres, 1988). Research in the area of self-concept and its relationship to LD is relatively thorough, indicating that both global and academic self-concepts affect an LD student's classroom achievement (Cooley & Ayres).

Similarly, the self-concepts of children who are both gifted and LD are lower than the self-concepts of their normally achieving peers (Waldron, Saphire, & Rosenblum, 1987). But how do students who are gifted/LD compare with those who are only LD? Children who are gifted/LD face the same academic challenges that students with LD face; however, students who are gifted/LD have additional challenges. Most children who are gifted are highly critical of themselves and tend to set extremely high goals (Waldron et al.). A student's view of his or her academic work strongly influences his or her self-concept, making students who are gifted/LD even more vulnerable (Winne, Woodlands, & Wong, 1982).

The expectations of parents and teachers further complicate students' development of self-concept. Although parents and teachers may set high standards because of the giftedness, they often lower their expectations because of the learning disability, regardless of the student's talents (Swesson, 1994). These mixed messages are hard to interpret. Therefore, students who are gifted/LD often have conflicting thoughts concerning their capabilities in the classroom and the expectations of their performance; such thoughts tend to result in a low self-concept (Waldron et al., 1987).

The expectations of parents and teachers further complicate students' development of self-concept.

Waldron and colleagues (1987) found that students who are gifted/LD had lower self-concepts than gifted students and believed that they were less intelligent than their peers. Twice-exceptional students rated themselves as more anxious and personally dissatisfied than their gifted peers, appearing to internalize their perception of academic behavior (Waldron et al.). Even when students who are gifted/LD hide their learning difficulties, they may be doing so at the expense of a lower self-concept.

Social Concerns of Gifted/LD Students

Students with LD have more social problems than their peers without LD. These problems include difficulty using appropriate social skills, generating solutions to social problems, and interpreting social cues (Stormont, Stebbins, & Holliday, 2001). In fact, students with LD are less likely to be leaders in their peer group, are less likely to be popular, and are often more rejected than their nondisabled peers (Flicek, 1992; Flicek & Landau, 1985). What about students who are both gifted and LD? Does giftedness serve as a protective factor in social situations? Actually, research has found the opposite to be true. Students who are both gifted and LD are at even more risk than their LD peers (Moon & Dillon, 1995; Vespi & Yewchuk, 1992).

Because twice-exceptional children seem to possess characteristics of both giftedness and LD, they often struggle with perceptions of being different and feeling isolated. One study that interviewed four twice-exceptional boys concluded that these children seemed to know how to make and keep friends but were often unable to put that knowledge to use in social situations (Vespi & Yewchuk, 1992). All four boys in the study reported being frustrated with their peer relationships, and three of the four appeared to relate better to adults than to their peers (Vespi & Yewchuk). Students who are gifted/LD may also experience anger, frustration, and resentment because of recognizing the discrepancy between their potential and their social and academic problems, which can further influence relations with peers (Brody & Mills, 1997; Moon & Dillon, 1995). To nurture the whole child, teachers and parents must recognize the social and emotional needs of students who are gifted/LD.

Supporting the Needs of Gifted/LD Students

The essential element in meeting the educational needs of students who are gifted/LD is providing instruction that emphasizes these students' strengths and interests while remediating their learning deficits (Nielsen & Mortorff-Albert, 1989). However, many schools offer only remediation designed for LD only students, that is, it focuses only on improving a child's weaknesses. One study investigating the effects of special education on the global self-concept of students who are gifted/LD found that the self-concept scores of students receiving gifted services were significantly higher than those receiving services for learning disabilities only (Nielsen & Mortorff-Albert). This study concluded that the self-concepts of students who are gifted/LD appear to vary according to the type of special education services they receive. When students' services included gifted programming that focused on their strengths, the self-concepts of students who are gifted/LD matched those of their nondisabled peers (Nielsen & Mortorff-Albert).

Why is remediation alone not helpful for students who are gifted/LD? Remediation offers few opportunities for a twice-exceptional child to demonstrate his or her gifts and talents and often focuses on weaknesses at the expense of developing gifts. This set of circumstances can result in low self-esteem, a lack of motivation, depression, and stress (Baum, 1994). Therefore, students who are gifted/LD require a program designed to develop their strengths, interests, and superior intellect as well as remediate their deficits. Students who are gifted/LD need an educational environment that circumvents problematic academic areas, such as reading, arithmetic, and writing, and highlights abstract thinking and creativity (Baum, 1994).

Strategies for Supporting the Social and Emotional Needs of Gifted/LD Students

Support services for twice-exceptional children must treat the whole child—that is, must include not only academic interventions but also strategies to address these students' social and emotional needs (see box, "Guidelines for Developing Programs for Gifted/LD Students"). Following is a list of strategies that will likely benefit the students who are gifted/LD in your classroom:

1. Foster a clear understanding of their disability as well as their strengths to promote self-understanding and self-acceptance. If students are aware of their abilities, strengths, and weaknesses, they will be better prepared to make decisions about their future (Stormont et al., 2001).

2. Continually encourage gifted/LD students to succeed, and enlist the support of their parents and other teachers in this endeavor. Teach students to set realistic goals, accept their limitations, and reward their accomplishments.

3. Teach students coping strategies to use when they become frustrated. Learning ways to cope will help reinforce a student's commitment to persist with challenging tasks (Stormont et al., 2001).

4. If needed, encourage counseling to effectively monitor each student's emotions that accompany frustrations and perceived failures. Group counseling may also be beneficial, especially if students can speak with other students who are experiencing the same difficulties and frustrations (Brody & Mills, 1997).

5. Remind yourself and encourage others to recognize the unique needs of twice-exceptional students. Think of these children not only as having a disability or as being gifted but as having individual needs.
   a. Think twice about why a student may avoid a task or rush through an assignment. Does this child always avoid the same type of assignment?
   b. Offer multiple ways in which students can learn and demonstrate their knowledge in the classroom (e.g., presentations, projects, skits).

c. Encourage and positively reinforce students' efforts, especially on challenging tasks.
   d. Recognize and support the social and emotional needs of these children while also nurturing their academic strengths.

6. Provide support in establishing and maintaining social relationships by
   a. Introducing a structured learning environment that encourages positive social interactions with peers in the classroom (Vespi & Yewchuk, 1992);
   b. Increasing the opportunities for peer interactions in the classroom and supporting students in the appropriate use of social skills (Stormont et al., 2001); and
   c. Giving students who are gifted/LD opportunities to act in leadership roles with peers, especially in areas in which they excel.

7. Ensure parents' understanding of their child's giftedness and disability, emphasizing the child's potential. Build a collaborative relationship with parents to create a school–home partnership that supports the child.

8. Support students who are gifted/LD with future goals and career planning. Make sure that students are aware of their potential and do not sell themselves short.

9. Provide a mentorship with an adult who is also gifted/LD. This relationship can lend encouragement and hope to those who are frustrated with their school experiences (Swesson, 1994).

Final Thoughts

Twice-exceptional students have great potential to succeed. However, many become incredibly frustrated and have difficulty coping with the discrepancy between their giftedness and their learning disability. Their struggle to cope with frustration often leaves them feeling inadequate, disappointed, and angry, all of which negatively affect their self-concept. Many twice-exceptional students are also confused about where they fit in

Support services for twice-exceptional children must treat the whole child.

Guidelines for Developing Programs for Gifted/LD Students

- Focus attention on developing students' talents and strengthening their abilities through enrichment activities.
- Provide a nurturing environment in which students feel valued and their individual differences are respected.
- Teach compensation strategies after efforts to remediate skill deficits have helped students reach a level of proficiency.
- Encourage students' awareness of their individual strengths and weaknesses.

Source: Baum, 1990.

among their peers, and they often struggle with the social skills needed to maintain positive peer relationships.

Teachers, administrators, and parents must first acknowledge the individual gifts as well as the needs of students who are gifted/LD. These students must then be encouraged to recognize their own strengths and limitations so that they can better prepare for their future. Teachers must aim to strengthen these students' academic abilities and nurture their gifts while also supporting the social and emotional struggles that twice-exceptional students face inside and outside the classroom. By providing support that targets the whole child, we have the opportunity to tap the full potential of gifted students with learning disabilities.

References

Baum, S. M. (1984). Meeting the needs of learning disabled gifted students. *Roeper Review, 7*(1), 16–19.

Baum, S. M. (1990). *Gifted but learning disabled: A puzzling paradox.* Council for Exceptional Children: Reston, VA. ERIC Digest #E479.

Baum, S. M. (1994). Meeting the needs of gifted/learning disabled students: How far have we come? *The Journal of Secondary Gifted Education, 5*(3), 6–22.

Bong, M., & Skaalvik, E. M. (2003). Academic self-concept and self-efficacy: How different are they really? *Educational Psychology Review, 15*(1), 6.

Brody, L. E., & Mills, C. J. (1997). Gifted children with learning disabilities: A review of the issues. *Journal of Learning Disabilities, 30*(3), 282–296.

Coleman, M. R. (1992). A comparison of how gifted/LD and average/LD boys cope with school frustration. *Journal for the Education of the Gifted, 15*(3), 239–265.

Coleman, M. R. (2001). Surviving or thriving? *Gifted Child Today, 24*(3), 56–64.

Cooley, E. J., & Ayres, R. R. (1988). Self-concept and success-failure attributions of nonhandicapped students and students with learning disabilities. *Journal of Learning Disabilities, 21*(3), 174–178.

Fetzer, E. A. (2000). The gifted/learning-disabled child. *Gifted Child Today Magazine, 23*(4), 44–51.

Flicek, M. (1992). Social status of boys with both academic problems and attention-deficit hyperactivity disorder. *Journal of Clinical Child Psychology, 14,* 353–366.

Flicek, M., & Landau, S. (1985). Social status problems of learning disabled and hyperactive/learning disabled boys. *Journal of Clinical Child Psychology, 14,* 340–344.

Harter, S., Whitesell, N. R., & Junkin, L. J. (1998). Similarities and differences in domain-specific and global self-evaluations of learning-disabled, behaviorally disordered, and normally achieving adolescents. *American Educational Research Journal, 35*(4), 653–680.

McCoach, D. B., Kehle, T. J., Bray, M. A., & Siegle, D. (2001). Best practices in the identification of gifted students with learning disabilities. *Psychology in the Schools, 38*(5), 403–411.

Moon, S. M., & Dillon, D. R. (1995). Multiple exceptionalities: A case study. *Journal for the Education of the Gifted, 18(2),* 111–130.

Nielsen, M. E., & Mortorff-Albert, S. (1989). The effects of special education service on self-concept and school attitude of learning disabled/gifted students. *Roeper Review, 12*(1), 29–36.

Rivera, D. B., Murdock, J., & Sexton, D. (1995). Serving gifted/learning disabled. *Gifted Child Today Magazine, 18*(6), 34–37.

Schiff, M. M., Kaufman, A. S., & Kaufman, N. L. (1981). Scatter analysis of WISC-R profiles for learning disabled children with superior intelligence. *Journal of Learning Disabilities, 14*(7), 400–404.

Stormont, M., Stebbins, M. S., & Holliday, G. (2001). Characteristics and educational support needs of underrepresented gifted adolescents. *Psychology in the Schools, 38*(5), 413–423.

Strop, J. (2003). The affective side: Programming beyond the label. *Understanding Our Gifted, 15*(2), 27–29.

Swesson, K. (1994). Helping the gifted/learning disabled: Understanding the special needs of the "twice-exceptional." *Gifted Child Today, 17*(5), 24–26.

Vespi, L., & Yewchuk, C. (1992). A phenomological study of the social/emotional characteristics of gifted learning disabled children. *Journal for the Education of the Gifted, 16*(1), 55–72.

Waldron, K. A., Saphire, D. G., & Rosenblum, S. A. (1987). Learning disabilities and giftedness: Identification based on self-concept, behavior, and academic patterns. *Journal of Learning Disabilities, 20*(7), 422–432.

Winne, P. H., Woodlands, M. J., & Wong, B. Y. L. (1982). Comparability of self-concept among learning disabled, normal, and gifted students. *Journal of Learning Disabilities, 15*(8), 470–475.

EMILY WILLIAMS KING (CEC NC Federation), Doctoral Student, School Psychology, University of North Carolina, Chapel Hill. Address correspondence to Emily Williams King, 8 Weathergreen Court, Durham, NC 27713. (e-mail: eaw18@yahoo.com)

From *Teaching Exceptional Children*, by Emily Williams King, Vol. 38, No. 1, September/October 2005, pp. 16–20. Copyright © 2005 by Council for Exceptional Children. Reprinted by permission.

Creating a Personal Technology Improvement Plan for Teachers of the Gifted

KEVIN BESNOY

There is a high incidence of today's gifted students independently interacting with their global community through technology tools. Teachers of the gifted (GT teachers) must possess an understanding of technology processes and concepts in order to engage their students through instructionally meaningful and appropriate lessons (Bybee & Loucks-Horsley, 2000). Although many educators would like to use technology tools as an instructional medium, two obstacles prevent GT teachers from integrating technology into the curriculum: access to resources and continuous professional development.

The first obstacle to technology integration is access to resources (Minkel, 2004; Wilson & Notar, 2003). During the past decade, United States school systems have spent more than $19 billion on developing technology systems for local schools. Furthermore, national groups have set standards aimed at improving teachers' use of technology as an instructional tool (National Council for Accreditation of Teacher Education [NCATE], 2003; No Child Left Behind Act [NCLB], 2001; Preparing Tomorrow's Teacher's to Use Technology [PT³], 2005; International Society for Technology Education [ISTE], 2005). The goal of these efforts is to increase the amount of needed resources so that educators can more frequently and efficiently integrate technology into curricula.

Yet, despite the allocation of funds and creation of standards, there has been only modest technology integration into 21st-century classrooms (Minkel, 2004; Wilson, Notar, & Yunker, 2003). Minkel (2004) conducted a study to determine students' (ages 6–17) satisfaction with computer and Internet access at school. The results showed that almost half of the students (49%) were dissatisfied with the amount of time spent online. According to Minkel, "this represents a doubling of dissatisfaction on the part of children since 2000" (p. 26). Interestingly, even with the increased spending

on resources, students are not satisfied with amount of computer integration into instruction. Perhaps the solution to inadequate integration of technology can be found in teacher training.

The second obstacle to more frequent technology integration is strategic planning that provides continuous professional development and allows GT teachers to learn how to integrate technology resources as an instructional tool. According to Shaunessy (2003), 81% of GT teachers report receiving fewer than 10 hours of staff development in technology integration. Staff development content generally is outlined by district and school administrators and designed for an entire faculty (school and/or district). Unfortunately, many professional development opportunities unsuccessfully meet the technology needs of GT teachers and gifted students (Karnes & Shaunessy, 2004).

As a result of the one-size-fits-all aspect of technology-focused professional development opportunities, GT teachers cannot afford to wait for districtwide staff development sessions to teach them how to integrate computer resources. Rather, they must independently seek professional development opportunities that meet their specific instructional technology (IT) needs. A Personal Technology Improvement Plan (PTIP) facilitates this by allowing GT teachers to create an individualized professional development plan (Karnes & Shaunessy, 2004; see Appendix A).

Based on research conducted by Dettmer and Landrum (1998), a PTIP is a personalized, strategic professional development plan used to help GT teachers analyze and identify their professional technology needs and create a plan that allows them to meet those needs. PTIPs serve three purposes. First, they provide GT teachers with a continuous strategic plan to follow that will guide perpetual development and produce an able implementer of classroom technology

(Al-Weshail et al., 1996). In addition, they permit teachers to individualize their own technology development and allow them to progress at a self-determined pace. Finally, PTIPs represent a concerted effort by GT teachers to meet the "ambitious learning goals we hold for all students" (Bybee & Loucks-Horsley, 2000, p. 34).

PTIPs are similar to other professional development plans except that they focus on an individual teacher's technology needs. Although each PTIP will be uniquely designed to suit an individual teacher, all PTIPs are created along the same guidelines. According to Kelly and McDiarmid (2002), professional development plans should (a) support continuous learning, (b) meet individual teacher's needs, (c) promote collaboration among educators, (d) reflect student learning, and (e) evaluate teacher proficiency. Individualizing a technology plan transforms a one-size-fits-all plan to one that a teacher of the gifted can use to improve classroom pedagogy.

Creating a Personal Technology Improvement Plan

In order to create a PTIP, GT teachers must conduct a needs assessment and identify professional development resources that enable them to enhance their technology integration skills (Dettmer & Landrum, 1998). Although Dettmer and Landrum did not specifically mention IT skills, this suggestion is prudent in light of the work of other researchers in the field of gifted education (Shaunessy, 2003; Siegle, 2005; Southern & Spicker, 1989; Subhi, 1999).

Whether the GT teacher is a novice or an expert at integrating technology into the gifted education classroom, PTIPs can help improve his or her ability to use computers as an instructional tool. In order to create an effective plan that provides continual development over a 5-year period, GT teachers should follow a step-by-step process. The five steps include: (a) conduct a needs assessment, (b) write short- and long-term goals, (c) identify and access resources, (d) implement learned skills, and (e) evaluate progress.

Conduct a Needs Assessment

Conducting a needs assessment determines which resources and skills a teacher of the gifted has and which ones he or she needs. Furthermore, it provides a teacher with a direction that will guide the PTIP and maximize professional development opportunities. In order to conduct a needs assessment, a teacher should obtain a needs assessment survey. According to Thurlow (1999), the Teacher Computer Ability Profile (TCAP; http://www.johnthurlow.com/usm/emt/emt.html) is an easy-to-use survey that GT teachers can complete in a few minutes. The needs assessment survey should be conducted at least once a year to measure progress and reevaluate specific needs.

With this survey, GT teachers can determine their technology skills and needs. Each of the seven subscales (Basic Computer Skills; Managing Computer Files; Using Word Processing Software; Use of Other Software; Use of Multimedia, CD-ROM, and Educational Software; Use of the Internet; and Curriculum Integration of Computer Technology) allows teachers to determine their proficiency level (nonuser, novice, basic, advanced, or expert) and helps to prioritize areas of greatest need (Thurlow, 1999).

Unfortunately, the TCAP does not have a section for determining the type and number of available computer resources. However, GT teachers can answer the following questions to quickly determine the available resources: (a) How many computers are in my classroom?; (b) Is there a computer lab? If so how many computers are there?; and (c) What type of software do I already have access to? These basic questions will serve as a good beginning for developing a needs assessment.

What do I do if I am a nonuser or novice? Individuals whose IT skills are at the beginning stage will create a needs assessment that addresses the most basic skills. It is imperative to identify an individual in the school building or district who can act as an IT mentor. Much like a personal trainer, an IT mentor will help the nonuser or novice work through technophobia situations. In addition, seek out peers who share the same basic IT skill set and form an IT support group. This allows individuals to share resources, frustrations, and successful experiences.

Write Short- and Long-Term Goals

As with any good professional development plan, a PTIP must have short- and long-term goals. There should be several short-term goals that can be accomplished in 4 to 5 months. On the other hand, there should only be a couple of long-term goals that are to be accomplished during the life of the plan. It is imperative to base the goals on the results of the needs assessment. According to Al-Weshail et al. (1996), a good flexible plan can be adapted to meet the changing needs and resources of both the teacher and his or her students.

Short-Term Goals. There are two types of short-term goals that GT teachers need to set for themselves: skill acquisition goals and hardware and software acquisition goals. Skill acquisition goals focus on specific abilities. Examples of short-term skill acquisition goals include:

- I want to have an organized filing system for my electronic documents,
- I want to know how to run basic software programs,
- I want to teach others how to use presentation software in their classrooms, and
- I want to be able to use technology to meet the National Association for Gifted Children's Program Standards.

Table 1 Instructional Technology Professional Development Websites

4Teachers (http://www.4teachers.org)
4Teachers is a comprehensive Web site that provides educators with a portal to numerous IT tools and professional development opportunities. Interested individuals even can access an education technology-planning guide. Additionally, there are links to grant opportunities that specifically target K-12 classroom settings.

ALTEC (http://pd.altec.org)
ALTEC is for teachers who are interested in locating IT-focused professional development opportunities. This site offers help with learning basic and advanced IT tools. Teachers can register for online opportunities.

Beginning Teacher's Tool Box
(http://www.inspiringteachers.com/bttindex.html)
This site is a wonderful resource for teachers who are looking to learn new technology integration skills. It provides access to mentors, resources, and advice. Furthermore, this site has a collection of articles describing best practices for integrating IT tools into the classroom.

STAR Tech Professional Development Program
(http://www.startechprogram.org)
This program is open to anyone interested in learning how to integrate IT tools into their classroom. It guides teachers through a professional development program. Interested teachers can learn a range of skills for their individual classrooms.

Each of these goals is stated specifically and can be achieved easily in a brief time period.

Additionally, a teacher of the gifted should set goals that include acquiring newer and more robust hardware and software. Examples of short-term hardware and software acquisition goals include:

- I want to attain a new desktop publishing program to use with my students,
- I want another computer for my classroom, and
- I want to purchase a microscope that connects to the computer.

Although achieving these goals might seem costly, there are several professional development Web sites available for teachers that provide funding that make these aspirations attainable (see Table 1).

Depending on the teacher's starting point determined by the needs assessment, both skill and hardware and software acquisition goals can be achieved within a few months. It is important to be realistic about current skill level, available resources, and expertise. For instance, a novice might not be able to create a Web page for the entire school within a short time frame. However, he or she can learn how to set up a simple Web page and post classroom information in just a few weeks.

Long-Term Goals. In order to maintain a cohesive PTIP, a long-term goal should be an extension of several short-term goals. GT teachers should consider skill and hardware and software long-term acquisition goals that will transform their classroom into a student's learning dream world. Examples of long-term skill acquisition goals include:

- I want to learn how to teach my students to create a series of learning podcasts,
- I want to learn how to integrate multimedia-rich activities and distance learning to deliver Web-based classroom instruction,
- I want to learn how to incorporate low-level video chat software to connect my classroom with other classrooms across the globe,
- I want to earn a higher degree in instructional technology, and
- I want to develop and implement a technology improvement plan for my school district's gifted education program.

Attaining these achievable goals requires a teacher of the gifted to commit to a sustained PTIP.

Many of these goals cannot be achieved without acquiring new hardware. As such, GT teachers might need to consult IT specialists as to the specific hardware and software required to complete the long-term goals. Examples of hardware and software acquisition goals include:

- I want to expand the number of computers in the school's computer lab,
- I want to acquire Web cams for each classroom, and
- I want to put all student work into an electronic portfolio.

Although the goal(s) can be as grand as a teacher envisions, they should be consistent with the other stated PTIP goals.

Identify and Access Resources

After conducting a needs assessment and writing goals, the GT teacher needs to implement the PTIP. It is important to identify a number of professional development opportunities and select the ones that match interests and needs. There are several resources available that can aid in this step. Many universities offer courses in instructional technology. Another resource is professional organizations, including the International Society for Technology Education (http://www.iste.org). Each year they host the National Educators Computer Conference (NECC), where experts in the field of instructional technology present the latest strategies. Finally, many local educational agencies and state educational agencies offer IT workshops that develop skills, which easily can be implemented into current lesson plans.

Identifying resources is just half the battle. GT teachers will not progress through their PTIP successfully if they do not access the identified resources. Take the time and register for professional development opportunities. It is best to take one opportunity at a time and then progressively get more involved as time allows (Thurlow, 1999).

Implement Learned Skills

This section of the PTIP is exciting because it represents the culmination of a lot of hard work. According to Kelly and McDiarmid (2002) teachers should implement new strategies as they are learned. GT teachers should not wait until the end of a staff development to integrate new skills; rather, these should be implemented as they are learned. This will increase the value of the staff development sessions because teachers will understand what works and what does not work. It also provides an opportunity to ask the instructor tangible questions about specific strategies during the professional development session rather than waiting until it is too late.

Another benefit of implementing the new skills is that the gifted students immediately will see their teacher's dedication to using technology in the classroom. This realization helps to improve learning and teacher/student relationships. Moreover, the students will be given an opportunity to utilize computers in their learning.

Evaluate Progress

It is important to constantly evaluate progress. As a new skill is learned and implemented, the teacher of the gifted should evaluate how effective it was to integrate it into the gifted education classroom. According to Thurlow (1999), evaluation informs the teacher what worked and how to improve upon what did not work. Moreover, it provides feedback for the teacher as to what skills need to be learned to further progress through the PTIP. There are two forms of evaluation that GT teachers should conduct: student feedback and personal reflection.

The easiest method for gauging student opinions about implemented IT skills is to ask them directly. GT teachers should survey their students to determine if the implemented IT tools were successful. Students poignantly will opine whether or not the newly implemented IT skills were effective.

Furthermore, GT teachers should participate in the reflective teaching process. They need to reflect on the effectiveness of the implemented skills and how to improve them the next time. Implementing new skills always is difficult, but practicing them in authentic situations makes for more efficient instruction.

Final Thoughts

GT teachers must take the time to evaluate their ability to integrate technology into the gifted education classroom. Gifted students want to use computers as a learning tool, and understanding how to incorporate technology into the classroom is a 21st-century skill. By creating a PTIP, GT teachers can evaluate their current ability to integrate technology into the curriculum, and ascertain the best method for improving their skill.

References

Al-Weshail, A. S., Baxter, A. L., Cherry, W., Hill, E. W., Jones, C. R., Love, L. T., et al. (1996). *Guidebook for developing an effective instructional technology plan.* Starkville, MS: National Center for Technology Planning.

Bybee, R. W., & Loucks-Horsley, S. (2000). Advancing technology education: The role of professional development. *The Technology Teacher, 60*(2), 31–34.

Dettmer, P., & Landrum, M. (1998). *Staff development: The key to effective gifted education programs.* Waco, TX: Prufrock Press.

International Society for Technology in Education (ISTE). (2005). *The NETS project.* Retrieved August 18, 2006, from http://cnets.iste.org/nets_overview.html

Karnes, F. A., & Shaunessy, E. (2004). The application of an individual professional development plan to gifted education. *Gifted Child Today, 27*(3), 60–66.

Kelly, P. P., & McDiarmid, G. W. (2002, April). *Professional development under KERA: Teachers' decisions and dilemmas.* Paper presented at the annual meeting of the American Educational Research Association, New Orleans, LA.

Minkel, W. (2004). Kids not getting the Web access they want. *School Library Journal, 50*(1), 26.

National Council for Accreditation of Teacher Education (NCATE). (2003). *Program standards and report forms: Technology education.* Retrieved August 18, 2006, from http://www.ncate.org/public/programStandards.asp?ch=4#ITEA

No Child Left Behind Act, 20 U.S.C. § 6301 (2001).

Preparing Tomorrow's Teachers to Use Technology (PT[3]). (2005). *The PT[5] project.* Retrieved August 18, 2006, from http://pt3.org

Shaunessy, S. E. (2003). *Attitudes of teachers of the intellectually gifted in Mississippi toward information technology.* Unpublished doctoral dissertation, The University of Southern Mississippi.

Siegle, D. (2005). Six uses of the Internet to develop students' gifts and talents. *Gifted Child Today, 28*(2), 30–36.

Southern, W. T., & Spicker, H. H. (1989). The rural gifted online: Bulletin and electronic curriculum. *Roeper Review, 11,* 199–202.

Subhi, T. (1999). Attitudes towards computers of gifted students and their teachers. *High Ability Studies, 10*(1), 69–84.

Thurlow, J. P. (1999, May). *Teachers as technologists: Professional development for technology integration.* Paper presented at the annual meeting of the International Reading Association, San Diego, CA.

Wilson, J., & Notar, C. (2003). Use of computers by secondary teachers: A report from a university service area. *Education, 123,* 695–704.

Wilson, J., Notar, C., & Yunker, B. (2003). Elementary in-service teacher's use of computers in the elementary classroom. *Journal of Instructional Psychology, 30,* 256–263.

Appendix A

Personal Technology Improvement Plan

Needs Assessment *These are based on your current computer needs/abilities.*	How many computers do I have in my classroom? _____ How many computers are in the lab? _____ Do these computers allow me to utilize all of my computer skills? _____ How many technology specialists are there in my school? _____ Which software programs do I have access to? _____ What are the computer skills of my students? _____	What computer skills do I currently have? _____ What e-mail skills do I currently have? _____ What Internet skills do I currently have? _____ What multimedia skills do I currently have? _____ Which software programs do I currently know how to use? _____ How can I use my skills to integrate technology into the curriculum? _____	Prioritize your needs 1. _____ 2. _____ 3. _____ 4. _____ 5. _____
Short-Term Goals *These are goals that can be achieved within a few months.*	Acquiring hardware/software goals • _____ • _____ • _____ • _____ • _____	Acquiring computer skills goals • _____ • _____ • _____ • _____ • _____	Prioritize your short-term goals 1. _____ 2. _____ 3. _____ 4. _____ 5. _____
Long-Term Goals *These are goals that take a year or more to achieve*	Acquiring hardware/software goals • _____ • _____ • _____ • _____ • _____	Acquiring computer skills goals • _____ • _____ • _____ • _____ • _____	Prioritize your long-term goals 1. _____ 2. _____ 3. _____ 4. _____ 5. _____
Resources *Identify sources of funding to acquire specific technologies and locations/details of professional development opportunities*	Sources of grant funding • _____ • _____ • _____ • _____	Location/details of professional development opportunities • _____ • _____ • _____	Prioritize acquisition of resources 1. _____ 2. _____ 3. _____ 4. _____ 5. _____

(continued)

Implementation *Create a timeline of the steps required to achieve your goals.*	Implementation of short-term goals Month 1: _____ Month 2: _____ Month 3: _____ Month 4: _____ Month 5: _____	Implementation of long-term goals Year 1: _____ Year 2: _____ Year 3: _____ Year 4: _____ Year 5: _____	
Evaluation	Reflect on how successful you were in completing and implementing your short-term goals	Reflect on how successful you were in completing and implementing your long-term goals	

Test-Your-Knowledge Form

We encourage you to photocopy and use this page as a tool to assess how the articles in *Annual Editions* expand on the information in your textbook. By reflecting on the articles you will gain enhanced text information. You can also access this useful form on a product's book support website at *http://www.mhcls.com*.

NAME:

DATE:

_____

TITLE AND NUMBER OF ARTICLE:

_____

BRIEFLY STATE THE MAIN IDEA OF THIS ARTICLE:

_____

LIST THREE IMPORTANT FACTS THAT THE AUTHOR USES TO SUPPORT THE MAIN IDEA:

_____

WHAT INFORMATION OR IDEAS DISCUSSED IN THIS ARTICLE ARE ALSO DISCUSSED IN YOUR TEXTBOOK OR OTHER READINGS THAT YOU HAVE DONE? LIST THE TEXTBOOK CHAPTERS AND PAGE NUMBERS:

_____

LIST ANY EXAMPLES OF BIAS OR FAULTY REASONING THAT YOU FOUND IN THE ARTICLE:

_____

LIST ANY NEW TERMS/CONCEPTS THAT WERE DISCUSSED IN THE ARTICLE, AND WRITE A SHORT DEFINITION:

We Want Your Advice

ANNUAL EDITIONS revisions depend on two major opinion sources: one is our Advisory Board, listed in the front of this volume, which works with us in scanning the thousands of articles published in the public press each year; the other is you—the person actually using the book. Please help us and the users of the next edition by completing the prepaid article rating form on this page and returning it to us. Thank you for your help!

ANNUAL EDITIONS: Educating Children with Exceptionalities 10/11

ARTICLE RATING FORM

Here is an opportunity for you to have direct input into the next revision of this volume.
We would like you to rate each of the articles listed below, using the following scale:

1. **Excellent: should definitely be retained**
2. **Above average: should probably be retained**
3. **Below average: should probably be deleted**
4. **Poor: should definitely be deleted**

Your ratings will play a vital part in the next revision.
Please mail this prepaid form to us as soon as possible.
Thanks for your help!

RATING	ARTICLE	RATING	ARTICLE
	1. The Issues of IDEA		16. Young Women in Jail Describe Their Educational Lives
	2. Learn about Your New Students		17. Classroom Problems That Don't Go Away
	3. Use Authentic Assessment Techniques to Fulfill the Promise of No Child Left Behind		18. Assessment and Intervention for Bilingual Children with Phonological Disorders
	4. Does This Child Have a Friend?		19. A Speech-Language Approach to Early Reading Success
	5. Rethinking Inclusion: Schoolwide Applications		20. The Debate over Deaf Education
	6. Children of Alcoholics: Risk and Resilience		21. Using Tactile Strategies with Students Who Are Blind and Have Severe Disabilities
	7. What Can You Learn from Bombaloo?		22. Writing Explicit, Unambiguous Accommodations: A Team Effort
	8. Dyslexia and the Brain: What Does Current Research Tell Us?		23. ADHD and the SUD in Adolescents
	9. Build Organizational Skills in Students with Learning Disabilities		24. Trick Question
	10. Inclusion by Design: Engineering Inclusive Practices in Secondary Schools		25. Monitor That Progress!: Interpreting Data Trends for Assistive Technology Decision Making
	11. Reading Disability and the Brain		26. Addressing the Social and Emotional Needs of Twice-Exceptional Students
	12. Autism, the Law, and You		27. Creating a Personal Technology Improvement Plan for Teachers of the Gifted
	13. Heading Off Disruptive Behavior		
	14. Understanding and Accommodating Students with Depression in the Classroom		
	15. Rethinking How Schools Address Student Misbehavior and Disengagement		

ABOUT YOU

Name

Date

Are you a teacher? ☐ A student? ☐
Your school's name

Department

Address

City

State

Zip

School telephone #

YOUR COMMENTS ARE IMPORTANT TO US!

Please fill in the following information:
For which course did you use this book?

Did you use a text with this ANNUAL EDITION? ☐ yes ☐ no
What was the title of the text?

What are your general reactions to the Annual Editions concept?

Have you read any pertinent articles recently that you think should be included in the next edition? Explain.

Are there any articles that you feel should be replaced in the next edition? Why?

Are there any World Wide Websites that you feel should be included in the next edition? Please annotate.

May we contact you for editorial input? ☐ yes ☐ no
May we quote your comments? ☐ yes ☐ no

NOTES

NOTES

NOTES

NOTES

NOTES

NOTES

NOTES

NOTES